NON-COMPENSATORY DAMAGES IN ENGLISH LAW

This book gives the first detailed analysis of non-compensatory damages ('NCDs') as a category in English tort and contract law.

The book argues that most NCD awards are defined as those justified by damage to public interests and that they are in contrast to compensatory awards. The author argues that NCDs should be treated as a distinct class of awards. It shows how such a collective approach could be implemented in practice, without compromising the core tenets of the doctrines governing the award of NCDs. Offering both a unique theoretical framework and an emphasis on practical application, this will be of interest to both scholars and practitioners of English private law.

Volume 60 in the series Hart Studies in Private Law

Hart Studies in Private Law

This monograph series brings together in one place two types of book: works which examine in-depth the fundamental doctrines and principles of private law, and works which engage with the theoretical underpinnings of private law. The series thus aims to contribute to ever-evolving debates about the nature of private law such as problems of classification and taxonomy, remedies, the relationship with public law and the boundaries of private law generally.

The series includes, but is not confined to, works on contract, tort, unjust enrichment, equity, property and the conflict of laws, welcoming work which intersects with other fields of study to enable a deeper understanding of private law theory and practice.

Non-Compensatory Damages in English Law

A Reinterpretation

Václav Janeček

•HART•
OXFORD • LONDON • NEW YORK • NEW DELHI • SYDNEY

HART PUBLISHING

Bloomsbury Publishing Plc

Kemp House, Chawley Park, Cumnor Hill, Oxford, OX2 9PH, UK

1385 Broadway, New York, NY 10018, USA

Bloomsbury Publishing Ireland Limited, 29 Earlsfort Terrace, Dublin 2, D02 AY28, Ireland

HART PUBLISHING, the Hart/Stag logo, BLOOMSBURY and the Diana logo are trademarks of Bloomsbury Publishing Plc

First published in Great Britain 2026

A catalogue record for this book is available from the British Library.

A catalogue record for this book is available from the Library of Congress.

ISBN: HB: 978-1-50998-143-4
ePDF: 978-1-50998-145-8
ePub: 978-1-50998-144-1

Typeset by Compuscript Ltd, Shannon

ACKNOWLEDGEMENTS

This monograph was produced during my role at the University of Bristol Law School – a home to some of the best private law scholars in the common law world, both established and emerging. I was very lucky to have joined such a strong intellectual environment back in 2022, and I should like to thank the Law School for supporting me in finalising the book and the project which preceded it.

The book intellectually originates from my doctoral (DPhil) project at the University of Oxford (2018–2023) which, in turn, originates from my master's research project, also at the University of Oxford (2016–17). The research behind the project, as well as the formulation of my ideas, has benefited enormously from the detailed feedback by a range of experts with whom I discussed the present work since around 2016. Most notably, my thanks are due to Professors James Goudkamp (my doctoral supervisor), Professor Eric Descheemaeker (my external examiner) and Professor Sandy Steel (my internal examiner).

For various forms of support, I would like to thank my wife, family, friends, academic colleagues and fellow research students. Amongst my fellow research students, I want to express my thanks to Dr Tom Kohavi in particular.

Parts of my research were presented at academic events, and my work has therefore benefited from the feedback of the participants in those events, namely the Oxford Graduate Legal Research Conference (April 2017), the Oxford Obligations Discussion Group's seminar in Oxford (May 2018), the Obligations IX Conference in Melbourne (July 2018), the Oxford Philosophy of Private Law Working Group's workshops (April and November 2018), the 110th SLS Annual Conference in Preston (September 2019), the 'Public Interest in Law' Conference in Prague (October 2019), and the 115th SLS Annual Conference in Bristol (September 2024).

Parts of my research were published under the following peer-reviewed titles: V Janeček, 'CPR Pt 36: Enhanced Interest Should Not Function as Punitive Damages for Malicious Defence' (2019) 38 *CJQ* 168; V Janeček, 'Public Interest Damages' (2020) 40 *LS* 589; V Janeček, 'Data Protection, the Value of Privacy and Compensable Damage' (2020) 79 *CLJ* 417; V Janeček, 'Three Problematic Assumptions about Public Interests in Law' in L Tichý and M Potacs (eds), *Public Interest in Law* (Cambridge, Intersentia, 2021); and V Janeček, 'Mass Compensation Claims for Illegal Online Tracking' (2022) 138 *LQR* 205. The present book adopts some of the key arguments made in those publications.

The research project behind this book (2016–2023) was partially supported by the Oxford Law Faculty Scholarship and Pontigny Scholarship (St Edmund Hall), and specific research travels were sponsored by the Max Planck Scholarship, the Czech Science Foundation, the Postgraduate College Grant for Academic Purposes (St Edmund Hall), the MCR 50th Anniversary Grant (St Edmund Hall) and the Graduate Travel Grant (Faculty of Law, University of Oxford). I am grateful for this support.

CONTENTS

PART II
PUBLIC INTEREST DAMAGES

TABLE OF CASES

UNITED STATES

AUSTRALIA

CANADA

EUROPE

UNITED KINGDOM

TABLE OF STATUTES

TABLE OF DELEGATED LEGISLATION

TABLE OF OTHER SOURCES

INTERNATIONAL TREATIES

EU LAW

1

Introduction

Damages are not all of a kind. Take, for instance, the doctrinal categories of compensatory, aggravated, negotiating, user, liquidated, expectation, reliance, exemplary and nominal damages; the scholarly categories of substitutive, restorative, transformative, replicative, redressive and preventive damages; and those categories that straddle doctrine and theory, such as disgorgement and restitutionary damages. The labelling of different types of damages – which has been one of the dominant features of the law of damages over the last 50 years[1] – makes this area of the law very complex. Unfortunately, this level of complexity means that the area is not easy to analyse and that it is difficult to apply the relevant doctrines coherently.

At least one thing is very clear, though: compensatory damages are the key remedy in tort and contract. They are by far the most important kind of damages. According to the orthodox position, compensatory damages are designed to put the claimant in the position he would have been in had the wrong not occurred and are measured by reference to the claimant's loss.[2] Compensation so conceived is made on the *restitutio in integrum* principle: the aim is to put the claimant, as far as money can do so, in the original position as if the wrong had not occurred. In both contract and tort, the aim of compensatory damages is to rectify what was lost due to the wrong, be it a performance interest (as in contract law)[3] or other types of protected interest. As put by Friedmann, 'the basic principle as to damages is identical in contract and tort, though there may be some variations in its application'.[4]

Accepting the category of compensatory damages as the Archimedean point in the law of damages, one could try to make sense of all the various types of

[1] A Burrows, 'Damages and Rights' in D Nolan and A Robertson (eds), *Rights and Private Law* (Oxford, Hart Publishing, 2012) 277.

[2] See *Livingstone v Rawyards Coal Co* (1880) 5 App Cas 25 (HL) 39 (Lord Blackburn). See also *Owners of Dredger Liesbosch v Owners of Steamship Edison* [1933] AC 449 (HL) 459 (Lord Wright).

[3] *Robinson v Harman* (1848) 1 Exch 850, 855, (1848) 154 ER 363, 365.

[4] D Friedmann, 'The Performance Interest in Contract Damages' (1995) 111 *LQR* 628, 639 (footnote omitted). It is sometimes said that tort damages look backwards while contract damages look forward, because tort law compensatory damages put the claimant in a position he would have been in had the wrong not occurred, whereas contract law compensatory damages are designed to put the claimant in the same position as if the contract had been performed. But as Friedmann correctly observes '[t]his analysis is based on a misconception which derives from the failure to adequately distinguish between rights and remedies' – ibid.

damages by drawing a contrast between compensatory and non-compensatory damages. Intuitively, such a division makes perfect sense and is easy to understand. Indeed, the leading publication on the subject, *McGregor on Damages*, has for long considered some damages as exceptions to 'the true compensatory role of damages'.[5] Similarly, in *Street on Torts*, it is said that '[a]lthough the vast majority of damages … are intended to compensate the claimant … occasionally other forms of award are made'.[6] And in Kramer's *The Law of Contract Damages*, for example, we read that contract law too recognises '[d]amages awards not based on compensation'.[7] Apparently, the elementary contrast between compensatory and non-compensatory damages is thus firmly rooted in our understanding of damages in English private law.

That said, the contrast between compensatory and non-compensatory damages is itself normally not the object of legal studies. A number of basic questions are thus left unanswered in the literature. What exactly are these non-compensatory damages? Is there any stable meaning of the term 'non-compensatory damages'? Can we make any claims about non-compensatory damages collectively? Do non-compensatory damages fulfil a truly distinctive remedial function? And is this function radically unconcerned with the *restitutio in integrum* principle? The present book tackles these questions. It suggests a systematic reinterpretation of the legal sources governing the award of non-compensatory damages, partly as a way to overcome hidden tensions in the law of damages stemming from a fragmentary approach to this area of English law.

To be sure, this book does not simply describe the law controlling the award of individual non-compensatory damages (NCDs). Instead, it offers an interpretive theory of NCDs that, as far as possible, fits with the existing doctrines that govern the award of NCDs and that better reflects the important overlaps among individual types of NCDs. In doing so, it tests the orthodox view that all the various kinds of NCDs stand in contrast with compensatory damages and works out the doctrinal implications of this dividing line, including the implications concerning the availability, quantum and (in)compatibility of different forms of damages.

This introductory chapter first outlines the book's main claims (section I). Then it surveys, in a descriptive mode, the primary and secondary sources so that the reader can see how the term 'NCDs' has been used and understood so far and, accordingly, what the scope (section II) and subject matter (section III) of this book is. Section IV highlights the contribution this book makes, relative to the existing scholarship. Finally, section V outlines the book's structure, explains the nature of claims made in individual chapters and discusses the book's methodology.

[5] J Edelman, J Varuhas and A Higgins (eds), *McGregor on Damages*, 22nd edn (incorporating 1st supplement, London, Sweet & Maxwell, 2025) para 1-008.

[6] C Witting (ed), *Street on Torts*, 16th edn (Oxford, OUP, 2021) 677.

[7] A Kramer, *The Law of Contract Damages*, 3rd edn (Oxford, Hart Publishing, 2022) 567.

I. The Book in a Nutshell

The book shows that the category of NCDs is most typically associated with the awards of punitive, nominal, contemptuous, vindicatory, restitutionary and disgorgement damages. There is no suggestion in the sources that all these different types of non-compensatory damages have anything significant in common with each other save that they are not compensatory. Thus, NCDs are currently seen as a group of disparate remedies. The book challenges this view.

The book demonstrates that punitive, nominal, vindicatory and disgorgement (not restitutionary) damages can be collectively defined as damages justified by violations of public interests. In short, most types of NCDs can be collectively defined as 'public interest damages'. Public interests are understood in this book as matters that are significant for the functioning of our society, and they are explored and defined in detail in chapter five. It is contended that if we reinterpret NCDs as 'public interest damages', we can clearly understand their contrast with compensatory awards. This is because public interest damages are unconcerned with the *restitutio in integrum* principle and because, unlike compensation for loss, they are not justified by violations of private interests or underpinned by the norms of corrective justice.

It is also contended that, properly understood, contemptuous and restitutionary damages stand next to (rather than in contrast with) compensatory damages. In particular, we will see that both contemptuous and restitutionary damages are probably best understood as damages that are made on the *restitutio in integrum* principle and that protect the claimant's private interests. In this regard, neither contemptuous nor restitutionary damages can be defined as 'public interest damages'. Moreover, and contrary to the established linguistic convention in the law, the book argues against labelling these awards as NCDs because such labelling suggests a fundamental contrast with compensatory damages, even though there is none.

More generally, and in line with this qualification about contemptuous and restitutionary damages, the book advocates a systematic approach to damages based on what they are, rather than based on what they are not. In this vein, chapter five argues that we should start using the phrase 'public interest damages' to collectively refer to punitive, nominal, vindicatory and disgorgement damages, and that we should stop using the unstable, internally inconsistent and negatively defined term 'NCDs'. The 'NCDs' label (as opposed to the 'public interest damages' label) has no obvious explanatory or practical advantages, and it conceals rather than reveals the positive justifications of the non-compensatory awards in question. The proposed reinterpretation and relabelling of NCDs *qua* public interest damages is far from radical, especially since no primary legal source (as opposed to secondary sources) uses the term 'NCDs' in relation to contemptuous or restitutionary damages, as will be shown in section III.

Importantly, the book claims that public interest damages, ie, the coherent subset of what we now call 'NCDs', differ from compensatory awards in a profound way. This difference springs from a contrast between two fundamental justifications for awarding damages: those giving effect to individual rights and the protection of private interests (which underpin compensatory damages) and those giving effect to non-rights-based considerations, namely the protection of public interests (which underpin public interest damages). It is argued that all justifications of damages awards are reducible to either of these two broad categories. In theory, this would mean that the whole law of damages could be reinterpreted as consisting of two (and only two) broad categories: private interest damages and public interest damages. Such a reinterpretation of the law is, however, not the aim of the present book. Instead, the monograph focuses on a more modest set of implications. For example, as the second justification is not based on rights held by individuals, this implies that public interest damages should not be available as of right. Highlighting several other important doctrinal implications, the book contends that the law would do better to recognise these two fundamental justifications.

The book shows that the similarities and overlaps amongst individual types of public interest damages and the distinctions between compensatory and non-compensatory damages (*qua* public interest damages) are too important to be ignored. Thus, it is recommended that we understand and develop public interest damages collectively as a distinct class of awards. Dealing with potential counter arguments, the book sketches how this collective approach could be implemented in practice and reconciled – by way of reinterpretation, not change of the law – with the existing doctrines governing the award of NCDs. It also reveals the benefits of approaching public interest damages collectively.

Overall, by advancing a new interpretation of the law of NCDs, the book also contributes to our understanding of the English law of damages more generally and of the typically overlooked, yet significant role of public interests in the law of damages.

II. The Scope of the Book

The book's main claims are about NCDs in English law. Although the book draws on some cases from other jurisdictions, it does not make claims about the law elsewhere. The book substantiates its main claims in relation to tort and contract damages. This limitation of the book's scope is not always easy to maintain unless we adopt an inclusive view of what falls within these two general areas of law. That is because different forms of wrongdoing, such as administrative wrongdoing, competition law wrongs, and intellectual property wrongs, attract tortious forms of liability, and because many contractual obligations are nowadays specified in statutes, and so a breach of a contractual provision is by definition also a breach of a contractual duty. One thus cannot draw a simple line between tort and contract law remedies on the one hand and these special areas of the law on the other hand.

For this reason, and to ensure that the findings of this book are relevant to the study of the English law of damages more generally, the book will adopt an inclusive view of what amounts to tort and contract damages.

Thus, while the book does not make claims about statutory 'damages', this does not mean that statutes are irrelevant to the analysis. Significant portions of tort and contract are governed by statutory law, and so the book cannot ignore statutory provisions that might control or inform the award of damages in tort and contract. It would thus be misleading to draw a categorical line between common law and statutory damages. Of course, statutes do not always use the term 'damages' in the same sense as common law. For example, the Consumer Protection Act 1987 uses the word 'damages' as a shorthand for compensation which is not dependent on a wrong. But where the statute merely refers to damages in the common law sense as wrongs-based remedial awards (see more on the definition of 'damages' in chapter two, section I), there is no reason to exclude that statute from the scope of this book insofar as it can trigger tortious or contractual liability. The book thus discusses statutory awards when surveying the usage of the term 'NCDs' (section III), when defining the concept of 'damages' (chapter two, section I) and when exploring the so-called Category 3 punitive damages, ie, punitive damages expressly authorised by a statute (chapter four, section I).

Equitable 'damages' are, by contrast, excluded from the scope of this book, and the book does not make any claims in this regard. The book does not feature any special chapter on equitable wrongdoing, nor does it discuss equitable wrongdoing in any systematic way throughout the book. This is, first, because the present work is a monograph, not a handbook. Its purpose is not comprehensively to restate the law of non-compensatory money awards. Instead, its purpose is to analyse non-compensatory 'damages' (which equitable remedies are technically not). The lack of a discussion regarding equitable wrongdoing is thus not a weakness of this monograph.

Second, I make observations about equitable remedies (especially the account of profit) and draw arguments based on comparisons between common law and equity at various places in the manuscript. In this vein, the reader is not left in doubt as to what relevant overlaps and distinctions there are between my claims about 'damages' and the law regarding equitable money awards. In particular, the book discusses equitable remedies when defining the overall concept of 'damages' (chapter two, section I) and in relation to disgorgement damages – a category closely associated with equitable account of profits (chapter four, section VI). Indeed, as we will see shortly, the term NCDs is sometimes used to refer to disgorgement of profits – which is traditionally an equitable remedy – in a breach of contract situation (eg, in *Blake*[8]).

The discussion of disgorgement remedies in equity is particularly relevant because, as stated in section 49(1) of the Senior Courts Act 1981, 'wherever there

[8] *AG v Blake* [2001] 1 AC 268 (HL) (Blake case).

is any conflict or variance between the rules of equity and the rules of the common law with reference to the same matter, the rules of equity shall prevail' and because, as Arden LJ clarified in *Devenish Nutrition Ltd v Sanofi-Aventis SA*,

> [t]he overall holding in *Blake* [was] that the law on remedies for interference with property, damages in lieu of an injunction, damages for breach of fiduciary duty and breach of contract should be coherent and that the same remedies should be available in the same circumstances, even if the cause of action is different.[9]

Third, if I extended the discussion to all non-compensatory monetary remedies (as opposed to just 'damages'), some of my main claims would lose their thunder. The prime example of this is the claim that non-compensatory damages should not be available as of right. That claim is possibly groundbreaking with respect to 'damages', but not in relation to equitable remedies.

Fourth, the analysis would probably imply that equitable 'compensation' should be available as of right. While interesting in its own right, a thorough examination of this claim would itself require a lot of conceptual unpacking beyond the scope of the present monograph. This unpacking would, in turn, divert the reader from the core arguments of the book to matters of unnecessary technical complexity. Equitable remedies follow a distinct logic, one which cannot be simply galloped over under the banner of 'damages'. I therefore decided to leave out monetary remedies for equitable wrongs outside of this book's scope.

III. The Current Usage of the Term 'Non-Compensatory Damages' and the Adjective 'Non-Compensatory'

It is necessary to recognise at the outset that the term 'non-compensatory damages' has been used rather loosely in the sources. In particular, there seems to be a failure to distinguish clearly between the use of the term NCDs, on the one hand, to describe various non-loss-based measures of damages and, on the other hand, damages which stand in contrast with compensation on the *restitutio in integrum* principle. This section shows how the term NCDs is used in the primary legal sources (ie, cases and statutes) and the secondary sources (ie, academic writings) before it evaluates what types of damages are best to be analysed under the NCDs umbrella in this book.

Only a handful of cases and statutes explicitly mentions NCDs, but none of them provides a definition or analysis of NCDs. As of 9 July 2025, for example, there were only 17 UK court decisions and pieces of UK legislation prohibiting NCDs awards in claims against air carriers which use the term NCDs.[10] Several

[9] *Devenish Nutrition Ltd v Sanofi-Aventis SA* [2008] EWCA Civ 1086, [2009] 3 WLR 198 [4].

[10] This data was retrieved from Westlaw UK, Nexis UK, BAILII, The National Archives, vLexJustis and EUR-Lex. There has been no significant new decision or legislation using the term NCDs since. The review of primary sources also shows that the term NCDs appears in six pre-Brexit judgments by the Court of Justice of the EU, five opinions of AG, one decision by the European Court of Human Rights,

other cases (not legislation) use the adjective 'non-compensatory', but merely 18 of them do so when discussing damages. This makes it difficult to assert that there would be any widely accepted doctrinal meaning of the term.

In English law, the term 'non-compensatory damages' seems to make its first appearance more than two decades ago in a dissenting opinion in *AG v Blake*.[11] In that case, Lord Hobhouse used this term to warn about the danger in introducing 'some more extensive principle … [of awarding account of profits, explicitly described by him as] non-compensatory damages … [,] for breach of contract … [in] commercial law'.[12] In particular, Lord Hobhouse used the term NCDs to describe a gain-based award that does not represent 'a [standard] substitute for performance'[13] of a contractual obligation that should have been performed.[14] This usage of the term NCDs in *Blake* was probably motivated by the need to highlight the contrast between damages awarded on the principle of *restitutio in integrum* (the substitute for performance) and non-compensatory damages that are not constrained by this principle. As summarised by Lord Reed in *One Step*, '[w]hat *Attorney General v Blake* decided was that in exceptional circumstances an account of [all] profits [gained by the defendant's wrong] can be ordered as a remedy for breach of contract'.[15]

Clearly, the term NCDs in *Blake* referred to some anomalous remedy, ie, anomalous relative to the standard remedy for a lost performance of a contractual obligation. To highlight the exceptionality of the remedy, Lord Nicholls, who gave the leading judgment in *Blake*, drew a parallel between punitive damages and account of profits, acknowledging that it 'is axiomatic … [that with] the anomalous exception of punitive damages, damages are compensatory'.[16] We can thus argue that the term NCDs in *Blake* was used to refer to the exceptional disgorgement of profits awarded against Mr Blake and, indirectly, also to punitive damages. Both punitive and disgorgement damages stand here in fundamental contrast to compensatory awards.

The term NCDs is used similarly, ie, as a shorthand for an exceptional remedy, by the courts and lawmakers in other cases as well. For example, in *R (Anam) v Secretary of State for the Home Department*, Walker J used the expression 'non-compensatory

the Rome II Regulation (European Parliament and Council Regulation (EC) 864/2007 on the law applicable to non-contractual obligations (Rome II) [2007] OJ L199/40) and the Trade and Cooperation Agreement between the European Union and the European Atomic Energy Community, of the one part, and the United Kingdom of Great Britain and Northern Ireland, of the other part [2021] OJ L149/10.

[11] *Blake* (n 8).

[12] ibid 299.

[13] ibid 298.

[14] His Lordship's usage of the term as a synonym for some type of non-substitutive damages was cited with approval in *Devenish Nutrition Ltd v Sanofi-Aventis SA* (n 9) [149] (Longmore LJ (dissenting)) and *Luxe Holding Ltd v Midland Resources Holding Ltd* [2010] EWHC 1908 (Ch) [54] (Roth J). Indirectly, the same understanding of the adjective 'non-compensatory' was adopted in *Less v Hussain* [2012] EWHC 3513 (QB), [2013] Med LR 383 [179]–[180].

[15] *One Step (Support) Ltd v Morris-Garner* [2018] UKSC 20, [2019] AC 649 [82].

[16] *Blake* (n 8) 282. See also *R (Abulbakr) v Secretary of State for the Home Department* [2022] EWHC 1183 (Admin), [2022] 5 WLUK 554 [23]: 'exemplary damages are non-compensatory'.

damages' to refer to a nominal and vindicatory award which was supposed 'to mark the abuse of power'[17] by the state, which had unlawfully detained the claimants. In *Gulati v MGN Ltd*, Mann J stated that the adjective 'vindicatory' is sometimes used 'in the sense of non-compensatory, intended to mark "the sense of public outrage, emphasize the importance of the constitutional right and the gravity of the breach, and deter future breaches"'.[18] In *Ashley v Chief Constable of Sussex*, Lord Scott argued that 'vindicatory damages, although not punitive in intent, are, in common with exemplary damages, extra- compensatory in character [and] … essentially non-compensatory'.[19] In *OMV Petrom SA v Glencore Intl AG*, Sir Geoffrey Vos C ruled that the court 'undoubtedly has a discretion to include a non-compensatory element to the award … of enhanced interest [on costs] under CPR'[20] if one party unjustifiably refuses to settle and thus deserves to be sanctioned for its malicious defence.[21] Elsewhere, the phrase 'non-compensatory damages' was also used to refer to a ban under section 5(2)(a) of the Protection of Trading Interests Act 1980 on the enforcement of foreign judgments for multiple damages (arrived at by doubling, trebling or otherwise multiplying a sum assessed as compensation for the loss or damage).[22] In such cases, the adjective 'non-compensatory' is being associated with punitive aspect of multiple damages awards.[23] Similarly, in a case concerning recital (32) of Rome II Regulation, the court discussed a ban on the applicability of the doctrines on 'non-compensatory … punitive damages'.[24] In yet another context, the term NCDs denoted awards

[17] *R (Anam) v Secretary of State for the Home Department (No 2)* [2012] EWHC 1770 (Admin) [30] (Walker J) (Anam case).

[18] *Gulati v MGN Ltd* [2015] EWHC 1482 (Ch), [2016] FSR 12 [127] (referring to *R (Lumba) v Secretary of State for the Home Department* [2011] UKSC 12, [2012] 1 AC 245 (Lumba case)).

[19] *Ashley v Chief Constable of Sussex* [2008] UKHL 25, [2008] 1 AC 962 [28].

[20] *OMV Petrom SA v Glencore Intl AG* [2017] EWCA Civ 195, [2017] 1 WLR 3465 (Petrom case) [38]. Note that there was a second Court of Appeal judgment on the same case concerning the measure of damages in deceit: *OMV Petrom SA v Glencore Intl AG (No 2)* [2016] EWCA Civ 778, [2017] 3 All ER 157. The 'non-compensatory' element to the award was discussed only in the first *Petrom* decision. The ruling in *Petrom* concerning the enhanced non-compensatory interest rate has been applied in multiple judgments since 2017.

[21] I analyse this decision in more detail in V Janeček, 'CPR Pt 36: Enhanced Interest Should Not Function as Punitive Damages for Malicious Defence' (2019) 38 *Civil Justice Quarterly* 168.

[22] *SAS Institute Inc v World Programming Ltd* [2018] EWHC 3452 (Comm), [2019] FSR 30 [213]; *SAS Institute Inc v World Programming Ltd* [2020] EWCA Civ 599, [2020] 1 CLC 816 [43]. See also *Hangzhou Jiudang Asset Management Co Ltd v Hung* [2022] EWHC 3265 (Comm) [32], [43] and [47]. According to the Protection of Trading Interests Act 1980, s 5(2)(a): 'no court in the United Kingdom shall entertain proceedings at common law for the recovery of any sum payable [under a judgment] for multiple damages'.

[23] See, eg, *British Airways Board v Laker Airways Ltd & Ors* [1985] AC 58 (HL) 89; *Pace Europe Ltd v Dunham* [2012] EWHC 852 (Ch), [2012] BPIR 836 [17]–[18]; *Motorola Solutions Inc v Hytera Communications Corp Ltd* [2024] EWHC 2891 (Comm) [62].

[24] *KMG Intl NV v Chen* [2019] EWHC 2389 (Comm) [54]; *Begum v Maran (UK) Ltd* [2021] EWCA Civ 326, [2021] 1 CLC 514 [95]. According to recital (32) of Rome II Regulation: 'Considerations of public interest justify … the possibility … [of] overriding mandatory provisions. In particular, the application of a provision of the law … which would have the effect of causing non-compensatory exemplary or punitive damages of an excessive nature to be awarded may … be regarded as being contrary to the public policy (ordre public) of the forum.'

of punitive damages against air carriers.[25] In this last-mentioned context (and prior to Brexit), the Court of Justice of the European Union has also explicitly referenced NCDs in some of its judgments concerning damages against air carriers.[26]

Without going into much detail about all these different examples, there are two key lessons we can learn from the primary sources. First, there are indeed several types of award that are expressly referred to as NCDs, and these awards do not seem to be animated by the *restitutio in integrum* principle in any meaningful sense. We can thus observe, in a descriptive mode, that these awards are referred to as 'non-compensatory' because they stand in some fundamental contrast with damages that give effect to the *restitutio in integrum* principle, namely compensatory damages. Taking stock of these use cases and linking them with the established doctrinal categories, we can see that they span:

- punitive damages in various contexts,
- exceptional account of profits in contract law,
- nominal damages in tort law,
- vindicatory damages in various contexts (although we should keep in mind that vindicatory damages are currently not available in English law[27]),
- multiple damages in a foreign judgment (which are punitive in effect[28]), and
- the order of enhanced interest rate on costs (which are also punitive in effect, although we should keep in mind that the enhanced interest order is not strictly speaking an award of damages).

The second lesson is that primary legal sources neither define nor explain the meaning of the term NCDs. This is probably not surprising. Bound as they are

[25] *Hall v Heart of England Balloons Ltd* [2010] 1 Lloyd's Rep 373 (CCt (Birmingham)) [35]; *Hook v British Airways Plc* [2011] EWHC 379 (QB), [2011] 1 All ER (Comm) 1128 [5]; *Hook v British Airways Plc* [2012] EWCA Civ 66, [2012] 2 All ER (Comm) 1265 [2]; *Stott v Thomas Cook Tour Operators Ltd* [2014] UKSC 15, [2014] AC 1347 [31]. See also *O'Carroll v Ryanair* [2008] ScotSC 23, (2009) SCLR 125 [2], [8], [10], [12], [16] and [17]; *Caldwell v easyJet Airline Co Ltd* [2015] ScotSC 64, (2015) SCEDIN 64 [7]; *Akulinina v Ifly SA* [2022] EWHC 166 (QB) [11]; *Mather v easyJet Airline Co Ltd* [2022] CSOH 40, 2022 SLT 631[5].

[26] Given that these judgments interpret EU law which is applicable also in the UK, the ECJ judgments might arguably be seen as relevant to certain questions of English law. See C-344/04 *R (IATA) v Department for Transport* EU:C:2005:530, [2006] 2 CMLR 20, Opinion of AG Geelhoed, para [4]; C-396/06 *Kramme v SAS Scandinavian Airlines Danmark A/S* EU:C:2007:555, Opinion of AG Sharpston, para [6]; joined cases C-581/10 and C-629/10 *Nelson v Deutsche Lufthansa AG* EU:C:2012:657, [2013] 1 CMLR 42, paras [8], [20], [28]–[40]. See also joined cases C-581/10 and C-629/10 *Nelson v Deutsche Lufthansa AG* EU:C:2012:295, [2013] 1 CMLR 42, Opinion of AG Bot, paras [6], [21] and [51]; C-12/11 *McDonagh v Ryanair Ltd* EU:C:2013:43, [2013] 2 CMLR 32, para [5]; C-240/14 *Prüller-Frey v Brodnig & Anor* EU:C:2015:325, [2015] 1 WLR 5031, Opinion of AG Szpunar, para [5]; C-240/14 *Prüller-Frey v Brodnig & Anor* EU:C:2015:567, [2015] 1 WLR 5031, para [5]; C-429/14 *Air Baltic Corporation AS v Lietuvos Respublikos specialiųjų tyrimų tarnyba* EU:C:2016:88, [2016] Bus LR 623, paras [10] and [25]; C-532/18 *GN v ZU* EU:C:2019:1127, [2020] 1 WLR 3059 [8].

[27] See *Lumba* (n 18) [101] (Lord Dyson).

[28] See *SAS Institute Inc v World Programming Ltd* (HC Comm) (n 22) [2], [20], [223] and [244].

by particular precedents, and confronted as they are with particular claims, it is understandable why judges do not posit or theorise some overarching category of NCDs. This does not mean, of course, that the term NCDs cannot have any stable and useful meaning. On the contrary, since primary legal sources rely on our implicit understanding of the term NCDs, one may assume there is a common rationale to all these use cases. And if any meaningful and justifiable overarching category of NCDs exists, it just needs to be uncovered, defined and expressly articulated – which is what this book seeks to do.

Let us now turn to the literature. Generally speaking, doctrinal scholarship uses the term NCDs to signal that the remedy in question pursues some distinctive non-compensatory function. Thus, practically all doctrinal texts confirm the distinctive non-compensatory functions of punitive and nominal damages.[29] Most doctrinal scholars further separate contemptuous damages from nominal damages, for they presumably rest on distinct justificatory reasons and pursue slightly distinct non-compensatory goals.[30] Next, some academic writings also attest to the non-compensatory distinctiveness of vindicatory damages.[31] (The category of vindicatory damages will thus be explored in this book as a type of NCDs, although vindicatory damages are not an award that would ever be expressly made under the English law and English courts generally hold a sceptical view of this type of award.[32]) Many texts also single out the awards of gain-based damages as pursuing distinct non-compensatory goals, but it is sometimes unclear whether they draw a line between gain-based restitutionary damages and gain-based disgorgement damages.[33]

Sometimes, the scholarship uses the term NCDs also more loosely as a shorthand for various other-than-loss-based damages, without regard to whether such

[29] Kramer (n 7); J Goudkamp and D Nolan (eds), *Winfield & Jolowicz on Tort*, 20th edn (London, Sweet & Maxwell, 2020); R Mulheron, *Principles of Tort Law*, 2nd edn Cambridge, CUP, 2020); Witting (n 6); C Brennan, *Tort Law Concentrate: Law Revision and Study Guide*, 7th edn (Oxford, OUP, 2024) ch 17; P Giliker, *Tort*, 8th edn (London, Sweet & Maxwell, 2023); NJ McBride and R Bagshaw, *Tort Law*, 7th edn (London, Pearson, 2024); M Chen-Wishart, *Contract Law*, 7th edn (Oxford, OUP, 2022) 532; J O'Sullivan, *O'Sullivan's & Hillard's The Law of Contract*, 11th edn (Oxford, OUP, 2024) 452; S Green and J Gardner, *Tort Law*, 2nd edn (Oxford, Hart Publishing, 2024) 557–58; Edelman, Varuhas and Higgins (n 5).

[30] PH Winfield, *A Text-Book of the Law of Tort* (London, Sweet & Maxwell, 1937) 151; H Street, *The Law of Torts* (London, Butterworth & Co Publishers, 1955) ch 28; Goudkamp and Nolan (n 29) paras 23-007 to 23-008; Giliker (n 29) ch 17; Witting (n 6) 654.

[31] McBride and Bagshaw (n 29) ch 27; Edelman, Varuhas and Higgins (n 5) ch 18. But, for example, Goudkamp and Nolan think that 'there is no such thing as an award of "vindicatory damages" in private law' (Goudkamp and Nolan (n 29) para 23-039 (footnote omitted)). According to others, vindicatory damages may play the same role as punitive damages. See, eg, R Stevens, 'Torts, Rights and Losses' (2006) 122 *LQR* 565, 568; D Pearce and R Halson, 'Damages for Breach of Contract: Compensation, Restitution and Vindication' (2008) 28 *OJLS* 73, 86; ED Ventose, 'Damages for Constitutional Infringements: Compensation and Vindication' [2010] *Commonwealth Law Bulletin* 223, 245.

[32] See, eg, *R (NAB) v Secretary of State for the Home Department* [2011] EWHC 1191 (Admin) [6] (Irwin J). I will return to vindicatory damages in Section 4.4.

[33] eg, Kramer (n 7) ch 23; Goudkamp and Nolan (n 29) paras 23-032 to 23-038; Giliker (n 29) ch 17; Mulheron (n 29) ch 11. I will attend in more detail to the relation between the gain-based restitutionary and the gain-based disgorgement damages in ch 4.

damages have any distinctive non-compensatory function.[34] The most prominent example of this kind of approach is *McGregor on Damages*. To the extent that *McGregor on Damages* aspires to be the leading descriptive account of the law, this is surprising because there is a clear tension between how this publication and primary sources use the term NCDs. *McGregor on Damages* uses the label NCDs as a convenient title for Part 2, comprising chapters on: (i) nominal damages, (ii) exemplary damages, (iii) licence fee (negotiating or user) damages, (iv) account and disgorgement of profits, (v) liquidated damages and penalties and (vi) vindicatory damages.[35] In *McGregor on Damages*, the line between NCDs and compensatory damages thus seems to be drawn according to the distinction between loss-based and non-loss-based damages, which is not exactly how the primary sources use the term NCDs. How else would we be able to explain that negotiating damages, for example, are labelled as NCDs in *McGregor on Damages*? If we look into the law's own way to describe negotiating damages, we can clearly see that they are characterised as compensatory, not as NCDs. As ruled by the Supreme Court in *One Step*, negotiating damages are compensatory because the hypothetical negotiation is merely 'a tool'[36] for arriving at the relevant figure to compensate the claimant, even though they do not compensate the claimant for any actual loss (as I will go on to explain in chapter two, negotiating damages can be said to compensate the claimant for loss if we accept a broad interpretation of the term loss, but such interpretation will be rejected for the purposes of defining NCDs in favour of a broader term 'damage' which will be defined in chapter three). So the term NCDs in *McGregor on Damages* must mean something different from awards that stand in contrast with compensatory damages.

One way to explain the approach in *McGregor on Damages* is that the label 'NCDs' is not itself important for the authors. Indeed, the authors do not try to identify how the primary sources use the term NCDs. They are interested in the individual types of NCDs and the doctrines governing their award. In relation to licence fee (negotiating or user) damages, the doctrine has evolved over the past years, and so there may be some historical reasons why it is still meaningful to classify these measures as NCDs. To explain, in previous editions of the book, these

[34] See, eg, AI Ogus, *The Law of Damages* (London, Butterworths, 1973) ch 2; A Burrows, *Remedies for Torts and Breach of Contract*, 1st edn (London, Butterworths, 1987) 236; A Burrows, *Remedies for Torts and Breach of Contract*, 2nd edn (London, Butterworths, 1994) 269; A Burrows, 'Reforming Non-Compensatory Damages' in W Swadling, GH Jones and RG Goff of Chieveley (eds), *The Search for Principle: Essays in Honour of Lord Goff of Chieveley* (Oxford, OUP, 1999); G Samuel, *Law of Obligations and Legal Remedies*, 2nd edn (London, Cavendish Publishing Ltd, 2001) 204–07; J Varuhas, *Damages and Human Rights* (Oxford, Hart Publishing, 2016) 116–17; Kramer (n 7) ch 23 (who all have a separate chapter on 'Non-compensatory damages'). Other authors, though, simply put them in the 'other' category – eg, T Dorgan and P McKenna, *Damages* (Dublin, Thomson Reuters Ireland Limited, 2015) ch 2, entitled 'Awards of damages other than ordinary damages'.

[35] See Edelman, Varuhas and Higgins (n 5) part 2.

[36] *One Step (Support) Ltd v Morris-Garner* (n 15) [91]. See also ibid [95]; *Lunn Poly Ltd v Liverpool & Lancashire Properties Ltd* [2006] EWCA Civ 430, [2006] 2 EGLR 29 [22]; *Abbar v Saudi Economic & Development Co (SEDCO) Real Estate Ltd* [2013] EWHC 1414 (Ch) [224].

remedies were discussed in *McGregor on Damages* under the banner of 'restitutionary damages',[37] ie, a gain-based award. And as was explained above, the academic literature still regards gain-based restitutionary damages as a remedy that pursues a distinct non-compensatory aim. Another way to explain *McGregor on Damages*'s current approach is to say that the term 'NCDs' is used solely as a convenient label for 'damages not falling strictly within compensation',[38] some of which are best thought of as 'additional types of damages rather than as exceptional'.[39] Thus, the main body of *McGregor on Damages* explores the cases and principles concerning different measures of damages, without suggesting that there would be any doctrinal category of NCDs as such. Each of these non-loss-based 'NCDs' is analysed in *McGregor on Damages* as a disparate category.

This loose usage of the term NCDs will not be relied on in this book for two main reasons. First, it does not track the usage of the term we find in primary sources. Second, if taken seriously, it would probably require us to define NCDs as all awards labelled other than 'compensatory damages' or assessed by reference to something else than loss in the strict sense. This, again, is too detached from the law's own usage of the term NCDs and also from the explanations offered in the academic literature, which seeks to compare and contrast NCDs with compensatory damages based on their overarching functions, rather than just based on how they are labelled (see more on this approach in section II).

For example, if taken seriously, the approach adopted in *McGregor on Damages* would probably require us to say that aggravated damages are also a kind of NCDs. Indeed, it is common for textbooks to devote a separate chapter to aggravated damages, as they are a somewhat special case and are not labelled as 'compensatory damages'.[40] So it would be logical to conclude that aggravated damages are a kind of NCDs. But the same textbooks observe – in line with authority – that aggravated damages are in essence compensatory and their distinctiveness stems mainly from how the award is measured,[41] ie, from its being compensation for the claimant's 'feelings of distress or outrage'.[42] Similarly, the awards of liquidated,[43]

[37] eg, J Edelman, J Varuhas and S Colton (eds), *McGregor on Damages*, 20th edn (London, Sweet & Maxwell, 2017) ch 14.

[38] Edelman, Varuhas and Higgins (n 5) para 1-010.

[39] ibid para 1-010. *cf* ibid para 1-008.

[40] eg, Goudkamp and Nolan (n 29) paras 23-025 to 23-032; Mulheron (n 29) ch 11; Witting (n 6) 664–65; Giliker (n 29) ch 17.

[41] eg, P Cane, 'Exceptional Measure of Damages: A Search for Principles' in P Birks (ed), *Wrongs and Remedies in the Twenty-First Century* (Oxford, Clarendon Press, 1996) 305; Edelman, Varuhas and Higgins (n 5) paras 44-012 to 44-014.

[42] *Ashley v Chief Constable of Sussex* (n 19) [102] (Lord Neuberger). See also *Khodaparast v Shad* [2000] 1 WLR 618 (CA) [40]–[45]; Law Commission, *Aggravated, Exemplary and Restitutionary Damages* (Law Com No 247, 1997) 3 (para 1.8 and para 1.9); A Beever, 'The Structure of Aggravated and Exemplary Damages' (2003) 23 *OJLS* 87; J Murphy, 'The Nature and Domain of Aggravated Damages' (2010) 69 *CLJ* 353.

[43] *cf* Edelman, Varuhas and Higgins (n 5) who put liquidated damages under the NCDs heading mainly because of their close connection with contractual penalties and because it is sometimes hard to distinguish the two (ibid ch 17).

delay,[44] negotiating (sometimes also called user[45] or Wrotham Park damages),[46] reliance and expectation damages[47] are not measured by loss in the strict sense and they are other-than-compensatory by their name, but as a matter of their justificatory rationale all of them are typically regarded as compensatory. In other words, these awards are typically seen as distinctive manifestations of the same *restitutio in integrum* principle.

For these reasons, this book will not adopt *McGregor's* broad understanding of NCDs as damages not concerned with loss in the strict sense (ie, as 'actual loss') or as damages labelled other than 'compensatory damages'. Instead, it will understand NCDs as awards that statedly pursue a distinct non-compensatory function. Thus, it will focus only on measures of damages that, according to primary and secondary sources, stand in contrast with (rather than next to) compensation on the *restitution in integrum* principle. Following this approach, the previous review of primary sources tells us that the term NCDs refers to the exceptional disgorgement of profits (eg, in *Blake*[48]), nominal damages (eg, in *Anam*[49]), vindicatory damages (eg, in *Ashley*[50]) and punitive damages (eg, in *Stott*[51]). Based on the secondary sources, then, the category of NCDs could additionally include contemptuous and gain-based restitutionary damages, both of which purportedly pursue distinct non-compensatory functions. It is probably unnecessary to create a separate subcategory of NCDs for: (i) multiple damages under statute, and (ii) enhanced interest orders, because, as was shown above, in relation to both of these types of award the term 'non-compensatory' is used in primary sources as a shorthand for their punitive function. Thus, insofar as these awards are functionally equivalent to punitive damages, it will suffice to explore their non-compensatory nature under the punitive damages heading.

Conveniently, NCDs can thus be tentatively defined by a reference to a closed list of awards, which will be the prime focus of this book:

(i) punitive damages,
(ii) nominal damages,
(iii) vindicatory damages,
(iv) disgorgement damages,
(v) restitutionary damages,
(vi) contemptuous damages.

[44] Recently, see, eg, *J Murphy and Sons Ltd v Beckton Energy Ltd* [2016] EWHC 607 (TCC), [2016] BLR 448 [6], [20]; *Vinci Construction UK Ltd v Beumer Group UK Ltd* [2017] EWHC 2196 (TCC), [2017] BLR 547 [5].

[45] *One Step (Support) Ltd v Morris-Garner* (n 15) [3], [25]–[30] (Lord Reed), [128] (Lord Carnwath). See also *Blue Sky One Ltd v Mahan Air, PK Airfinance US Inc v Blue Sky Two Ltd* [2010] EWHC 631 (Comm) [58].

[46] *Wrotham Park Estate Co Ltd v Parkside Homes Ltd* [1974] 1 WLR 798 (Ch) 815. See A Burrows, 'One Step Forward?' (2018) 134 *LQR* 515.

[47] In more detail, see Edelman, Varuhas and Higgins (n 5) paras 5-036 to 5-043.

[48] n 16.

[49] n 17.

[50] n 19.

[51] n 25.

Each of these awards and the doctrines governing them arguably qualify as NCDs, although the primary sources (unlike secondary sources) only use the term NCDs in relation to the first four measures. This qualification is important because, as will be argued, restitutionary and contemptuous damages do not go so well with the other four NCDs categories. Strictly speaking, the NCDs class (later defined as 'public interest damages') should thus only include the first four categories of damages. The inclusion of restitutionary and contemptuous damages under the NCDs umbrella can therefore be seen as a weakness of the secondary sources (academic literature) and not a problem for the law's own understanding of NCDs.

IV. A Contribution to the Scholarship

Although everyone would probably agree that damages are either compensatory or non-compensatory, there is virtually no study that tries to understand NCDs collectively.[52] In practice, compensatory damages are much more important terms than NCDs and so there is obviously little incentive to study NCDs systematically. The tacit assumption of the judges and doctrinal scholars is that all the various kinds of NCDs, including punitive, nominal, vindicatory and disgorgement damages are wholly or largely unrelated species of damages. This is a mistake because, as the book shows, there is in fact a unity to these types of NCDs. Specifically, they are united under the banner of violations of public interests.

Not only is this book the first analysis of NCDs collectively,[53] but also a first focused exploration of the role of public interests in the law of damages. Although some related issues have already been explored in the literature, such as the interplay between private and public wrongs,[54] the relevance of public interest considerations to private law remedies,[55] remedies against public law bodies,[56]

[52] A notable exception in this regard is Cane (n 41), although his work does not address NCDs directly. Cane searches for justifying principles of exceptional measures of damages which he understands as measures that are 'not' justified by correlative gain or loss. Note that Cane does not explore ordinary (let alone exceptional) measures of NCDs as such.

[53] See also V Janeček, 'Public Interest Damages' (2020) 40 *Legal Studies* 589, where I published some early results of my research into this area.

[54] eg, M Dyson (ed), *Unravelling Tort and Crime* (Cambridge, CUP, 2014); M Dyson (ed), *Comparing Tort and Crime* (Cambridge, CUP, 2015); J Wall, 'Public Wrongs and Private Wrongs' (2018) 31 *Canadian Journal of Law & Jurisprudence* 177.

[55] *cf*, eg, A Georgiou and S Steel, 'Remedies and the Public Interest' in A Robertson and JW Neyers (eds), *Private Law and the State* (Oxford, Hart Publishing, 2024) 222–27.

[56] eg, C Harlow, '"Public" and "Private" Law: Definition without Distinction' (1980) 43 *MLR* 241; H Woolf, 'Public Law – Private Law: Why the Divide? A Personal View' (1987) *PL* 220; J Beatson, '"Public" and "Private" in English Administrative Law' (1987) 103 *LQR* 34; G Samuel, 'Governmental Liability in Tort and the Public and Private Law Division' (1988) 8 *Legal Studies* 277; D Oliver, *Common Values and the Public-private Divide* (London, Butterworths, 1999); CD Campbell, 'The Nature of Power as Public in English Judicial Review' (2009) 68 *CLJ* 90; Varuhas (n 34) ch 4.

the limits of courts' reasoning in private law,[57] whether there is a public justification of punitive damages,[58] and the public law nature of certain areas of tort law,[59] no work has yet been focused on the justificatory role of public interests in the law of damages generally. By revealing the importance of public interests in the assessment and availability of NCDs, the book challenges those approaches that view damages as fundamentally 'private' law remedies. The book also reveals the distinct role of NCDs in identifying matters of radical significance for the functioning of our society, ie, matters of public interest.

Further, by exploring NCDs and the public interests that justify their measures, this book also advances our understanding of the law of damages more generally. There are, of course, numerous studies that also seek to improve our understanding of the law of damages by, for example, reconciling it with broader ideas of justice and private law.[60] Others try better to understand damages within the law of remedies at large.[61] Some try to describe the law by fleshing out the doctrines and justifications that, in their view, underpin distinct categories of damages at large.[62] Others do so only in individual parts of law, such as contract and tort law.[63] Some try to advance the law of damages by pointing out commonalities and differences in damages awards at large.[64] Others point out such commonalities and differences only in limited areas of law.[65] Some seek better to understand the distinct measures of damages at large,[66] while others focus on specific measures of damages such as compensatory,[67] disgorgement,[68] punitive,[69] or gain-based

[57] eg, C Conte, 'From Only the "Bottom-up"? Legitimate Forms of Judicial Reasoning in Private Law' (2014) 35 *OJLS* 1; J Plunkett, 'Principle and Policy in Private Law Reasoning' (2016) 75 *CLJ* 366.

[58] eg, BC Zipursky, 'A Theory of Punitive Damages' (2005) 84 *Texas Law Review* 105.

[59] eg, D Priel, 'A Public Role for the Intentional Torts' (2011) 22 *King's Law Journal* 183; D Nolan, 'Tort and Public Law: Overlapping Categories?' (2019) 135 *LQR* 272.

[60] eg, R Stevens, *Torts and Rights* (Oxford, OUP, 2007) ch 4; EJ Weinrib, *Corrective Justice* (Oxford, OUP, 2012) 87–98; PB Miller and J Oberdiek (eds), *Civil Wrongs and Justice in Private Law* (Oxford, OUP, 2020); A Slavny, *Wrongs, Harms, and Compensation: Paying for our Mistakes* (Oxford, OUP, 2023).

[61] eg, R Zakrzewski, *Remedies Reclassified* (Oxford, OUP, 2005); SA Smith, *Rights, Wrongs, and Injustices: The Structure of Remedial Law* (Oxford, OUP, 2019); K Barnett and S Harder, *Private Law Remedies* (Cheltenham, Edward Elgar, 2025).

[62] eg, A Burrows, *Remedies for Torts, Breach of Contract, and Equitable Wrongs*, 4th edn (Oxford, OUP, 2019); Edelman, Varuhas and Higgins (n 5).

[63] This concerns mostly textbooks. In more detail, see the literature referenced in n 575.

[64] eg, S Harder, *Measuring Damages in the Law of Obligations: The Search for Harmonised Principles* (Oxford, Hart Publishing, 2010).

[65] eg, D Winterton, *Money Awards in Contract Law* (Oxford, Hart Publishing, 2015).

[66] eg, J Stapleton, 'A New "Seascape" for Obligations: Reclassification on the Basis of Measure of Damages' in P Birks (ed), *The Classification of Obligations* (Oxford, Clarendon Press, 1997).

[67] eg, A Burrows, 'Comparing Compensatory Damages in Tort and Contract: Some Problematic Issues' in S Degeling, J Edelman and J Goudkamp (eds), *Torts in Commercial Law* (London, Thomson Reuters, 2011).

[68] eg, K Barnett, *Accounting for Profit for Breach of Contract: Theory and Practice* (Oxford, Hart Publishing, 2012).

[69] eg, J Goudkamp and E Katsampouka, 'An Empirical Study of Punitive Damages' (2018) 38 *OJLS* 90; J Goudkamp and E Katsampouka, 'Form and Substance in the Law of Punitive Damages' in A Robertson and J Goudkamp (eds), *Form and Substance in the Law of Obligations* (Oxford, Hart Publishing, 2019).

damages.[70] The present work is distinct from all those accounts in that it focuses on all NCDs in a way that distinguishes them from compensatory awards but not from the remedial category of damages at large. By doing so, the book shows that all measures of damages are reducible to two fundamentally distinct types (those giving wholly or predominantly effect to the protection of private interests and those giving wholly or predominantly effect to the protection of public interests) and works out the doctrinal implications that flow from this distinction.

V. A Book Outline and Methodology

The book has two parts: Part I ('Non-Compensatory Damages'), which seeks to analyse the doctrines governing the award of NCDs and identify their commonalities; and Part II ('Public Interest Damages'), which seeks to reinterpret NCDs as public interest damages, explore the implications associated with this interpretive account of the law, and show how this interpretive theory of NCDs can be adopted in practice.

Part I comprises chapters two to four. The ground-clearing chapters two and three can be read relatively swiftly, as they are not the centre of gravity in this book. They introduce a framework based on which individual types of NCDs can be analysed collectively and in contrast with compensatory awards, namely the framework of correlative and non-correlative justifying reasons for measures of damages. Thus, chapter two first consolidates the current law and doctrinal writings to explain what compensatory and non-compensatory damages have in common with each other. We see that, according to the established view, both compensatory and non-compensatory damages belong to the remedial category of damages, although the meaning of the term 'damages' gives rise to some complexities in relation to different measures of damages. The concept of 'damages' is thus explored. Next, chapter two turns to what distinguishes the two types of measure. Drawing on the existing literature, we see that the contrast is typically discussed with regard to the compensatory and non-compensatory *functions* of damages, rather than their specific doctrinal forms. The shortcomings of the existing functional approaches to different measures of damages are then discussed. It is proposed that if we want a robust method to compare and contrast different measures of damages by reference to their functions, we need to fix the meaning of a function of damages relative to the harm they seek to remedy. This way, we will be able to interpret both compensatory and non-compensatory damages at the same level of analysis and, thus, compare and contrast them with each other.

Chapter three argues that the harm (relative to which functions of damages can be ascertained and compared with each other) is best characterised as 'damage'

[70] eg, J Edelman, *Gain-Based Damages: Contract, Tort, Equity and Intellectual Property* (Oxford, Hart Publishing, 2002); E Hondius and A Janssen (eds), *Disgorgement of Profits: Gain-Based Remedies throughout the World* (Cham, Springer, 2015).

to protected interests. Chapter three defends this slightly idiosyncratic usage of the term 'damage' and then shows that all the various measures of damages in English law should, in principle, be reducible to just two discrete types: (i) measures justified by damage to private interests (in other words, measures justified by considerations giving effect to individual rights), or (ii) measures justified by considerations not based on individual rights, such as damage to public interests. Using the popular corrective justice terminology, these two types of justifying reason for measures of damages can be referred to as correlative and non-correlative damage. It is contended that – if the distinction between the two types of harm is actually present in the cases – the law should acknowledge these two fundamental justifications because the distinctions between them could have important doctrinal implications. Finally, it is concluded that if compensatory damages stand in contrast with NCDs, then NCDs could tentatively be defined as damages justified by non-correlative damage or, in other words, as damages justified by considerations that do not give effect to individual rights (such as public interests).

Chapter four tests the tentative definition of NCDs, ie, whether they are justified by non-correlative reasons. We see in chapter four that most types of NCDs are indeed so justified or, to be more precise, that the reasons that justify those NCDs can collectively be interpreted as non-correlative reasons. We see that these reasons are sometimes even expressly referred to as public interests. We see that the usage of the term NCDs in the primary sources is fully consistent with the idea that NCDs can be interpreted as damages justified by non-correlative reasons and that these remedies stand in sharp contrast with compensatory damages. Importantly, chapter four confirms that the distinction between the two fundamental justifications for measures of damages is real, although it is not yet clear at this stage in the book whether all the non-correlatively justified damages are in fact justified by damage to public interests. The analysis in chapter four also tackles some difficulties concerning the established understanding of nominal, contemptuous, vindicatory and restitutionary damages and suggests how to deal with those difficulties.

Part II of the book, as was stated, offers a positive account of NCDs *qua* public interest damages; it works out the implications thereof and discusses pathways to its practical adoption. Part II comprises chapters five to seven. Chapter five advances the theory of NCDs *qua* public interest damages. It focuses on the idea of public interests and explores whether the 'non-correlativity' and 'publicness' of protected interests are two sides of the same coin and, relatedly, whether all non-correlatively justified NCDs can be defined as damages justified by damage to public interests, or as 'public interest damages' for short. Chapter five answers both of these questions in the affirmative. It is argued that the 'public interest damages' category should be the focal point of our attention if we want to understand damages that stand in contrast with compensatory awards. The somewhat unstable category of NCDs should thus be reinterpreted in terms of 'public interest damages'. A clear advantage of the 'public interest damages' definition is that it informs us about the nature of these awards independently of our understanding of compensatory damages, ie, it tells us what the non-correlative justifying reasons are (as opposed to what they are not). This, in turn, helps us to focus on the questions concerning when such public interest damages are justified (as opposed to when they are not justified).

To achieve its aims, chapter five starts by analysing the notion of public interest and the role of public interests in interpersonal disputes. It does so by observing and analysing the law's own well-established use of public interests when adjudicating interpersonal disputes. It then suggests a method of determining whether the matters in dispute are matters of public interest. The accuracy of the method – which I call a 'hypothetical waiver' method – is then tested against the leading cases concerning damages with a view to seeing whether the theory of NCDs *qua* public interest damages would lead to the same outcomes as the current doctrines and whether we can thus say that all non-correlatively justified damages are damages justified by damage to public interests. It is concluded in chapter five that the method is accurate and that the 'public interest' definition of NCDs is thus consistent with the authorities.

To be sure, the definition of NCDs *qua* public interest damages is interpretive in nature (I will say more on this book's methodology shortly), as it respects central uses of a term, but can be stipulative on others. By central uses, I mean the law's own uses of the term. By other uses, I mean the scholarship's treatment of the term NCDs in relation to contemptuous and restitutionary damages. The book's definition of NCDs *qua* public interest damages thus captures punitive, nominal, vindicatory and disgorgement damages, but not contemptuous and restitutionary damages. As such, the definition fits with the core uses of the term NCDs and successfully explains the meaning of the NCDs term as it appears in the primary legal sources. It is thus no objection to the 'public interest' definition of NCDs that it is stipulative or even prescriptive in relation to the literature's (and in this sense non-core) understanding of the term NCDs.

Chapter six then advances a normative argument about why we should seek to apply and develop 'public interest damages' collectively, rather than as a series of unrelated public interest awards. The book demonstrates that the similarities amongst public interest damages and the distinctions between compensatory and non-compensatory damages (*qua* public interest damages) are too important to be ignored. We see that various forms of public interest damages overlap very significantly with each other even though they are statedly unrelated remedies. We also see that public interest damages attract distinctive ethical considerations which require us to argue for or against these remedies in a different way from how we argue for or against compensatory awards. The difference is explained in chapter six with a view to advancing the law of NCDs in a fair, consistent and principled manner. It is argued that we should approach them collectively as a distinct class of remedies, but without unifying them altogether. Rather, the overlaps amongst different forms of public interest damages require us to re-think how we quantify the specific measures of NCDs and how we co-ordinate those measures and their availability.

Chapter seven works out several other doctrinal implications of the public interest analysis of NCDs, and, by doing so, it shows a possible way forward for the law of damages. It argues, inter alia, that public interest damages should not be available as of right and that the courts should be more active when identifying the non-correlative reasons for those awards. The text also discusses whether this normative claim can be reconciled with the law as it stands. Finally, chapter seven deals with possible objections to the theory of NCDs *qua* public interest damages. It concludes that all of those objections can be met and that there are good reasons to adopt the public interest analysis of NCDs, especially since the collective approach to public interest damages does not require us to compromise the key doctrines governing the award of NCDs.

Chapter eight concludes by highlighting the main claims and the key tensions that emerged from the book's findings. It also evaluates the success of the theory of NCDs *qua* public interest damages as a whole. Overall, it is recommended that the interpretive account of NCDs *qua* public interest damages be accepted as a better way to understand this otherwise piecemeal and obscure area of the law.

Methodologically, as is probably clear to the reader by now, the book's main approach is theoretical: I theorise about an area of the law, and I do that with a particular methodological framework in mind. Namely, this book pursues an interpretive theory. An interpretive theory of law (if we were to rely on Smith's well-known account of: (i) historical, (ii) prescriptive, (iii) descriptive and (iv) interpretive theories),[71] results from 'a constant back and forth between theory and facts. A theorist's understanding of which facts are relevant is continually revised by the theorist's attempts – which themselves are continuously being revised – to understand those facts.'[72] Indeed, while Parts I and II work with the cases concerning NCDs and with the doctrines that govern their award, they do not discuss those cases and doctrines indiscriminately, without regard to the observables that can be meaningfully contrasted with similar observables in the case of compensatory awards and doctrines of compensation. Much of the theoretical groundwork that frames the interpretation (and hence the selection of the relevant facts) is done in chapters two and three.

Both the interpretive theory of NCDs and, relatedly, the definition of NCDs as 'public interest damages' can be evaluated against all four main success criteria as suggested by Smith – ie, the criterion of 'fit', 'coherence', 'morality' and 'transparency'.[73] The 'fit' of the theory with the data can be evaluated by reference to data about the usage of the term NCDs, data about the doctrines governing the types of damages referred to as NCDs and data about awards which are not easily explicable in compensatory terms.[74] The 'coherence' of the interpretive theory can be evaluated by looking at the unity of the core justifications behind NCDs and at

[71] S Smith, *Contract Theory* (Oxford, OUP, 2004) ch 1.
[72] ibid 11.
[73] ibid 7.
[74] See, especially, section III, ch 4, and ch 5, sections II, V and VI of the book.

the non-contradictoriness of explanations pertaining to individual types of NCDs as compared with compensatory awards.[75] The 'morality' of the theory can be evaluated based on how well the suggested interpretation portrays the law of NCDs as morally justified, intelligible and practically appealing.[76] And the 'transparency' of the theory can be assessed based on how well the interpretive theory accords with the law's internally stated explanations and justifications of NCDs.[77]

By the end of the book, I hope to persuade the reader that the suggested theory of NCDs *qua* public interest damages and the book's definition of NCDs are successful because they fit with the law's own usage of the term, explain the law of NCDs coherently, reveal the inner morality of NCDs in an appealing light, and increase the transparency of the law's own explanations and justifications of NCDs.

[75] See, especially, ch 3, section V, chs 5 and 6, and ch 7, section I.
[76] See, especially, chs 5 to 7.
[77] See, especially, chs 2 to 4.

PART I

Non-Compensatory Damages

2

Defining Damages and Their Functions

According to the scholarly literature, NCDs are united by the fact that they are not compensatory.[78] This observation, though, is as circular and empty as observing that all males are not non-males. Our definitional strategy must be better than that if we want to explore what can be said positively about NCDs as a category (rather than as a shorthand for a collection of unrelated awards). We need to find: (i) what NCDs have in common with compensatory awards; and (ii) how they differ.

To answer what NCDs and compensatory awards have in common, we need to understand what it means that NCDs are 'damages'. This is done in section I, which defines damages as remedial rights arising from court decisions in response to a civil wrong and wrongful consequences thereof. This definition will be relied on throughout the book. By defining 'damages', this book will thus exclude certain types of award from the scope of the overall inquiry, although those awards might in other contexts be labelled as damages by lawyers. That is not a weakness of the present endeavour. As put by Smith, '[i]ndeed, one of the aims of interpretive inquiries is to suggest how borderline cases should be classified'.[79] The main reason to limit the scope of the book in this way is to avoid the risk that the book would inadvertently end up comparing damages with non-damages – which would be, of course, a major methodological weakness.

To answer how NCDs and compensatory damages differ, we need to find the correct level of analysis at which all NCDs can be meaningfully compared and contrasted with compensatory awards. This is done in section II. In particular, it explains the conventional approach to classifying measures of damages by reference to their functions (also referred to as 'goals' or 'aims' in the literature). In this light, NCDs have arguably distinct non-compensatory functions or goals, albeit they are still 'damages', ie, albeit they have in common with compensatory awards that they rectify damage to some protected interests. Section II explores the benefits and limitations of this functional approach, and suggests that if compensatory awards respond to damage to private interests of the claimant (they are designed to put the claimant in a position he would have been in, with respect to his protected interests, had the wrong not occurred or

[78] See the text accompanying n 34.
[79] Smith (n 71) 9.

had the contract been performed), then NCDs must respond to something else than damage to the claimant's interests.

Section III concludes and sets the scene for the next chapter.

I. Non-Compensatory Damages as 'Damages'

NCDs are 'damages', provided that labels are being taken at face value. It is obvious that courts award punitive damages or nominal 'damages', for instance, and so it would be incorrect to exclude these non-compensatory awards from the 'damages' category. In this vein, this book assumes that both compensatory and non-compensatory damages are indeed 'damages', ie, that they share some common features. This starting point seems uncontroversial, perhaps even trivial, as nearly all writings discuss NCDs as a special category of 'damages' rather than a distinct kind of remedy altogether.

Of course, the label 'damages' is sometimes used as a shorthand for compensatory awards. For example, in *Leeds Industrial Co-Operative Society Ltd v Slack*, the House of Lords stated that 'the word "damages" means money compensation for wrong done'.[80] Similarly, it is not uncommon for legal dictionaries to define damages as a 'sum of money awarded by a court as compensation for a tort or a breach of contract'.[81] You may thus object to any systemic attempt to analyse both compensatory and non-compensatory damages, in view of the biased understanding of 'damages' in the sources.

Some may be even prepared to argue that the category of 'damages' ought to include only compensatory awards, but this book does not accept that position. According to Weinrib, for example, we should classify damages in full accord with 'a normative idea' of private law to which the present law may or may not fully conform.[82] It can be inferred from Weinrib's writings that damages ought to be justified by (and only by) correlative reasons. Weinrib argues why it is good that compensatory awards have this correlative rationale, and also why damages awards generally should not be justified by non-correlative reasons.[83] He claims that, as a matter of private law concerning relations between equals, the award of damages must (analytically) be only about these correlative reasons. According to Weinrib, '[t]he idea of correlativity shows, negatively, that the rights of private law cannot coherently be based on non-correlative notions'.[84] Hence, for Weinrib, NCDs do not even qualify as 'damages' because they do not fit the normative idea

[80] *Leeds Industrial Co-Operative Society Ltd v Slack* [1924] AC 851 (HL) 868.

[81] eg, J Law (ed), *A Dictionary of Law*, 9th edn (Oxford, OUP, 2018), entry 'damages'. Similarly, see J Simpson and E Weiner (eds), *The Oxford English Dictionary*, 2nd edn (Oxford, OUP, 1989), entry 'damage' ('the sum of money claimed or adjudged to be paid in compensation for loss or injury sustained').

[82] EJ Weinrib, 'The Juridical Classification of Obligations' in P Birks (ed), *The Classification of Obligations* (Oxford, Clarendon Press 1997) 37. See also Weinrib (n 60) 9–37.

[83] See, especially Weinrib (n 60) 87–98; EJ Weinrib, *The Idea of Private Law*, rev edn (Oxford, OUP, 2012) 133, 142, 226–27.

[84] Weinrib (n 60) 34.

of private law and therefore do not fit the 'distinctive internal rationality' of such private law.[85]

The analysis of NCDs in the present book is not dependent on any such normative view of private law or of the category of damages. For the purposes of this book, nothing follows from whether we characterise specific measures of damages as 'private law' remedies or not. Rather, this book starts from the undeniable (descriptive) fact that current English law contains certain types of award that cannot be understood in compensatory terms and that are sometimes referred to as NCDs. It is thus sensible to define the term 'damages' in a way that: (i) accords with the conventional understanding of the term, but which (ii) does not exclude NCDs from the overarching category of damages.

So what do I mean by 'damages' in this book? As per the conventional understanding, 'damages' are a monetary award for a civil wrong and wrongful consequences thereof.[86] I will adopt this conventional understanding, although it gives rise to some complexities.

In particular, since this book focuses on damages in tort and contract, it needs to be acknowledged that this conventional understanding captures also wrongs-based monetary remedies outside tort and contract. In *Hall Bros Steamship Co Ltd v Young*, for example, the Court of Appeal observed that

> [t]he word "damages" is one which to an English lawyer conveys a sufficiently precise meaning. … "Damages" to an English lawyer imports this idea, that the sums payable by way of damages are sums which fall to be paid by reason of some breach of duty or obligation, whether that duty or obligation is imposed by contract, by the general law, or legislation.[87]

It follows that 'reparative' equitable compensation (ie, a personal remedy in equity dependent on proof of a loss which requires 'the trustee or custodial fiduciary to make good the loss resulting from the relevant breach'[88]) would fit this broad understanding of 'damages', albeit courts do not normally refer to such awards as 'damages'.[89] Similarly, a court-ordered account of profits gives rise to rights that are, from the claimant's perspective, effectively the same as rights arising from the order of damages.[90]

However, for reasons explained in chapter one, this broad understanding of damages should not be put to the book's debit. On the contrary, this understanding

[85] See Weinrib (n 82) 37.

[86] See, eg, Edelman, Varuhas and Higgins (n 5) paras 1-001 and 1-015 and *BPE Solicitors v Hughes-Holland* [2017] UKSC 21, [2017] 2 WLR 1029 [38].

[87] *Hall Bros Steamship Co Ltd v Young* [1939] 1 KB 748 (CA) 756.

[88] J Ward, 'Equitable Compensation – An Overview' in S Degeling and J Varuhas (eds), *Equitable Compensation and Disgorgement of Profit* (Oxford, Hart Publishing, 2019) 74 (footnote omitted). See also W Tan, 'Unpacking the Enigma of Equitable Compensation for Breaches in Equity' [2022] *Journal of Business Law* 407.

[89] *Main & Ors (Giambrone & Law (a firm) & Ors* [2017] EWCA Civ 1193 [45]–[64] (discussing structural similarities between equitable compensation and damages, yet distinguishing between the two remedies). See also Edelman, Varuhas and Higgins (n 5) 1-011.

[90] *cf* S Watterson, 'An Account of Profits or Damages? The History of Orthodoxy' (2004) 24 *OJLS* 471.

will help us to better grasp the category of disgorgement damages (which are arguably found in both common law and equity). It will also help us to investigate the nature of punitive damages under statute. By 'damages' I will thus refer to all judicial monetary remedies, regardless of the claim, awarded to the claimant in response to relevant wrongdoing and wrongful consequences thereof.

Broad as it may seem, this conventional definition of 'damages' is limited to awards based on a civil wrong (a breach of a legal duty owed to another).[91] Owing to this limitation, the meaning of 'damages' does not, contrary to what some authors argue, mean mere 'pecuniary satisfaction obtainable by success in an action'.[92] In this sense, the line between damages and other court-ordered money awards can be drawn alongside the division between wrongs-based and non-wrongs-based awards.

This has important implications for the scope of the book. The conventional definition of 'damages' does not include non-wrongs-based awards such as court-ordered costs, interest, statutory reimbursement, restitution of unjust enrichment, debt, an award of an agreed sum and generally any compensation not dependent on a wrong.[93] It is now well established, for example, that restitution of unjust enrichment (unlike restitution of gains obtained by wrongfully taking something from the claimant) is distinct from 'damages' because the liability-establishing event that underpins restitution of unjust enrichment is not a civil wrong.[94] Similarly, all the various awards of statutory compensation which are unconcerned with wrongdoing should not be classified as 'damages'. For instance, in *Harpur v The Mayor, Aldermen, and Burgesses of Swansea*, undertakers who laid down water pipes were obliged to pay compensation for any damage which they caused in the execution of their powers. The works were carried out in compliance with the Waterworks Clauses Act 1847, and the compensation duty in that case was thus prescribed even though there was no civil wrong.[95] And similarly, the fact that an award of costs or interest fulfils some compensatory function does not imply that the award is to be classified as 'damages'.

Importantly, it follows from the wrongs-based definition of 'damages' that the non-compensatory element to the award of enhanced interest on costs under CPR (see chapter one, section III[96]) should not be analysed under the heading of

[91] For the purposes of this book, I will not dispute that the concept of a civil wrong includes both fault-based wrongs and wrongs that trigger liability regardless of one's fault (including no-fault liability). *cf*, eg, P Jaffey, 'Liabilities in Private Law' (2008) 14 LEG 233, 239–40 and J Goudkamp and J Murphy, 'The Failure of Universal Theories of Tort Law' (2015) 21 *Legal Theory* 47, 80–81 (pointing out that strict liability is not always understood as liability based on a breach of a duty, ie, on a wrong).

[92] F Gahan (ed), *Mayne's Treatise on Damages*, 10th edn (London, Sweet and Maxwell, 1927) 1.

[93] *cf* R Blackburn, A Tettenborn and A Wilson (eds), *Halsbury's Laws*, 5th edn (London, LexisNexis, 2019) vol 29, para 304.

[94] eg, *Lipkin Gorman v Karpnale Ltd* [1991] 2 AC 548 (HL) 572. See also P Birks, *Unjust Enrichment*, 2nd edn (Oxford, OUP, 2005) 9; G Virgo, *The Principles of the Law of Restitution*, 3rd edn (Oxford, OUP, 2015) 427; R Stevens, *The Laws of Restitution* (Oxford, OUP, 2023) Part VI.

[95] See *Harpur v The Mayor, Aldermen, and Burgesses of Swansea* [1913] AC 597 (HL) 602, 604 and 607.

[96] Especially the text to n 20.

'damages', unless we are prepared to say that the award in *Petrom* – which was the case where the non-compensatory function of the award was identified – in fact functioned as an award of 'damages'.[97] The penal interest rate under CPR will thus not form part of the central subject matter of this book, although it is referred to as a 'non-compensatory' award in the primary sources.[98]

One may argue that the wrongs-based definition of 'damages' is underinclusive because, sometimes, 'damages' are awarded as compensation for harms regardless of whether the harm is caused by a civil wrong. For example, the award of 'damages' in *Rylands v Fletcher* (the House of Lords expressly stated that the Court of Exchequer Chamber had awarded 'damages' to the claimant[99]) was not clearly linked to breach of any particular duty. Rather, the cause of action was the defendant's risky and 'non-natural use [of land]'[100] which had resulted in harm to the claimant's property. The harm was caused by 'the evil … of the escape of the water'[101] kept by the defendant on his land for his own purposes and at his own peril. One way to deal with this example might be to state that, insofar as the rule in *Rylands v Fletcher* gives rise to a tort, the award in *Rylands* must be wrongs-based because every tort is conceptually a wrong. Another way to deal with this example might be to say that the award was not one of damages, but simply compensation for the harm caused by a risky activity. It is not necessary to resolve the tension in this work because the book is primarily about NCDs. Yet it is good to keep in mind that the conventional wrongs-based definition of damages raises similar issues and has normative implications for where we draw the line between damages and non-damages.[102]

Finally, it needs to be clarified that this book discusses damages in a specific sense as remedial rights that 'arise from a particular class of events, namely, the making of certain judicial commands or statements'.[103] This is because the decision to award punitive damages is discretionary, according to the House of Lords

[97] In more detail, see Janeček (n 21), where it is argued that while the enhanced interest award in *Petrom* (n 20) can be seen as a functional equivalent of punitive damages, this functional interpretation must be wrong because the decision in *Petrom* would be at odds with the House of Lords authority in *Rookes v Barnard* [1964] AC 1129 (HL) (Rookes case).

[98] This new penal type of CPR sanction has been already confirmed in several cases: *Jordan v MGN Ltd* [2017] EWHC 1937 (Ch), [2017] 4 Costs LR 687; *Mohammed v Home Office* [2017] EWHC 3051 (QB), [2018] 1 WLR 1780; *Bruma v Hassan* [2018] EWHC 248 (QB); *Triple Point Technology, Inc v PTT Public Company Ltd* [2018] EWHC 45 (TCC), [2018] 1 Costs LR 111 [18]; *Assetco Plc v Grant Thornton UK LLP* [2019] EWHC 592 (Comm) [30]–[50]; *Price v Saundry* [2019] EWHC 1039 (Ch) [61]; *Hochtief (UK) Construction Ltd & Anor v Atkins Ltd* [2019] EWHC 3028 (TCC) [16].

[99] *Rylands v Fletcher* (1868) LR 3 HL 330, 338.

[100] ibid 339.

[101] ibid 339.

[102] A similar argument about the non-wrongs-based nature of some 'damages' can be made, for example, about 'damages' under the Consumer Protection Act 1987. The Act uses the word 'damages' in the sense of compensation for the harm caused, rather than in the sense of a remedy for a civil wrong. See also *Vincent v Lake Erie Transp Co* (1910) 109 Minn 456, 124 NW 221 and MS Bedke, 'Explaining compensatory duties' (2010) 16 *Journal of Legal Theory* 91.

[103] Zakrzewski (n 61) 46–47. See also R Halson and D Campbell (eds), *Research Handbook on Private Law Remedies* (Cheltenham, Edward Elgar, 2019); Smith (n 61) especially ch 4.

decision in *Rookes*,[104] and the court will always need to consider whether the compensation payable is adequate to serve the punitive aims.[105] When analysing NCDs, it is thus descriptively accurate to rely on the definition of damages as remedial rights that arise from a judgment. So while some may want to define 'damages' as a pre-judgment right (or a duty)[106] that may arise directly from the relevant wrong, this definition would be too narrow because it would exclude punitive damages (which never arise independently of a court decision). By implication, the understanding of damages adopted in this book therefore leaves open the question whether individual types of damages are owed to the claimant as of right or not. This particular question will be addressed in chapter seven.

II. Compensatory and Non-Compensatory Functions of Damages

Now that we have seen what NCDs have in common with compensatory awards, let us turn to what is distinct about NCDs. According to the literature, various measures of damages are typically distinguished from each other by reference to their functions. Thus, the literature typically highlights that NCDs do not have compensation as their (main) function. In particular, the literature most often distinguishes between the remedial functions of: (i) compensation on the one hand, and (ii) restitution, (iii) punishment, (iv) deterrence and (v) declaration on the other hand.[107]

But how far does this functional approach take us? Is the functional approach well suited to defining NCDs in contrast with compensatory awards? Let us try to unpack some answers to these questions. Adopting this functional understanding of damages, we could say that NCDs (as opposed to compensatory awards) pursue restitution, punishment, deterrence and/or declaration as their main aim. This is a fairly conventional understanding of NCDs.

Here are three difficulties with the functional approach (I will talk about them in more detail throughout this section). First, there is no universal agreement as to how we divide the functions of damages. Second, while individual categories of damages may pursue certain functions, they are not defined by those functions. And so the line between compensatory and non-compensatory categories of damages cannot be the same as the line drawn according to the supposed dividing line between distinct functions of damages. Third, it is unclear what a 'function' of damages means and therefore whether we can meaningfully compare the stated

[104] *Rookes* (n 97) 1160.
[105] ibid 1227–28.
[106] *cf* S Smith, 'Why Courts Make Orders (and What This Tells us About Damages)' (2011) 64 *Current Legal Problems* 51; J Gardner, 'Damages without Duty' (2019) 69 *University of Toronto Law Journal* 412; S Steel and R Stevens, 'The Secondary Legal Duty to Pay Damages' (2020) 136 *LQR* 283.
[107] See, eg, AS Burrows, 'Judicial Remedies' in AS Burrows (ed), *English Private Law*, 3rd edn (Oxford, OUP, 2013) 1257.

five functions of damages to each other. This means that we run into the risk that the compensatory and non-compensatory functions of damages could overlap, making it impossible to use them as the basis for clearly distinguishing compensatory from non-compensatory damages.

I think we can avoid these difficulties, at least partly, by pinning down more precisely what we mean by a 'function' of damages. I will show that the 'functions' can be compared with each other at the same level of analysis if we define them relative to how they respond to some harmful interference with protected interests. This way, the functions may vary, but the element relative to which they are defined will be fixed. Building on the definition of 'damages' from section I, it is thus argued that functions of damages can be defined relative to the harm caused by the civil wrong which the award is supposed to remedy. Different conceptions of compensable harm are then discussed to explore what understanding of compensation is best suited to drawing a line between NCDs and compensatory awards. This will, by way of implication, lead us to a tentative definition of NCDs on which further chapters will build.

The first difficulty with the functional definition of NCDs is that there is no agreement as to how we characterise and organise all the various functions that damages can fulfil and, more importantly, which list of functions is the most accurate and exhaustive. This raises the question as to which list of functions is best suited to defining NCDs. For example, Stevens would contrast a substitutive function of damages with a compensatory function. Stevens holds that all damages (including nominal and punitive) can be at least partly explained as the 'next best' substitute for the primary right infringed[108] and that they need to be distinguished from additional 'consequential damages [awarded] as compensation'.[109] On this view, it would seem that 'substitutive damages' are not compensatory, but it would be a stretch to say that substitutive damages and NCDs are synonyms.[110] Stevens's rights-based theory helpfully puts all damages at the same level of analysis: they are all justified by a violation of the claimant's right. However, his rights-based interpretation of damages denies the very distinction this book seeks to analyse: the distinction between compensatory and non-compensatory types of damages. According to Stevens, the distinction between compensatory damages (in the sense of consequential damages) and substitutive damages is similar to the distinction between damages for 'consequential loss' and damages for 'direct loss'.[111] Under his framework, substitutive damages thus include awards that compensate direct losses.

In this light, Stevens's substitutive function of damages cannot be seen as equivalent to non-compensatory functions of damages. If it were so seen, we

[108] Stevens (n 60) ch 4.
[109] ibid 60.
[110] See ibid ch 4.
[111] See ibid 62. Although this is a bit misleading because substitutive damages are 'available even though no [direct] loss is suffered as a matter of fact' – ibid 62.

would be committed to saying that NCDs are in the same class with damages that have compensatory functions. And so while Stevens argues that substitutive damages are 'not compensatory for [consequential] loss at all',[112] it would be misleading to make any association between NCDs and substitutive damages in this book. Indeed, Stevens himself does not say that all substitutive damages are NCDs in any established sense of the term 'non-compensatory'. For example, writing about damages for breach of contract awarded where '[a] purchaser of goods is entitled to the difference in value between the goods he was promised and those he received',[113] Stevens claims that the substantial award is a next-best substitute for the right to the promised goods, but he does not claim that the award is non-compensatory. True, the quantum of the award is, according to Stevens, not affected by the absence of any actual loss.[114] But this does not mean that we cannot analyse the same award as compensation for the loss (or diminution) of a right to obtain the promised performance. Thus, in order to define the NCDs in contrast with compensatory awards, we cannot simply rely on Stevens's rights-based approach and the contrast between substitutive and compensatory functions.

Another classification of functions can be found in Zakrzewski's *Remedies Reclassified*, where all remedies are said to have either replicative or transformative functions.[115] But again, such a division of functions – while insightful in its own right – is not well suited to defining NCDs. This is because the distinction between replicative and transformative functions does not (at least not directly) acknowledge the very distinction that this book tries to understand, ie, the distinction between compensatory damages and NCDs. It may be the case that all replicative awards are compensatory and all transformative awards are non-compensatory. But if we want to analyse NCDs, it seems methodologically problematic to start by looking at functions which the law does not yet expressly acknowledge.

Thus, if we are to adopt a functional definition of NCDs, it is good to begin with the law's own categories. Accordingly, we will focus on the five functions (compensation, restitution, punishment, deterrence and declaration) because these trace the law's own language when it comes to functions of damages.[116] Besides, the doctrinal scholarship cited in chapter one, section III also typically discusses these five functions as distinct objectives of damages. It is thus preferable to take this conventional classification of functions as our starting point.

[112] ibid 62.
[113] ibid 70.
[114] ibid 70.
[115] See Zakrzewski (n 61) ch 5.
[116] *cf* PBH Birks, 'The Law of Restitution at the End of an Epoch' (1999) 28 *University of Western Australia Law Review* 13, 17 (discussing the functions of restitution, compensation, punishment, perfection and other goals); or G Calabresi, *The Cost of Accidents: A Legal and Economic Analysis* (New Haven, Yale University Press, 1970) 16, (stating that the two principal goals of accident law are justice and cost reduction, and that spreading of costs and general deterrence are approaches or methods for achieving goals).

The second difficulty is that, while we may identify the stated non-compensatory functions of damages, it would be wrong to replace the question about what NCDs have in common with the question about what non-compensatory functions of damages have in common. Related as they are, those two questions must not be confused because a single damages award may have multiple functions. In other words, the disparate doctrinal categories of damages cannot be perfectly mapped onto disparate functions of damages. So while we may agree that restitution, punishment, deterrence and declaration can be distinguished from 'compensatory' functions of damages, it does not mean that compensatory damages cannot have punitive functions or, vice versa, that punitive damages cannot have compensatory functions. For example, what one sees as punishment (relative to his epistemic perspective), another person may understand as compensation and vice versa. Punishment can be a goal intended by the court when it grants punitive damages, but also an effect perceived by the defendant when he has to pay damages.[117] Indeed, it is clear from *Rookes* that punitive damages can be awarded only if the compensation payable to the claimant is inadequate to serve the punitive goals,[118] which means that compensatory damages can have punitive functions. And vice versa, punitive damages can have compensatory effects when, for example, the compensatory award is insufficient to eliminate the loss for one reason or another (eg, when part of the claim is time-barred). The root of this difficulty is, I think, that the stated five functions do not map onto a single framework and can hardly be compared with each other at the same level of analysis.[119]

This brings us to the third difficulty with the functional approach to defining NCDs. It remains unclear how the five functions relate to each other, whether they overlap and why, or when they are (in)compatible with each other.[120] We may try to overcome this difficulty by specifying in detail what we mean by a 'function' of damages and how such functions are ascertained. For example, in his book *The Anatomy of Tort Law*, Cane writes that functions are purposes or goals.[121] But then we run into further questions. How do we define a 'goal', say the purpose to create compensatory rights through a court order? Are there any objective criteria for such a definition? Is the purpose what the judge aims to achieve by the award?

[117] See also K Barker, 'Punishment in Private Law – No Such Thing (Any More)' in E Bant, W Courtney and J Goudkamp (eds), *Punishment and Private Law* (Oxford, Hart Publishing, 2021) 41–43.

[118] *Rookes* (n 97) 1227–28. See also *Rees & Ors v Commissioner of Police of the Metropolis* [2019] EWHC 2339 (QB) [12] (stressing that the test applies to inadequacy of both compensatory and aggravated damages).

[119] See more in P Birks, 'Definition and Division: A Meditation on *Institutes* 3.13' in P Birks (ed), *The Classification of Obligations* (Oxford, Clarendon Press, 1997) who argues that '[i]ntersecting categories cause chaos and injustice' (ibid 23). The functional approach to private law and remedies is also contested by, eg, Weinrib (n 83) 3–8 and Stevens (n 60) 36.

[120] Though it is true that we know, for instance, that compensatory and gain-based damages cannot be obtained in respect of a single wrong. See *Ministry of Defence v Ashman* (1993) 25 HLR 513 (CA) 519 (discussed also in Goudkamp and Nolan (n 29) 23-036).

[121] P Cane, *The Anatomy of Tort Law* (Oxford, Hart Publishing, 1997) 206.

Is the purpose what the claimant seeks to obtain by filing a claim? No satisfactory answer to these questions has yet been provided in the literature.

A better way to understand the functions of damages is then, I think, to assess them relative to some objective feature of all damages awards. By doing so, we would at least put all damages and their functions on a level playing field. Let us try to do that, using the definition of 'damages' from section I as the starting point. If 'damages' are defined as a monetary award for a civil wrong and wrongful consequences thereof, we can assume that the function of damages can always be assessed relative to harmful consequences of the civil wrong. That seems straightforward. To put the same point more briefly, let us assume that the function of all damages is to remedy some damage to protected interests and that the function can thus be ascertained relative to that damage.

So in the case of compensatory damages, for example, the damage relative to which the award fulfils its compensatory function is typically the claimant's actual loss. Actual loss is understood here as being factually (rather than normatively) worse off. Indeed, the orthodox function of compensatory damages is to put the claimant in a position he would have been in, with respect to his actual loss, had the wrong not occurred or had the contract been performed. The compensatory function can thus be ascertained here by looking at the relationship between the award and the claimant's actual loss which flows from the civil wrong (be it a loss of performance, loss of amenity, loss of earnings, loss of property, etc).

Now, accepting that the function of all 'damages' is to rectify damage to some protected interests,[122] we can start seeing that individual categories of damages can rectify damage to a wider range of protected interests. This could help us to see that individual categories of damages can fulfil multiple functions. That said, accepting the orthodox definition of the compensatory damages – associated with the main function of compensatory awards – it would follow that NCDs must not put the claimant into the position he would have been in, with respect to his loss, had the wrong not occurred. To put the same point positively, it would follow that NCDs must either:

(i) fulfil this purpose (ie, that NCDs put the claimant in a position he would have been in had the wrong not occurred) with respect to something else than the claimant's loss, or
(ii) fulfil a different purpose, but still function as a remedy for damage to some protected interests.

Both of these functional definitions of NCDs are promising in that they put NCDs in direct contrast with compensatory awards and in that these two definitions are clearly comparable with the functional definition of compensatory damages. However, the first suggested definition must be rejected because it is at odds with individual types of NCDs. On the one hand, we could apply the first definition

[122] In more detail on this idiosyncratic usage of the word 'damage', see ch 3.

of non-compensatory functions to restitutionary damages: the purpose of restitutionary damages (the term 'restitutionary damages' will be explored in more detail in chapter four, section V) can be said to be to put the claimant in a position he would have been in, with respect to the defendant's gain (and not the claimant's loss), had the wrong not occurred. On the other hand, the same definition does not work for punitive damages. There is observably nothing with respect to which punitive damages would be designed to put the claimant in a position he would have been in had the wrong not occurred. Yes, punitive damages can have restorative or compensatory side-effects, but they are not designed to restore the claimant's position with respect to anything.

Another problem with the first suggested definition of NCDs is that while it may be sometimes difficult to conceptualise the claimant's suffering in terms of actual loss or provide evidence of such loss, '[s]uch difficulties do not justify the abandonment of any attempt to measure loss', as was explained by Lord Reed in *One Step*.[123] The gist of this statement is that damages can have compensatory functions even if there is no actual loss, because compensation rectifies loss in a broader sense. Thus, in *One Step*, it was ruled that negotiating damages are compensatory, even though they are not measured by actual loss.[124] As famously stated by Lord Shaw, 'wherever an abstraction or invasion of property has occurred … the law ought to yield a recompense [under the user principle of price or hire, even if] I restore the [property and t]here is no loss'.[125] Damages for such an infringement do not respond to actual loss but rather to loss of control over some right or asset. Such kind of loss is not loss 'proper' in that such loss is not experienced in the real world, and the fact of the loss (ie, whether it is true or not that the loss has occurred) is wholly dependent on the norms which created the valuable control rights in the first place. As put by Lord Reed, negotiating damages are awarded 'for the loss of the value of the exercise of that right'.[126] Thus, it can be argued that negotiating damages are compensatory, but they are compensatory in relation to normative loss rather than actual loss.

In order to retain the conventional meaning of loss as being factually worse off (ie, as 'actual loss'), it is then useful to describe the compensatory function in these cases as a goal to rectify, as far as money can do so, the damage to the claimant's protected interests. This will help us to avoid the confusing notion of loss (which sometimes means only actual loss and sometimes both actual and normative loss) when discussing the line between compensatory and non-compensatory damages.[127]

[123] *One Step (Support) Ltd v Morris-Garner* (n 15) [73] (Lord Reed (with whom Baroness Hale, Lord Wilson and Lord Carnwath agreed)).

[124] ibid [91] and [95]. See also J Senu, 'Negotiating Damages and the Compensatory Principle' (2020) 40 *OJLS* 110.

[125] *Watson, Laidlaw & Co Ltd v Pott, Cassels & Williamson* [1914] SC (HL) 18, 31 (Lord Shaw).

[126] *One Step (Support) Ltd v Morris-Garner* (n 15) [95].

[127] For a detailed analysis of the analytical difficulties with the current notion of loss in the law of damages, see, S Steel, 'Damages without Loss' (2023) 139 *LQR* 219.

Thus, instead of the notion of 'loss', this book will rely on the notion of 'damage to protected interests' as a way to describe the consequential harm relative to which the function of damages can be ascertained. The idea of protected interests, or more precisely damage to protected interests, is relatively familiar[128] and well explains why awards made when a person's right has been interfered with, but not necessarily through causation of actual loss,[129] are often characterised as compensatory. This applies not only to negotiating damages as discussed above but also to, for example, aggravated damages. By recognising the compensatory function of aggravated damages (and despite the law's own rhetoric that might otherwise resemble the language of punitive damages), English law has made it clear that injury to dignity, and the claimant's feelings of distress and outrage are compensable by these awards.[130] A convenient way to describe this compensation through aggravated damages, alongside compensation for any actual loss that the claimant may have suffered, is thus to say that it is a remedy for damage to the claimant's private interests.

All this demonstrates that a key part of the difficulty with contrasting compensatory with non-compensatory functions of damages is the concept of loss itself. For example, a single incident that sets back the claimant's protected interests – let us imagine loss of money – can be analysed as either actual loss (loss of cash) or normative loss (diminution of monetary rights), depending on our level of abstraction.[131] As is observed in the scholarship, the law's own understanding of compensable harm can be explained not only as compensation for 'being factually worse off',[132] but also as some kind of remedy for normative loss, or diminution of a right.[133] In other words, compensation is not necessarily restricted to 'loss' in the strict sense of 'actual loss'. Yes, compensation is made on the *restitutio in integrum* principle (the principle that the claimant should be put in a position he would have been in but for the wrong[134]) and this principle is associated with all loss-based compensation.[135] In fact, some argue that '[w]ith the exception of exemplary damages, … the function of all heads of damage is to compensate the plaintiff on the principle of

[128] See, eg, Goudkamp and Nolan (n 29) para 7-007.

[129] For this conception of 'damage', see D Nolan, 'Rights, Damage and Loss' (2016) 36 *OJLS* 1.

[130] Indeed, aggravated were formally distinguished from exemplary damages in *Rookes* in 1964 as 'a by-product of the [House of Lords'] rationalisation of the law of exemplary damages', when it was clarified that aggravated damages are compensatory (M Tilbury, 'Aggravated Damages' (2018) 71 *Current Legal Problems* 215, 220 (cited according to N Sinanis, 'Punishment in Tort: The Context of Ideas in *Rookes v. Barnard*' (2022) 15 *Journal of Tort Law* 29, 30)).

[131] See also E Descheemaeker, 'The Standardisation of Tort Damages' (2021) 84 *MLR* 1, 9–16 and E Descheemaeker, 'Pecuniary and Non-pecuniary Loss: A Reinterpretation' (2022) 138 *LQR* 79, 89 and 90.

[132] See, especially, Stevens (n 60) 59 and 78.

[133] In more detail, see E Descheemaeker, 'Unravelling Harms in Tort Law' (2016) 132 *LQR* 595, 613–14.

[134] *Livingstone v Rawyards Coal Co* (n 2) 39 (Lord Blackburn). See also *Owners of Dredger Liesbosch v Owners of Steamship Edison* (n 2) 459 (Lord Wright).

[135] See Edelman, Varuhas and Higgins (n 5) para 2-004.

restitutio in integrum'.[136] But this does not mean that the compensable harm cannot be construed more broadly than just as actual loss.

For example, Descheemaeker observes that there are two dominant conceptions of compensable harm in the English law of tort – a bipolar model under which compensation rectifies direct and consequential losses that flow from a civil wrong, and a unipolar model under which compensation rectifies any 'violation of the claimant's right or protected interest … [and thereby] conflate[s] the wrong and the loss'.[137] The first model compensates actual losses, and the second compensates normative losses, but both of these models are ultimately two sides of the same coin. As put by Descheemaeker, 'the (abstract) right-diminution, that is, the infringement of the claimant's right, is to be understood as the reverse side of these two (concrete) injuries, the economic loss and the emotional distress flowing from the wrong'.[138] Both of these alternative conceptions of compensable harm 'are interpretive frameworks capable, at least prima facie, of making sense of the entirety of tort law', states Descheemaeker.[139] It can be argued that both of these models are thus capable, in alternative ways, of defining the compensatory function of damages: one aiming to right the defendant's wrong with respect to the harmful consequences that the claimant has suffered; the other putting the claimant in a position he would have been in, with respect to his rights, had the wrong not occurred.

The problem is that compensation for actual loss and compensation for normative loss cannot be meaningfully analysed alongside each other because the two notions do not fight over the same territory: each of these conceptions of compensation operates at a different level of abstraction. Convenient as it may be for legal practice,[140] the flexible notion of 'loss' is thus highly problematic for the purposes of defining NCDs in this book. As we can see here, if we want our definition of a compensatory function of damages to capture different conceptions of compensable harm, we need to define it in a relatively abstract way. In this regard, it seems uncontroversial to define compensation in a broader sense as a function that seeks to put the claimant in a position he would have been in, with respect to damage to his legally protected interests (rather than just 'actual loss'), had the wrong not occurred.[141]

[136] H Street, *Principles of the Law of Damages* (London, Sweet & Maxwell, 1962) 3 (footnotes omitted).

[137] Descheemaeker (n 133) 598.

[138] ibid 600. Descheemaeker qualifies this statement by explaining that 'the diminution of the right *must* factor in the consequences – at least the direct consequences – of the wrong' (ibid, emphasis in original).

[139] ibid 603.

[140] See also V Janeček, 'Data Protection, the Value of Privacy and Compensable Damage' (2020) 79 *CLJ* 417, commenting on *Lloyd v Google LLC* [2019] EWCA Civ 1599, [2020] QB 747 where 'loss of control' was deemed to have resulted from the wrong regardless of proof of any actual damage or loss and where the court conflated various meanings of loss. See also *Lloyd v Google LLC* [2021] UKSC 50, [2021] 3 WLR 1268 [92] and [159] (noted in V Janeček, 'Mass Compensation Claims for Illegal Online Tracking' (2022) 138 *LQR* 205).

[141] For a powerful analytical critique of the conventional loss-based understanding of damages, demonstrating how descriptively unsustainable the loss-based account is, see A Summers, *Mitigation in the Law of Damages* (Oxford, OUP, 2024) 278.

This broadened understanding of the compensatory function has at least two important implications. One relates to our definition of non-compensatory functions and NCDs: they do not purport to remedy damage to the claimant's protected interests. Instead, NCDs probably serve some purpose other than to put the claimant in the position he would have been in had the wrong not occurred (I will return to this point later in this section), although they still function as a remedy for damage to some protected interests.

The second implication relates to how we should classify negotiating (sometimes also called user) damages cases. As rightly observed in a recent Australian decision in *Lewis*, 'the lack of any actual loss in … user principle cases has led numerous … English courts to describe these damages awards as restitutionary',[142] because the award is being calculated by reference to the objective value of the wrongful use of the claimant's property – ie, by reference to the defendant's gain. One might thus be tempted to believe that these awards have non-compensatory functions and, by the same token, that they are thus a type of NCDs. But such an understanding of non-compensatory functions is at odds with how the primary sources use the term NCDs (see chapter one, section III). In particular, primary sources do not label negotiating damages as a kind of NCDs. We should thus probably not classify these 'restitutionary damages' cases as cases of NCDs either. Chapter four will address this in more detail.

In fact, it is possible that the suggested understanding of the compensatory function of damages means that the restitutionary function of damages (if defined as putting the claimant in a position he would have been in, with respect to the defendant's gain, had the wrong not occurred) is, by implication, a redundant function. In *Experience Hendrix LLC v PPX Enterprises Inc*,[143] for example, the court made the award of so-called restitutionary damages by depriving the defendant of profits gained by their selling of Jimmy Hendrix's recordings, which profits were obtained by breach of a contract. Damages in this case reflected the defendant's gain (which is why the award is regarded as having a restitutionary function). But not all of the defendant's gain was taken from them. Instead, the aggrieved party only obtained a reasonable sum (user fee) in restitution for the wrongful use of Hendrix's recordings. The restitutionary award thus put the claimants in a position, with respect to their interests (as infringed by the wrongful gain), they would have been in had the wrong not occurred or as if a hypothetical user agreement had been concluded and performed. In other words, without going as far as to claim that the award in *Hendrix* should be labelled as compensatory damages, we could say that the award served a compensatory function (under the banner of the *restitutio in integrum* principle). In fact, this would not be so controversial. Stevens, for example, holds that compensation may be awarded for consequential 'loss to the claimant, or

[142] *Lewis v Australian Capital Territory* [2020] HCA 26, [2020] 271 CLR 192 [147] (footnote omitted).
[143] *Experience Hendrix LLC v PPX Enterprises Inc* [2003] EWCA Civ 323, [2003] 1 All ER (Comm) 830.

gain to the defendant'.[144] The compensable damage to the claimant's protected interests can be measured by actual loss or actual gain resulting from the wrong. This functional overlap between the two sub-types of compensation helps us to understand why, for instance, a claimant will often have to elect between loss-based and gain-based compensation.[145]

The correct classification of awards which are sometimes labelled as restitutionary damages must be left for chapter four. The point of this chapter is simply to demonstrate that the broadened understanding of compensatory functions of damages should not be viewed as controversial and that we can thus rely on it for the purposes of defining NCDs.

Let us turn now to the remaining three functions (punishment, deterrence and declaration) in order to try to see whether they can be contrasted with compensation for damage to the claimant's protected interests. Since the first suggested definition of non-compensatory functions was rejected, then it seems fair to accept that these non-compensatory functions – if they are to be contrasted with the function of compensation – therefore cannot be based on the orthodox *restitutio in integrum* principle. We may thus define NCDs as awards the function of which is in some way unconcerned with damage to the claimant's private interests.

This finally brings us to the second suggested definition of NCDs and their functions, according to which NCDs are damages that '(ii) fulfil a different purpose [than to put the claimant in a position he would have been in had the wrong not occurred], but still function as a remedy for relevant damage'.[146] Indeed, it seems that NCDs are not concerned with the claimant's position or with rectifying damage to the claimant's protected interests, but since they are 'damages', they must still – by definition – be concerned with rectifying some kind of damage. It is thus logical to accept the second suggested definition and to conclude that the function of all NCDs, if defined relative to the harm caused by the wrong, can be described as the goal of rectifying damage to some other type of protected interests than the claimant's private interests. At first glance, this definition seems to fit the ideas of punishment, deterrence and declaration. Punishment, deterrence and declaration – at least in the case of punitive and nominal damages – seem all justified without particular regard to the claimant's individual position and the claimant's suffering, provided we understand declaration as dealing with the infringement of objective legal rules, rather than subjective legal rights. The best method to ascertain what types of protected interest justify NCDs is to look at the relevant types of damages and analyse them in detail. This will be done in chapter four.

Here we can say that, at least on a conceptual level, this tentative definition of non-compensatory functions allows us to compare and contrast damages the

[144] Stevens (n 60) 60.

[145] See, eg, *Tang Man Sit (Deceased) v Capacious Investments Ltd* [1995] UKPC 54, [1996] AC 514 (PC) 521. For a critique of that decision, see P Birks, 'Inconsistency between Compensation and Restitution' (1996) 112 *LQR* 375.

[146] See p 32 above.

function of which is to rectify damage to some other than the claimant's private interests with compensation on the *restitutio in integrum* principle. As such, this understanding of non-compensatory functions allows us to compare and contrast NCDs and compensatory damages at the same level of abstraction, which is critical if we are to draw any clear line between them.

III. Conclusion

This section explored: (i) what NCDs have in common with compensatory awards, and (ii) how they differ. We saw what it means that both compensatory and non-compensatory awards are 'damages'. The main conceptions of 'damages' were discussed in section I, and it was concluded that, for the purposes of this book, it is best to accept that 'damages' are remedial rights arising from court decisions in response to a civil wrong and wrongful consequences thereof. In this light, all measures of damages can be broadly understood as awards that rectify the harmful consequences of a civil wrong. The implication of this definition of 'damages' was that orders of penal interest rate on costs (referred to as 'non-compensatory' by the courts) are not 'damages'. The penal interest rate will thus not be analysed as part of this book, although the interest rate was identified in chapter one, section III as an example in relation to which primary sources use the word 'non-compensatory'.

In accordance with the conventional view, section II distinguished five functions of damages (compensation, restitution, punishment, deterrence and declaration) and explored how compensatory and non-compensatory functions can be distinguished from each other and what this means for our definition of NCDs. We saw that it is useful to stabilise the functions of damages by reference to the harm they are supposed to rectify. In this light, it was argued, the dividing line between compensatory and non-compensatory damages depends on our conception of compensable harm. To account for the varying conceptions of compensable harm, it was suggested that we can define the compensatory function of damages as the goal of putting the claimant in a position he would have been in, with respect to his actual as well as normative loss, had the wrong not occurred. It was then argued that, for the purposes of this book and in order to avoid the confusions associated with the dual meaning of the term 'loss' (actual loss and normative loss), a convenient way to describe this function is to simply say that the goal of compensatory damages is to remedy damage to the claimant's protected interests. Such a description of compensable harm helps to capture the breadth of compensatory awards and, at the same time, serves as a useful foundation for a definition of non-compensatory functions of damages.

In particular, section II concluded that NCDs, unlike compensatory awards, are in some way unconcerned with damage to the claimant's private interests. It was argued that the function of NCDs is to rectify some other type of protected interest, because NCDs are not designed to put the claimant in a position he would have been in, with respect to his protected interests, had the wrong not occurred. Chapter four will test whether individual types of NCDs can be explained as 'damages' that fulfil such functions, and it will try to identify the specific types of protected interest that justify the non-compensatory measure of damages.

Of course, the suggested division between damages justified by interferences with the claimant's private interests and damages justified by interference with other protected interests is not something expressly discussed in the law or literature. Rather, it is this book's own interpretation and combination of the positions we find in the law and literature. This approach is motivated by the need to identify a single level of abstraction where compensatory and non-compensatory damages can be analysed in contrast with each other. Thus, given the relative novelty of this approach, the following chapter will explain in more detail how we can interpret – for the purposes of this book – the various justifying reasons behind measures of damages so that they are comparable with each other.

3

Correlative and Non-Correlative 'Damage'

The chief aim of chapter three is to show that all the different justifications for measures of damages must, in principle, be reducible to: (i) justifications based on considerations giving effect to individual rights, such as damage to private interests, or (ii) justifications not based on individual rights, such as damage to public interests. Or, to use the popular language of corrective justice theory, all justifications of measures of damages must be reducible to: (i) correlative damage, or (ii) non-correlative damage. These two types of justifying reason will then be used as the key framework for analysing NCDs in chapter four with a view to seeing whether NCDs are justified by non-correlative damage.

The ideas discussed in this chapter are not new. Instead, they are borrowed from the existing literature, although it is fair to say that authors do not discuss those ideas specifically in relation to NCDs. In this sense, the burden of chapter three is to go over some of the terrain that we find in the literature and to explain what we should (and should not) take from several established theoretical positions. We will see how the framework adopted in this book (ie, the distinction between correlative and non-correlative damage) relates to established views. By doing so, chapter three clears the ground for the analysis in chapter four, where it will be tested whether NCDs are indeed justified by non-correlative considerations.

Chapter three proceeds in six steps. Section I explains why the book adopts a wrongs-based, rather than rights-based analysis of damages. This will help us to see why interferences with protected interests, rather than simply interferences with rights, are the preferred characterisation of the reasons that justify measures of damages. Section II defends a slightly idiosyncratic definition of 'damage' as interference(s) with legally protected interests. Section III briefly explains what is meant by 'protected interests', and section IV deals with Weinrib's objection that protected interests should be irrelevant to any coherent analysis of private law institutions. Section V shows why all measures of damages must be reducible to measures justified by correlative or non-correlative damage, and it argues that the law should recognise these two fundamental justifications. Section VI concludes by identifying the key to a successful interpretive definition of NCDs (that will be tested in chapter four) and by highlighting the ethical dimensions of the framework introduced in chapter three.

I. Justifying Reasons for Measures of Damages

Let me begin with a distinction. There are reasons that justify the defendant's remedial liability, and there are reasons that justify specific measures of damages (sometimes also referred to as reasons that implement the remedial liability).[147] This book focuses on the measures of damages, not the defendant's liability. Thus, I will not be concerned here with the first set of reasons and with the nature of the liability establishing civil wrongs. Chapter two, section I already showed that a wrong, ie, a breach of duty, is traditionally seen as a universal liability-establishing reason for all damages awards. The more interesting question is, for the purposes of this book, what reasons justify the different measures of damages?

If damages are defined as a remedy for a civil wrong and wrongful consequences thereof – and this is how this monograph defines them in accord with the existing literature – then it is apparent why this book will focus on these consequences and not the wrongs in their role of justifying reasons for the relevant measure of damages. Conceptually, the distinction between the wrong and its consequences is clear. It is clear because, at least conceptually, it is impossible for the cause (the wrong) and the effect (the harmful consequences) to be identical. But in concrete cases, it is not always easy to distinguish between the two. For example, how can we ascertain that nominal damages rectify the consequences of the wrong, rather than the wrong itself? Or how can we ascertain that damages for abstract harms (sometimes conceived of in terms of right diminution or right violation)[148] compensate the claimant only for the harm caused by the wrong and not the wrong itself, ie, for the violation of the victim's claim-right? These questions are difficult for a range of reasons. One difficulty is that the distinction between the wrong and the consequences thereof does not always map onto any clear distinction in the real world. The absence of any observable distinction makes it difficult to pin down the contrast between the wrong and the resulting harm. Another difficulty is that both the wrong and its abstract consequences can be interpreted in terms of a rights

[147] This distinction is parallel with the line between liability establishing causation and liability implementing causation here. In English literature, for instance, Steel describes this difference as of between causation 'establishing the infringement of a right and any liability arising in response to the infringement alone (wrong-constituting causation)' and causation 'determining the extent of consequential liability in respect of a wrong or cause of action (consequential-liability causation)'. See S Steel, *Proof of Causation in Tort Law* (Cambridge, CUP, 2015) 38. The distinction between so-called '*haftungsbegründende Kausalität*', ie, the liability establishing causation, and '*haftungsausfüllende Kausalität*', ie, the liability implementing causation, plays a pivotal role in German theory. See, in short, U Magnus, 'Causation in German Tort Law' in J Spier (ed), *Unification of Tort Law: Causation* (Alphen aan den Rijn, Kluwer Law International, 2000) 63–64.

[148] But *cf* Stevens (n 60) 4. Stevens's rights-based model limits the notion of 'rights' to correlative 'claim-rights'. This, in turn, leaves him no room to discuss the consequential loss in terms of right diminution or in terms of damage to protected interest; he 'insist on setting rights and loss against one another' (Descheemaeker (n 133) 602). In essence, Stevens's rights-based model thus mixes a unipolar interpretation with a bipolar interpretation of compensable harm, which is untenable.

violation. This interpretation then obscures the divide between the two because both of them would be characterised as a violation of a right.[149]

In order to avoid the risk of muddling up the divide between the wrong and the harmful consequences thereof, the book adopts a wrongs-based analysis (rather than a rights-based analysis) of damages. This seemingly cosmetic shift of emphasis from rights to wrongs will help us to hold the line between the reasons that justify the remedial liability (the wrongs) and the reasons that justify the specific remedial measure (harmful consequences arising from the wrongs), because the concept of 'civil wrong' is associated with the liability-establishing reasons only. So while we characterise the harmful consequences in terms of rights violations or rights diminution, we do not characterise them as civil wrongs. The emphasis on the wrongs-based nature of damages will thus help us consistently to analyse damages as remedies for harmful *consequences* of the wrong, ie, for the resulting damage.

II. Resulting 'Damage'

Chapter two described the consequences of a civil wrong as interferences with protected interests or, briefly, as damage to protected interests. Let me defend this idiosyncratic usage of the word 'damage'. After all, in the law's own language, we do not normally justify all measures of damages by reference to damage to protected interests.

The fact that the law does not expressly justify damages by reference to resulting 'damage' to protected interests does not imply that damages cannot be interpreted in those terms. As I will show, the usage of the term 'damage' in this book is consistent with the established terminology concerning wrongs-based harm. In particular, a reinterpretation of damages in terms of awards justified by damage to protected interests does not compromise the established meanings of the terms 'loss' and 'damage'.

Loss, standardly, is what occurs when a person is worse off in some legally recognised respect than if his right had not been violated. Loss thus standardly means being actually worse-off as a result of the wrong and being worse-off in a comparative or counterfactual sense.[150] Not all loss is, however, actual loss, as was demonstrated earlier in section II of chapter two. Sometimes, the notion of loss includes both actual and normative loss. The counterfactual exercise by which we identify loss therefore concerns not only loss of actual possessions, but also loss of more abstract types of protected interest. When we determine the extent of loss, the same type of protected interest is placed in two situations (one real and

[149] See also the text to nn 137–139.

[150] See *Johnston v NEI International Combustion Ltd* [2007] UKHL 39, [2008] AC 281 (Rothwell case) [7]; *One Step (Support) Ltd v Morris-Garner* (n 15) [36].

the other counterfactual), and we compare how much worse off in relation to that interest the victim is. That is also why loss so neatly fits the idea of compensation, ie, putting the claimant in a position he would have been in had the wrong not occurred.[151] The notion of 'loss' was relied on in chapter two in order to find the correct level of analysis of compensatory functions of damages in contrast with non-compensatory functions. But while it is still true that NCDs are somehow unconcerned with compensation for loss, the notion of loss does not tell us positively anything about NCDs, and so the analysis can dispense with that notion.

The notion of 'damage' is much better in this regard because both compensatory and non-compensatory damages arguably rectify some kind of wrongs-based damage to protected interests.[152] Standardly, damage is what occurs when a person's right has been detrimentally interfered with, but not necessarily through causation of actual loss.[153] Indeed, the unfortunate occurrence of harm only stands for damage if it frustrates someone's legal right or, more broadly, someone's legally protected interest. '[T]he world is full of harm for which the law furnishes no remedy', as Lord Rodger said.[154] Present English law, for example, does not recognise 'liability for seducing another person's husband, wife or partner', although it used to do so in the past.[155] Seducing another person's husband could, morally speaking, constitute terrible harm to that person, but it does not constitute damage in a legal sense because it does not violate (currently) protected interests. As observed by Nolan and Goudkamp, '[i]t is impossible to devise a general definition of damage that avoids circularity. The best we can do is to say that damage means a certain kind of interference with a person's protected interests.'[156]

The notion of damage thus standardly includes both actual and normative consequences of the wrong, and also the liability-establishing injury (ie, the civil wrong which also amounts to an interference with protected interests of another person). As such, the notion of damage is broader than the notion of actual loss. For example, if one party breaches his contractual obligations and causes the other party actual loss of money, this loss can be analysed in terms of the resulting damage to the victim's rights. But not all damage to the victim's rights needs to be represented by any actual loss. For example, if someone infringes your copyright by using your online publications as part of training data for their large language model, this inclusion of the copyright-protected material in the training data would amount to damage, but there would be no actual loss because the digital

[151] Similarly, see, eg, *Nykredit Mortgage Bank Plc v Edward Erdman Group Ltd* [1997] 1 WLR 162 (HL) 1631 (Lord Nicholls) or *One Step (Support) Ltd v Morris-Garner* (n 15) [36] (Lord Reed).

[152] This was discussed in chs 2, section II and 3, section I.

[153] See D Nolan, 'Rights, Damage and Loss' (2016) 36 *OJLS* 1.

[154] *JD v East Berkshire Community Health NHS Trust* [2005] UKHL 23, [2005] 2 AC 373 [100]. On the same note, see, eg, Birks (n 119) 26.

[155] K Oliphant, 'Basic Questions of Tort Law from the Perspective of England and the Commonwealth' in H Koziol (ed), *Basic Questions of Tort Law from a Comparative Perspective* (Vienna, Jan Sramek Verlag, 2015) 407. See also s 5 of the Law Reform (Miscellaneous Provisions) Act 1970.

[156] Goudkamp and Nolan (n 29) para 7-007 (footnote omitted).

copies of your work are non-rivalrous. In other words, your rights and protected interests can be damaged, even if you did not actually lose your work. We could say, of course, that there is some kind of normative loss (eg, that you lost the right to control the copyright-protected work and that this is the flipside of the victim's damage). But as was discussed in section II of chapter two, this broad understanding of loss will not be relied on in this book because it confuses the supposed division between (loss-based) compensatory and (non-loss-based) non-compensatory damages.

As shall be clear, the phrase 'damage to protected interests' – as it will be used in this book – can include both actual damage (eg, a physical injury in the sense of a concrete factual consequence of the wrong) and normative damage (eg, injury in the sense of a right infringement stemming from the wrong).[157] This is consistent with the established uses of the word 'damage'. For example, in *Rothwell*, the House of Lords used the term damage in the sense of 'being worse off in some material or economic sense'.[158] And as Holt CJ famously wrote, 'surely every injury imports a damage, though it does not cost the party one farthing'.[159] The word damage can thus describe some abstract harm in the sense of *injuria*. It is no surprise in this light why some authors believe that '[t]he slippery language of "damage" elides the distinction between injury and consequential harm'.[160] The notion of damage or the phrase 'damage to protected interests' can thus be viewed as an acceptable description of the harm resulting from the wrong. And while it can also be used as a description of the liability-establishing harm, we are concerned here with measures of damages and, relatedly, with analysing only the resulting damage which implements the remedial liability (see section II, chapter two and I in this chapter).

Now, given how close-knit the terms 'damage' and 'violation of protected interests' are, it seems useful – and consistent with the established use of the word 'damage' – to rely on the notion of damage as a shorthand for wrongs-based interferences with protected interests. This shorthand describes the reasons that justify all types of damages, not just compensatory awards. And while we may accept that interference with the claimant's right is a necessary condition for any measure of damages,[161] it does not follow that the claimant's right would also be a necessary justifying reason for all measures of damages. The harmful consequences of the wrong take different shapes, and the reasons why something amounts to wrongful damage vary because, as Steel puts it in his critical study of Weinrib's *Corrective*

[157] Nolan thinks that '"injury" is the slippery word here' (Nolan (n 153) 5). But *cf* T Weir, *A Casebook on Tort*, 1st edn (London, Sweet & Maxwell, 1967) 3: 'all legally protected interests, relevantly infringed, involve liability; but some damage (*e.g.*, grief), however produced, does not involve liability'.

[158] *Rothwell* (n 150) [7].

[159] In a similar sense, *Ashby v White* (1703) 2 Ld Raym 938 (KB) 955.

[160] R Stevens, 'Rights and Other Things' in D Nolan and A Robertson (eds), *Rights and Private Law* (Oxford, Hart Publishing, 2012) 121.

[161] In more detail on the nuances between the conceptions of remedies that see violations of rights as a formal 'condition' and as a material 'reason' for the award of damages, see EJ Weinrib, 'Two Conceptions of Remedies' in CEF Rickett (ed), *Justifying Private Law Remedies* (Oxford, Hart Publishing, 2008).

Justice, 'there is no *single* moral property which explains the wrongfulness of the wrongs in private law'.[162] 'Not all of the wrongs in private law are (or ought to be) wrongs against [individual] freedom',[163] argues Steel. And since the notion of damage is agnostic to the moral properties that explain the wrongfulness of the harm, it seems reasonable to rely on that notion for the purposes of our analysis.

Besides, I do not think there is any better alternative for how to describe the reasons that justify different measures of damages. One possible alternative could be the notion of 'wrongdoing'. We could say that different measures of damages are justified by different types of consequential 'wrongdoing'. After all, a civil wrong and its consequences can together be characterised as 'wrongdoing', and it seems uncontroversial to say that damages rectify some wrongdoing. What is more, the concept of 'wrongdoing' could be defined by stipulation in this book because it is less well established than the concept of 'damage'[164] and because 'wrongdoing' does not have any precise doctrinal legal meaning.[165] We may say that this is an advantage of the concept, as it could be deployed to explain what an established concept of 'damage' cannot explain. Well, I am not convinced by this argument. I think it would be even more confusing to rely on the unestablished meaning of 'wrongdoing' than to rely on the established concept of 'damage'. It would be confusing because we would need to reinterpret both compensatory and non-compensatory damages in terms of remedies for specific kinds of 'wrongdoing' and because such a reinterpretation would be too detached from the law's own language. Thus, what might be gained in precision would be lost in clarity. Besides, the word 'wrongdoing' might also obscure the dividing line between the wrong and the consequences thereof more than it is obscured by the phrase 'damage to protected interests'. On balance, while far from being perfect, the better option is thus to rely on the notion of 'damage' in this book.

III. Damage to 'Protected Interests'

One cannot write about damage to protected interests without explaining the concept of protected interests. English law straightforwardly accepts the justificatory role of protected interests in the law of damages. For example, the House of Lords tells us that the claimant must 'establish "an antecedent legal interest" or, as [Lord Millett] would prefer to put it, "a legally protected interest"'[166] in order

[162] S Steel, 'Private Law and Justice' (2013) 33 *OJLS* 607, 618 (emphasis in original).

[163] ibid.

[164] 'Wrongdoing' was a rare word before the 19th century and only came to be used more frequently from c. 1860 (Simpson and Weiner (n 81) entry 'wrong-doing'). See also ibid entry 'damage'.

[165] See, eg, *Edward John Giles v Caroline Bridget Towers Rhind* [2008] EWCA Civ 118 [37]–[38] (Arden LJ); *Emerald Supplies Ltd and Anor v British Airways plc* [2010] EWCA Civ 1284, [2011] Ch 345 [5]; or ME Newhouse, 'Two Types of Legal Wrongdoing' (2016) 22 *Legal Theory* 59.

[166] *Three Rivers District Council and Others v Governor and Company of the Bank of England (No 3)* [2003] 2 AC 1 (HL) 237.

to obtain damages for the alleged harm; in contract law, we normally talk about expectation (performance), reliance and restitution interests;[167] in tort literature, we read that foreseeability of harm is always linked with 'a legally protected interest of the plaintiff';[168] and we could continue with similar examples.

In fact, the role of protected interests is so deeply rooted in our thinking about law that some authors describe tort law as 'civil liability for harms to legally protected interests'.[169] These protected interests can take various forms, and not all legally protected interests must be expressed in the form of legal rights to have effects on damages awards.[170] Rather, interests serve as 'the means by which one could link descriptive categories of harm to normative principles of what a defendant ought to pay'.[171]

But what do we mean by 'protected interests'? Sometimes, an interest is 'more or less synonymous with … some sort of claim over or right in some [assets]'[172] such as property or contract. Sometimes, we think 'of a person's interests, or of the public interest, in a broader sense to mean simply objective or states of affairs which are, or would be, to the person's, or the public's, advantage', as Cane argues.[173] Interests of the first type are usually better protected by the law than interests of the second type, 'at least in the sense that interests [in assets] … often constitute legal "swords", whereas interests of the latter type are often only effective as "shields"'.[174] The 'swords' are typically referred to as claim-rights, because they entitle the right-holder actively to enforce his interests in court; the 'shields' are typically referred to as mere rights or, simply, as legally protected interests because they allow the relevant party merely to defend these interests against wrongful interferences.

In this book, my focus is on interests as those 'shields', ie, matters that are protected for one or more person's benefit and that are therefore in someone's interest. All these various interests could be generally characterised as 'demand[s] or desire[s] or expectation[s] which human beings, either individually or in groups or associations or relations, seek to satisfy', as Pound would put it.[175] Or they can be described as 'basic aspects of human well-being or flourishing, such as liberty and physical integrity; … [also] described loosely as "assets" or "resources"', as Varuhas

[167] See especially LL Fuller and WR Perdue, 'The Reliance Interest in Contract Damages' (1936) 46 *Yale Law Journal* 52; Friedmann (n 4).

[168] RFV Heuston, *Salmond on the Law of Torts*, 17th edn (London, Sweet & Maxwell, 1977) 223.

[169] FV Harper, *A Treatise on the Law of Torts: A Preliminary Treatise on Civil Liability for Harms to Legally Protected Interests* (Indianapolis, Bobbs-Merrill Co Publishers, 1933). Surveying the (mostly US) common law, Harper discusses invasions of interests in personality and property, economic relations and transactions, reputation, the domestic relations, freedom from unjustifiable litigation, the marketability of property, privacy, political activities and the interest in the life of a third person. *cf* Goudkamp and Nolan (n 29) para 2-019.

[170] See, especially, G Samuel, 'Should Jurists Take Interests More Seriously?' (2017) (August) *Law and Method* 1.

[171] ibid 21.

[172] P Cane, *Tort Law and Economic Interests* (Oxford, Clarendon Press, 1991) 3.

[173] ibid.

[174] ibid 3–4.

[175] R Pound, *Jurisprudence*, vol 3 (St. Paul, West Publishing, 1959) 16.

observes.[176] These descriptions of protected interests accord with an ordinary meaning of the term used by courts and do not seem to pose any practical difficulties, although they are relatively vague. The phrase 'damage to protected interests' (rather than damage to legal rights) will therefore be relied on for the purposes of comparing and contrasting the reasons that justify measures of damages.

IV. The Justificatory Role of Protected Interests

There is one obvious objection to the justificatory role of protected interests that needs to be addressed here. According to corrective justice theorists like Weinrib, protected interests should in principle be irrelevant to a coherent analysis of private law and, by implication, to the analysis of damages. He argues, for instance, that 'rights [which justify private law relationships] cannot be conceived merely as shorthand references to components of the plaintiff's welfare, for then rights will ultimately be as unexpressive of correlativity as welfare itself'.[177] Weinrib then adds that '[f]rom the standpoint of corrective justice, the advance achieved by introducing the notion of right and correlative duty would be undone by the non-correlative conception of the content of those rights as being based on welfare'.[178]

It is worth highlighting that Weinrib's approach is very distinct from the approach taken by this book, and his analysis could be set aside on this basis alone. His conceptual framework helps him to advance a unified normative account of private law (including private law remedies), not a descriptive (or interpretive) account of damages. From his perspective, it makes sense to adopt a specific language of rights *qua* claim-rights based on equality and individual freedom, rather than rights *qua* legally protected interests. But by accepting Weinrib's narrow view of damages *qua* correlatively justified remedies, we would too quickly dismiss the role of 'interests' as an expression of rights in a broader sense than 'claim-rights', ie, than rights that are always coupled with a correlative duty. Indeed, according to the interest theory of rights, it is neither necessary nor sufficient for holding a right that the right-holder be 'competent and authorized to demand or waive the enforcement of the duty that is correlative to the right'.[179]

[176] J Varuhas, 'The Concept of "Vindication" in the Law of Torts: Rights, Interests and Damages' (2014) 34 *OJLS* 253, 257 (footnotes omitted).

[177] Weinrib (n 60) 21.

[178] ibid 21–22. The same quote can be found in E Weinrib, *Reciprocal Freedom: Private Law and Public Right* (Oxford, OUP, 2022) 27.

[179] MH Kramer, 'Refining the Interest Theory of Rights' (2010) 55 *American Journal of Jurisprudence* 31, 32. See, also J Raz, *The Morality of Freedom* (Oxford, Clarendon Press, 1986) 166; VAJ Kurki, 'Rights, Harming and Wronging: A Restatement of the Interest Theory' (2018) 38 *OJLS* 430; M McBride, 'Preserving the Interest Theory of Rights' (2020) 26 *Legal Theory* 3.

Weinrib explains his position further in *Reciprocal Freedom*. He states that our understanding of the normative structure of private law should be independent of any one-sided considerations 'such as welfare or interests',[180] because the normative structure of private law is premised on equality of parties, and their freedom to pursue individual interests is thus also equal.[181] Private law rights, according to Weinrib, thus do not mandate any particular purpose, and private individuals are free to pursue their own interests.[182] Thus, private law rights 'serve as the juridical conduits through which persons interact on terms of their equal reciprocal freedom'.[183] Weinrib agrees that having a right 'contributes to a person's welfare by protecting some interest[s] from wrongful interference',[184] but he resists the idea that interests would have any significance for 'the rights and duties of private law'.[185] He dismisses 'those who accept the idea of correlativity but adopt an interest theory of right'.[186] Weinrib thinks this is supported by an observation that '[w]elfare serves only the secondary function … of *quantifying* the injury done to the object of the right'.[187] As Steel puts it in his interpretation of Weinrib, '[t]he idea of an "interest" is insufficiently relational in order to be consistent with correlativity'.[188]

But when it comes to damages, we need to be careful not to confuse the underlying normative structure – which may or may not be based exclusively on corrective justice – with concrete detriments caused by civil wrongs. Those detriments are directly linked with interests that individuals choose to defend as part of their claim. Thus, the question we should ask is not whether 'interests' are relevant in an interpretive or descriptive analysis of damages. They clearly are relevant. Instead, the question we should ask is whether and why specific interests deserve legal protection.

Weinrib's claim is precisely about the normative structure behind such legal protection and about the irrelevance of interests for that structure. By contrast, his claim is not about the irrelevance of the normative structure for the protection of specific interests or about the irrelevance of protected interests for the measures of damages. It is thus plausible to analyse damages by reference to the interests that they are designed to protect. In accordance with modern interpretations of the Kantian theory of right,[189] this book therefore accepts that protected interests have a legitimate role to play in the analysis of damages and their measures.

[180] Weinrib (n 178) 28.
[181] ibid 28.
[182] ibid 28.
[183] ibid 28.
[184] Weinrib (n 60) 22.
[185] ibid 23.
[186] Steel (n 162) 610 (footnote omitted).
[187] Weinrib (n 60) (emphasis added).
[188] Steel (n 162) 610.
[189] See, eg, G Beck, 'Immanuel Kant's Theory of Rights' (2006) 19 *Ratio Juris* 371.

V. Two Fundamental Justifications

Once we accept that damages need not be exclusively organised according to the corrective-justice-shaped idea of private law, it becomes clear that while the protection of some interests may give effect to individual rights based on the idea of reciprocal freedom, the protection of other interests may be non-rights-based. This section seeks better to explain why damage to protected interests can mean both: (i) interferences with interests that give effect to individual rights, and (ii) interferences with interests that give effect to non-rights-based considerations. In other words, it will be shown why measures of damages must in principle be always reducible to measures justified by damage to either: (i) correlative interests (giving effect to individual rights), or (ii) non-correlative interests (not giving effect to individual rights). Whether or not this division maps onto the compensatory versus non-compensatory damages divide is a separate question that will be answered in chapter four. However, it will be argued here that – provided that the division between the two fundamental justifications is real (and we will see in subsequent chapters that it is real) – the division should be duly acknowledged and properly articulated by existing legal doctrines because it has important implications.

The distinction between 'correlative' and 'non-correlative' reasons is not new. Inspired by a corrective justice theory of private law, Cane had already observed in his study of exceptional measures of damages that those measures are not justified by correlative reasons.[190] By doing so, Cane had implicitly alluded to the idea of 'non-correlative' reasons, although he did not explore if there is any common thread to all of those non-correlative reasons and did not try to define non-correlativity in positive terms. Similarly, Weinrib highlights that if justifying reasons are 'non-correlative, in that their normative force does not link the particular defendant who commits the injustice to the particular plaintiff who suffers it, then the law cannot coherently tie the defendant's liability to the plaintiff's entitlement'.[191] In this sense, compensable harm is explicable in terms of correlative damage, or damage to the claimant's private interests, because the protection of those interests is underpinned by the norms of corrective justice and because the protection of those interests is arguably based on a reciprocal freedom of the parties in dispute. But let us unpack this proposition in more detail, as it will help us better to understand the idea of 'non-correlative damage' as well.

To say that the compensatory measure is justified by correlative damage seems uncontroversial. The courts have discussed the correlative justification of compensatory awards since long ago.[192] The claimant's right to obtain

[190] Cane (n 41).
[191] Weinrib (n 83) xv.
[192] See, eg, *Blackett & Anor v Smith* (1809) 103 ER 1110 (KB) 1111; *M'Iver v Henderson* (1816) 105 ER 947 (KB) 949; *The Governor and Company of the Copper Miners of England v Fox* (1851) 16 QB 229, 237.

damages is correlated with the violation of the claimant's private interests, and, conversely, this damage to private interests is correlated with the defendant's duty to compensate for that detriment by way of reciprocally diminishing the defendant's monetary interests. Otherwise, the award would be unjust in the sense that there would not be a legitimate reason to divert the specific sum of money from the defendant's pocket into the claimant's pocket. What the claimant obtains from the defendant in damages – so the theory goes – correlates with what damage was caused by the defendant to the claimant's interests. The claimant's loss can be correlated with the defendant's duty to compensate for that loss. That is why we can say that the compensatory function of damages is to put the claimant into a position, with respect to his legally protected interests, in which he would have been had the wrong not occurred.

The compensatory function focuses on restoring the violated interests of the claimant and not of anyone else.[193] In this respect, compensation gives effect to the claimant's individual rights. The compensatory measure also gives effect to individual rights because the idea of compensable harm (ie, the claimant's loss or, more broadly, the claimant's damaged interests based on which the specific compensatory measure is justified) stems from the reciprocal freedom between the formally equal parties. In particular, these corrective justice considerations justify the extent to which the claimant's interests are protected against interferences by the defendant and, relatedly, the extent to which the claimant's harm is compensable. So far, we are discussing here the role of correlativity in justifying the measure of damages, not the role of correlativity in justifying the defendant's remedial liability at large.

There are, of course, other ways how correlativity is discussed in private law literature. The idea of correlativity appears more often to be discussed in relation to rights and duties, rather than in relation to wrongful consequences of interferences with those rights and duties. What those discussions tend to correlate are, for example in Weinrib's analysis, the claimant's private right and the defendant's correlative private duty.[194] This idea of correlativity mirrors the bipolar structure of private law relationships where two equal and free human individuals (the two poles of the bipolar relationship) have against each other rights and duties of a Kantian type.[195] As Cane puts it in his interpretation of Weinrib's work, '[i]n private law, one person's right is always a function of another person's duty, and vice

[193] See, eg, Burrows (n 62) 35–46 and the cases cited therein.

[194] See, eg, Weinrib (n 60) 3, 10, 17 and 35 or Weinrib (n 83) 115–26.

[195] According to the Kantian theory of rights, each person has an innate right to '[f]reedom (independence from being constrained by another's choice), insofar as it can coexist with the freedom of every other in accordance with a universal law' (I Kant, *The Metaphysics of Morals* (Cambridge, CUP, 1996) 6:237). For Weinrib, '[t]he claim is not … merely that Kantian right is one theory of rights *consistent* with correlativity, but rather that it is the *only* understanding of persons' rights and duties consistent with correlativity' (Steel (n 162) 610 (emphasis in original)).

versa'.[196] According to Weinrib, thus, correlativity is the 'general organizing feature for justifications of liability'[197] and the symmetrical structure of bipolar private law relationships implies that correlative considerations apply to both parties reciprocally, ie, in accord with the idea of reciprocal freedom between the equal parties.

In this light, it is then easy to see how such correlative considerations (that apply to both parties reciprocally) could justify not only the liability establishing rights and duties, but also the damage that implements the compensatory liability. In this light, it is also easy to see why correlativity helps us to distinguish liquidated damages clauses from similarly drafted – but non-correlatively justified – penalty provisions. In the eyes of the law, the provision constitutes a penalty if it 'imposes a detriment on the contract-breaker out of all proportion to any legitimate interest of the [claimant]'.[198] Similarly, the paradigm helps us to criticise punitive damages as an unjustified and anomalous windfall.[199]

Now, what does this tell us about non-correlativity? The idea that some justifying reasons for measures of damages can be non-correlative is a logical corollary of the claim that not all damages are necessarily justified by correlative reasons. And the example of punitive damages, at least, gives us the certainty that not all measures of damages are indeed justified by such correlative reasons.[200] The measure of punitive and possibly other non-compensatory damages must be justified by violations of protected interests, although not necessarily interests of the claimant, and the protection of these interests must be justified by norms of justice, although not necessarily by norms of corrective justice. Put in positive terms, we could say that some measures can, at least in theory, be justified by non-rights-based considerations such as public interests because the protection of those interests is not grounded wholly or predominantly in the reciprocal freedom between the parties.

This is why this book analyses all NCDs without prejudice to whether it is correlative or non-correlative reasons that justify their measure. It separates the question of the defendant's liability *to* the claimant for a civil wrong (which is typically at the forefront of corrective justice reasoning about private law) from the question of the defendant's liability *for* resulting damage (be it correlative or non-correlative damage). And as was explained earlier, this could mean that some

[196] P Cane, 'Corrective Justice and Correlativity in Private Law' (1996) 16 *OJLS* 471, 471.

[197] Weinrib (n 60) 19. See also Stevens (n 60) ch 4; Zakrzewski (n 61) 53–58 (both of them emphasising the rights-based nature of remedies); A Burrows, 'Judicial Remedies' in A Burrows (ed), *English Private Law*, 3rd edn (Oxford, OUP, 2013) 1255 (emphasising a primary duty (not right) with which the wrongdoer failed to comply). See also *Handbook of the New Private Law* (Oxford, OUP, 2020).

[198] *Cavendish Square Holding BV v Talal El Makdessi; ParkingEye Limited v Beavis* [2015] UKSC 67, [2016] AC 1172 [32] (Lords Neuberger and Sumption (with whom Lord Carnwath agreed)). See also S Rowan, 'The "Legitimate Interest in Performance" in the Law of Penalties' (2019) 78 *CLJ* 148.

[199] For an overview of these arguments, see, eg, V Janeček, 'Exemplary Damages: A Genuine Concept?' (2014) 6 *European Journal of Legal Studies* 189, 196–203.

[200] See also Steel (n 162) 624–25 (pointing out the difficulties of Weinrib's corrective-justice-based theory in relation to non-compensatory measures of damages) and ibid 618 (pointing out that 'not all wrongs in private law are (or ought to be) wrongs against [individual] freedom').

measures of damages can be justified by non-correlative reasons, even if the basis of the defendant's liability remains underpinned by correlative reasons.

Accordingly, it is more rigorous to consider from the outset the possibility that NCDs, unlike compensatory damages, can be (at least partly) justified by non-correlative reasons or, in other words, by reasons that do not give effect to individual rights or legally protected interests.[201] Chapter four will test this claim against the six types of damages that might theoretically fit the doctrinal scope of NCDs: punitive, nominal, contemptuous, vindicatory, restitutionary and disgorgement damages. By doing so, chapter four will seek positively to characterise the reasons that justify NCDs and highlight what all these different measures of damages have in common.

Importantly, provided that these non-correlative considerations are not a purely theoretical idea – and chapter four will show that this idea is real – then the law should recognise the said contrast between correlative and non-correlative measures of damages. Why? First, the contrast between the two fundamental justifications could imply whether certain measures should be available as of right or not. Surely, if a measure is justified by considerations giving effect to individual rights, then it should be available as of right, but if it is not so justified, then it should, arguably, not be available as of right. Second, it could help to confirm or deny the stated contrast between compensatory and non-compensatory awards and, hence, their mutual (in)compatibility. Surely, if different measures of damages are justified by the same reasons, then those measures probably discharge the same overarching function. And if different measures discharge the same overarching function, then such damages should not be awarded alongside each other because that would amount to double-counting. Third, it could help to confirm or deny the stated unrelatedness between individual types of NCDs. Surely, if measures of NCDs are justified by the same reasons, then their awards should be co-ordinated, or, at the very least, it would be sensible to approach them collectively. Fourth, it could help to increase the law's transparency. and such transparency could help better to identify areas ripe for a doctrinal change. Surely, if some measures of damages are justified by damage to public interests, then the public has the (moral) right to know about this because it is not necessarily up to the courts to decide what is and what should be in the public interest.

VI. Conclusion

Damages are clearly linked with considerations of justice.[202] In *Marathon Asset Management LLP & Anor v Seddon & Ors*, for example, Leggatt J confirmed that

[201] *cf* Georgiou and Steel (n 55) 202, who define 'public interests' as normative considerations 'not grounded wholly or predominantly in an individual's interest or moral status'.

[202] See, eg, J Gardner, 'What is Tort Law For? Part 1. The Place of Corrective Justice' (2011) 30 *Law & Philosophy* 1; SA Smith, 'Duties, Liabilities, and Damages' (2012) 125 *Harvard Law Review* 1727;

there is a strong and principled requirement 'to match the remedy to th[e] wrong'.[203] In the same vein, it can be said that the measure of the remedy should match the harm. Whether the remedy and the specific remedial measure is justified is to be assessed by norms of justice. John Gardner famously wrote that '[n]orms of justice are … norms for tackling *allocative* moral questions, questions about who is to get how much of what'.[204] Indeed, I agree with Gardner that the underlying considerations of justice allow us to tackle the questions about 'who' is to get 'what' if they are wronged (though in the case of damages the 'what' will always be money). I would also add that considerations of justice help us to ascertain 'from whom' the award should be obtained. Importantly, these questions help us to address the issue of liability, but not the specific remedial measure.

The 'who' and 'from whom' questions are the domain of theorists adopting the rights-based view. They teach us that the central norms of private law justice are norms of corrective justice. These norms tell us that, in relations between equal individuals – and the English law of damages is still firmly linked with the principles of rationality, individual freedom and human equality[205] – the right-holder can claim something back from a duty-bearer if that duty-bearer breaches his duty and if that duty is correlative to the right-holder's right. This idea has been widely explored in the literature and probably does not need further unpacking.[206]

The key for our understanding of the distinction between compensatory and non-compensatory damages then relates to the 'how much' question, ie, the question about the measure of damages. If we accept that all measures of damages are justified by wrongs-based damage to protected interests and if such justifications are governed by the norms of justice, then the key to our definition of NCDs turns out to be this: What norms of justice and what types of protected interest justify NCDs as compared with the norms of justice and types of interest that underpin compensatory awards? These questions will be answered in full by later chapters. In this chapter, it was merely demonstrated that measures of damages do not need to be exclusively underpinned by norms of corrective justice and that it is in principle possible that certain measures of damages do not give effect to individual rights. Instead, it is possible that such damages give effect to non-rights-based considerations.

J Gardner, 'What is Tort Law For? Part 2. The Place of Distributive Justice' in J Oberdiek (ed), *Philosophical Foundations of the Law of Torts* (Oxford, OUP, 2014).

[203] *Marathon Asset Management LLP & Anor v Seddon & Ors* [2017] EWHC 300 (Comm), [2017] ICR 791 [253].

[204] J Gardner, *Torts and Other Wrongs* (Oxford, OUP, 2019) 31.

[205] Generally, see, eg, M Lobban and J Moses (eds), *The Impact of Ideas on Legal Development* (Cambridge, CUP, 2012). See also 1 Bl Comm 38ff; 3 Bl Comm; DJ Ibbetson, *A Historical Introduction to the Law of Obligations* (Oxford, OUP, 1999) 153–54; M Lobban, 'English Jurisprudence and Tort Theory' in M Lobban and J Moses (eds), *The Impact of Ideas on Legal Development* (Cambridge, CUP, 2012). It has been also argued that the common law 'sets the highest value on its own great creation, *the liber et legalis homo*, "the reasonable man of the law," and on his free act of will' (R O'Sullivan, 'A Scale of Values in the Common Law' (1937) 1 *MLR* 27, 31).

[206] See, especially, Weinrib (n 60) ch 1.

Thus, we saw that there are – at least in theory – two fundamental justifications for measures of damages: (i) justifications based wholly or predominantly on considerations giving effect to individual rights grounded in reciprocal freedom of individuals or, put shortly, justifications based on damage to protected private interests of the claimant; and (ii) justifications not based wholly or predominantly on individual rights, such as damage to public interests. The justifications giving effect to individual rights are, in the popular language of corrective justice theory, to be understood as correlative considerations. Accordingly, the law can interpret the two fundamental justifications for specific measures of damages as: (i) correlative damage; and (ii) non-correlative damage. For reasons explained in section V, the law not only can but also *should* recognise these two justifications because the distinction between those justifications could have doctrinal implications. Let us now turn to the question of whether NCDs are truly justified by non-correlative damage (chapter four) and, if so, how best to describe that damage (chapter five).

4

Analysing Non-Compensatory Damages[207]

Now that we have pinned down the key analytical concepts and the analytical framework, we can test whether individual types of NCDs are justified by non-correlative damage. Throughout sections I to VI, this chapter analyses distinct measures of damages labelled as non-compensatory by both the primary legal sources (punitive, nominal, vindicatory and disgorgement damages) and the literature (restitutionary and contemptuous damages). Section VII summarises the key findings and concludes by highlighting the commonalities and distinctions amongst NCDs.

I. Punitive Damages

Punitive damages – sometimes also called exemplary damages[208] or, more archaically, vindictive damages[209] – seek to punish the defendant and to deter him and others from engaging in similar conduct in the future if the compensation payable to the claimant is inadequate to serve these goals.[210] While every legal sanction, including compensatory damages, may be seen as some sort of a punishment or deterrence,[211] the punitive aim of punitive damages is distinct in that it is the main aim or, according to some commentators, even 'the sole aim being pursued'.[212] In *Cavendish*, the Supreme Court acknowledged that 'deterrence is not penal if there is a legitimate interest in influencing the conduct of the contracting party'.[213] This clearly suggests that the punitive and deterrent goals of punitive damages can

[207] A distant version of this chapter was published in Janeček (n 53).

[208] *Rookes* (n 97).

[209] *Malik v Bank of Credit and Commerce International SA (in liq)* [1998] AC 20 (HL) 39. See also CG Addison, *Wrongs and Their Remedies: Being a Treatise on the Law of Torts*, 2nd edn (London, Stevens and Haynes, 1864) 905–07; Winfield (n 30) 151.

[210] *Rookes* (n 97) 1227–28. See also *Rees & Ors v Commissioner of Police of the Metropolis* (n 118) [12] (stressing that the test applies to inadequacy of both compensatory and aggravated damages).

[211] This position was held, eg, by Lord Devlin in *Rookes* (n 97) 1221 and P Birks, 'Civil Wrongs: A New World', *Butterworth lectures 1990–91* (London, Butterworths, 1992) 80.

[212] A Burrows, 'Reforming Exemplary Damages: Expansion or Abolition?' in P Birks (ed), *Wrongs and Remedies in the Twenty-First Century* (Oxford, Clarendon Press, 1996) 156.

[213] *Cavendish Square Holding BV v Talal El Makdessi; ParkingEye Limited v Beavis* (n 198) [99].

be contrasted with compensation by looking at whether the non-compensatory measure is or is not grounded in the claimant's legitimate private interests. In other words, *Cavendish* suggests that the penal function of damages is not justified by correlative damage.

Punitive damages can be awarded for a civil wrong[214] only if that wrong satisfies the categories test devised by Lord Devlin in *Rookes*. As per the categories test, punitive damages may be awarded in: Category 1 cases of 'oppressive, arbitrary or unconstitutional action by the servants of the government',[215] Category 2 cases where 'the defendant's conduct has been calculated by him to make a profit for himself which may exceed the compensation payable to the plaintiff',[216] and Category 3 cases where such award is 'expressly authorised by statute'.[217]

Under our framework, Category 1 punitive damages – ie, penal awards for wrongdoing by public officials – may be seen as a remedy for a civil wrong suffered by the private claimant, because it is the claimant whose claim-right was infringed. Under the framework from chapter three, the mere breach of such a claim-right is a correlative justifying reason and explains why the claimant can obtain *some* damages from the defendant. However, this civil wrong and the breach of the claimant's claim-right does not explain why the claimant can obtain *punitive* damages. Had the claimant suffered a consequential violation of his or her protected interests, such damage would be – in line with the current doctrine[218] – compensated before any punitive award could be contemplated. More importantly, the correlative damage to the claimant's protected interests would not trigger the extra-compensatory remedy, which is why it makes sense to ask what other interests have been damaged by the defendant's wrongdoing. Perhaps, the punitive measure is justified by the violation of some other interests than those of the claimant. Of course, the claimant 'cannot recover exemplary damages unless he is the victim of the punishable behaviour',[219] but this limitation seems merely to affect the claimant's standing and his ability to obtain the remedy, not the punitive aspect of the measure itself.

Indeed, it looks as though Category 1 punitive damages are not justified by giving effect wholly or predominantly to a reciprocal freedom of the parties. Take, for example, the reasoning in *Wilkes v Wood* – a case concerning an arbitrary exercise of investigatory powers by the Secretary of State.[220] It was made clear in that case that the

[214] In English law, there is no direct evidence that punitive damages can be awarded for breach of contractual rights. However, it is debatable whether contract law truly forbids these awards *en bloc*. See *Addis v Gramophone Co Ltd* [1909] AC 488 (HL) 496, 499 and the discussion in R Cunnington, 'Should Punitive Damages be Part of the Judicial Arsenal in Contract Cases?' (2006) 26 *Legal Studies* 369 and J Goudkamp, 'Exemplary Damages' in G Virgo and S Worthington (eds), *Commercial Remedies: Resolving Controversies* (Cambridge, CUP, 2017) 321–29.

[215] *Rookes* (n 97) 1226.

[216] ibid.

[217] ibid 1227.

[218] ibid 1227–28.

[219] ibid 1227.

[220] *Wilkes v Wood* (1763) Lofft 1, (1763) 98 ER 489.

power to issue a general search warrant on the basis of a mere suspicion 'certainly may affect the person and property of every man in this kingdom, and is totally subversive of the liberty of the subject'.[221] Such a practice was punished by a non-compensatory award of damages because the defendant's conduct was 'contrary to the fundamental principles of the constitution',[222] not because it was contrary to the private interests of the claimant. According to the court, the matters in dispute 'extended far beyond Mr. Wilkes personally … [as they indirectly] touched the liberty of every subject of this country … [and] if found to be legal, would shake that most precious inheritance of Englishmen'.[223] The non-correlative justification of the award in *Wilkes v Wood* seems clear in this case.[224]

The same point can be made as regards more recent Category 1 cases. For instance, in *Rees & Ors v Commissioner of Police of the Metropolis*, it was stated that 'public censure requires a separate award of exemplary damages to mark the court's denunciation of [the defendant's] unconstitutional behaviour as an agent of the state'.[225] The High Court made it clear that the punitive award made against the police officers 'is of public importance'[226] because their malicious prosecution and misfeasance in public office was in 'the need for public condemnation through the courts'.[227] Again, the non-correlative justification seems apparent here, as the punitive measure in *Rees* gives effect wholly or predominantly to some kind of public interest, rather than to the claimant's private rights or interests.

A possible reason why Category 1 justifying reasons are not so easy to conceptualise in terms of 'damage' is that such damage is not very specific. Unlike in the case of compensation, where the claimant's damage is typically pinned down with a degree of precision needed to quantify the measure, Category 1 punitive damages are justified by relatively generic and broad considerations. For example, in *Rookes v Barnard*, one of Lord Devlin's justifications for the punitive measure was that 'the servants of the government are also the servants of the people and the use of their power must always be subordinate to their duty of service'.[228] This statement can be interpreted as if Category 1 punitive damages protected the functioning of our society and the functioning of our legal system. His Lordship's view seems to have been underpinned by the principle of legality and the rule of law,[229]

[221] ibid 498.
[222] ibid 499.
[223] ibid 490. Similarly, see, eg, *Huckle v Money* (1763) 3 Wils KB 206, 206, 207, (1763) 95 ER 768, 768, 769; *Entick v Carrington & Ors* (1765) 2 Wils KB 275, 286, 292, (1765) 95 ER 807, 814, 818.
[224] An excellent, contextual account of the *Wilkes* case and the *Huckle* case can be found in N Sinanis, 'The North Briston No. 45 and the Doctrinal Origins of Exemplary Damages' (2023) 82 *CLJ* 321, 340. Sinanis colourfully portrays the relevant considerations – which I read to be considerations of public interest – which have led to extra-compensatory awards in these cases.
[225] *Rees & Ors v Commissioner of Police of the Metropolis* [2019] EWHC 2120 (Admin) [48].
[226] ibid [43].
[227] ibid [45].
[228] *Rookes* (n 97) 1226.
[229] According to some authors, the rule of law is but a grand term for the value of legality (eg, R Dworkin, 'Hart's Postscript and the Character of Political Philosophy' (2004) 24 *OJLS* 1, 24).

both of which are primarily beneficial for the functioning of our society, rather than for the individual claimant. These principles yield benefits to all members of the community, such as predictability of official activity and hence the possibility of better planning, protection from arbitrary and discriminatory actions by officials and enormous savings of energy that we would otherwise spend on thinking about the best way to regulate our lives.[230]

In this light, once we start thinking about the justifying grounds for Category 1 punitive damages in terms of 'damage to protected interests', it becomes clear they can be analysed as infringements of the public interest in an efficient and reliable operation of the principles of legality and the rule of law, or something along these lines.[231] The fact that such public interest is inflated to a very high degree of generality does not undermine the non-correlative nature of this justification. This public interest reason is clearly not grounded in individual rights, at least not wholly or predominantly grounded in those rights.

Another argument in support of the view that Category 1 punitive damages are justified by non-correlative damage comes from the Human Rights Act 1998 (HRA). This is because Category 1 wrongs committed by public authorities can often also be considered wrongful under section 8 of the HRA, and thus the arguments deployed in the HRA context might shed some light on the types of harm associated with Category 1 wrongs and resulting damage. Section 8 of the HRA allows for damages 'in relation to any act … of a public authority which the court finds is … unlawful'.[232] The award then must be 'necessary to afford just satisfaction',[233] which goal intellectually originates from article 41 of the European Convention for the Protection of Human Rights (the Convention) regulating the monetary remedy of 'just satisfaction'. The European Court of Human Rights, whose jurisprudence is relevant to our understanding of the Convention,[234] confirmed that the Court may award non-compensatory punitive damages under article 41 of the Convention on the basis of criteria such as

> the "absolute character" of the violated right, the "particularly serious character of the violations", the "gravity of the violations", or the "fundamental importance of that right" … [or where] the Court … finds [the award] to be fair in the particular case[, or on the basis of] general interest … taking into account … exemplary effect.[235]

Again, these reasons do not reflect merely a wrong against the claimant's claim-right or private interests. Rather, they reflect wrongdoing against non-correlative and presumably public interests which are infringed in parallel with the

[230] See SJ Shapiro, *Legality* (Cambridge, MA, Harvard University Press, 2011) 395–96.

[231] *cf* Nolan (n 59) 278–79 (highlighting the public law aspect of the doctrines of exemplary damages and misfeasance in public office).

[232] Human Rights Act 1998, s 8(1).

[233] ibid s 8(3).

[234] ibid s 8(4).

[235] *Cyprus v Turkey* (2014) 59 EHRR 16 [13] (footnotes omitted).

claimant's individual human rights.[236] One way to put it would be to say that there is an objective side to the fundamental right (its public significance) and a subjective side to the same right (its significance to the individual right-holder). The non-compensatory remedy responds to the violation of the objective and publicly significant aspect of the fundamental right, rather than the subjective side of the same right.

Let us now turn to Category 2 punitive damages. Category 2 awards punish the defendant's 'cynical disregard for [the] plaintiff's rights'[237] and for his aware calculation 'that the money to be made out of his wrongdoing will probably exceed the damages at risk'.[238] One could argue that there is a direct link between the level of recklessness on the defendant's side and the extent of damage to protected interests on the claimant's side: the more reckless the wrong, the bigger the damage to the claimant's rights and protected interests. This would mean that the penal award gives effect to the claimant's private rights and that it is ultimately justified by equal freedom and reciprocity between the parties. And this, in turn, would render Category 2 punitive damages indistinguishable from compensatory damages for such correlative harm. However, this is not how law treats Category 2 punitive damages.

Category 2 punitive damages must have a rationale distinct from awards of compensation because, as was already explained, they can only be awarded if compensation payable is not sufficient to achieve the deterrent goal. So, if Category 2 punitive damages are non-compensatory, then the defendant's cynical and profit-orientated conduct may better be understood as a one-sided (namely defendant-orientated) consideration that is unconcerned with how the aggravating factors (ie, the cynical disregard for the victim's rights and profit-seeking motive behind the wrongdoing) affect the claimant individually. The award may be better understood as being unconcerned with the correlative claimant-defendant relationship and the reciprocal rights and duties between the parties. In other words, it is a plausible interpretation of the law to say that the defendant's duty not to be cynical and profit-orientated whilst interfering with other people's private rights is not wholly or predominantly grounded in the victim's private rights. The defendant's motives can aggravate the claimant's distress, but since Category 2 punitive damages are available independently of any such distress, it seems clear that the punitive award must give effect to some non-correlative damage.

The more difficult question concerns the substance of the non-correlative damage. How shall we specify this non-correlative damage? The law gives us some indication, although the considerations which justified Category 2 awards are again discussed in fairly broad terms only. For example, in *John v MGN Ltd* – a libel case in which the defendant, with the intention of making a profit exceeding

[236] See also Zipursky (n 58) 107, 151ff (offering an explanation of the dual private/public nature of punitive damages).
[237] *Rookes* (n 97) 1227.
[238] ibid.

potential compensation, recklessly disregarded the claimant's rights and the truth or falsity of the defamatory publication – it was clearly stated that the punitive award 'fully secure[s] the public interest involved'.[239] The one-sided assessment of the defendant's behaviour was thus justified by damage to a non-correlative public interest. It was not a correlative private interest of the claimant, the violation of which justified the punitive measure of the award. Rather, it was a violation of a high-level public interest according to which members of the society do not treat each other with disrespect.

Further, we can say that the profit-seeking disregard for the law – which is a necessary ingredient of Category 2 awards – may cripple several other important public interests. For instance, the tortfeasor's conduct seems publicly troubling in unlawful eviction cases and cases involving a 'monstrous' violation of housing,[240] because protection of housing is a societal interest.[241] Another example might be the public interest in fair competition.[242] It is said to be 'necessary for the law to show [in these cases] that it cannot be broken with impunity'.[243] So, as is clear again, the justification for the punitive measure is not grounded wholly or predominantly in the claimant's private rights or interests, but in some non-correlative damage to protected public interests and in the courts' desire to mark that wrong, punish the defendant and deter others from engaging in similar conduct.

Category 3 punitive damages seem to be justified by non-correlative reasons as well. There are five statutes that explicitly permit this award, none of which has yet resulted in a reported case of such a penal award.[244] What follows is thus an attempt plausibly to interpret these statutes and also to understand them by analogy with similar awards under common law.

The first act is the Reserve and Auxiliary Forces (Protection of Civil Interests) Act 1951. The Act was enacted to 'provide for protecting the interests of persons called up or volunteering for certain naval, military or air force service, or doing work or training under the National Service Act 1948'.[245] In doing so, the Act poses a number of restrictions and conditions on the enforcement of a right or remedy

[239] *John v MGN Ltd* [1997] QB 586 (CA) 626D.

[240] eg, *Drane v Evangelou* [1978] 1 WLR 455 (CA); *Mafo v Adams* [1970] 1 QB 548 (CA); *Asghar v Ahmed* (1985) 17 HLR 25 (CA); *Millington v Duffy* (1985) 17 HLR 232 (CA); *Guppys (Bridport) Ltd v Brookling, Guppys (Bridport) Ltd v James* (1984) 14 HLR 1 (CA); *Design Progression Ltd v Thurloe Properties Ltd* [2004] EWHC 324 (Ch), [2005] 1 WLR 1.

[241] Similarly, LF O'Mahony, 'Eviction and the Public Interest: The Right to Respect for Home in English Law' in RP Malloy and M Diamond (eds), *The Public Nature of Private Property* (Farnham, Ashgate Publishing, 2011) 103, 110 (exploring public interests in housing and its link with Art 8 ECHR).

[242] *2 Travel Group Plc (in liq) v Cardiff City Transport Services Ltd* [2012] CAT 19, [2012] Comp AR 211 [593]–[596]; *Devenish Nutrition Ltd v Sanofi-Aventis SA* (n 9) [141].

[243] *Rookes* (n 97) 1227.

[244] As of 9 July 2025. cf *Phonographic Performance Ltd v Ellis* [2018] EWCA Civ 2812, [2019] Bus LR 542 [36]–[37] (Lewison LJ), labelling flagrancy damages pursuant to s 97(2) of the Copyright, Designs and Patents Act 1988 as an award '*sui generis*', rather than Category 3 punitive damages. See also *Original Beauty Technology Co Ltd & Ors v G4K Fashion Ltd & Ors* [2021] EWHC 3439 (Ch) [141] and [154].

[245] Reserve and Auxiliary Forces (Protection of Civil Interests) Act 1951, Introductory text.

against a tortfeasor who was 'for the time being performing a period of relevant service'.[246] Section 13(2) of the Act then permits punitive damages to be awarded in any action for damages for conversion or other proceedings 'which lie by virtue' of failing to observe the many restrictive conditions of the Act.[247] In essence, if someone converts the property or generally fails to observe the conditions of the Act when seeking to enforce their rights against a member of the reserve and auxiliary forces, then 'the court may take account of the conduct of the defendant with a view, if the court thinks fit, to awarding exemplary damages in respect of the wrong sustained by the plaintiff'.[248]

The relevant provision thus clearly points to one-sided considerations (namely the defendant's conduct) and, at least insofar as conversion in respect of goods is concerned, resembles the cause of action and the reasoning in *Borders*[249] – a case which allowed Category 2 punitive damages for conversion. Arguably, the provision is thus also based on a non-correlative rationale. In support of this view, it can be further argued that the aim of the Act is to help protect the integrity and functioning of naval, military or air force service and of the national service under the National Service Act 1948. This rationale points to a strong public interest in expressly allowing the award of punitive damages to be available against those who would undermine the functioning of these services by way of putting the servants in a difficult situation with regard to their civil interests, such as rent, debt, etc.[250]

The Crime and Courts Act 2013, which is our second example, permits punitive damages for publication of news-related material by someone who is not a member of an approved regulator and whose 'conduct has shown a deliberate or reckless disregard of an outrageous nature for the claimant's rights'.[251] Again, the justifying reason seems very similar to that of Category 2 punitive damages, and while the Crime and Courts Act 2013 does not explicitly require the profit-seeking motive as part of the conditions for the award, the court must take account of 'the nature and extent of any benefit the defendant derived or intended to derive from [the] conduct'[252] when determining the amount of punitive damages. Interestingly, section 36 states that the amount of punitive damages must be quantified with regard to 'the nature and extent of any loss or harm caused, or intended to be

[246] S 3(1)(a) of the Act.

[247] See s 13(2) of the Act.

[248] ibid. Of course if 'the court is satisfied that the defendant acted honestly and reasonably, and ought fairly to be excused for it, the court may relieve the defendant from liability in respect thereof' (s 13(3) of the Act).

[249] *Borders (UK) Ltd v Commissioner of Police of the Metropolis* [2005] EWCA Civ 197, [2005] Po LR 1 (Borders case).

[250] Ture, when addressing the relevant provision, Lord Kilbrandon doubted that the expression 'exemplary damages' here means anything else than aggravated damages, for by virtue of s 13(6) of the 1951 Act, this applies to Scotland, where exemplary damages are forbidden. But this contention is irrelevant, because it stems from a reading of the s 13(6) of the Act which is simply incorrect. The relevant section simply states the conditions under which s 13 applies to Scotland, but it does not say that it applies to Scotland only. See *Broome v Cassell & Co Ltd (No 1)* [1972] AC 1027 (HL) 1133.

[251] Crime and Courts Act 2013, s 34(6)(a). See also ss 34–39 of the Act.

[252] ibid s 36(3)(b).

caused, by the defendant's conduct', but it does not specify that this consideration would be limited to the claimant's private damage.

The idea that punitive damages can be awarded and quantified on the basis of such non-rights-based considerations supports the view that the punitive award under the Crime and Courts Act 2013 is justified non-correlatively. Besides, for the purposes of deciding whether to award punitive damages and in what quantum, the '[c]ourt may regard deterring the defendant and others from similar conduct as an object of punishment'.[253] Such deterrent considerations help the courts to stress the public disapproval and outrage against the defendant's conduct. After all, there is arguably a valid public interest in promoting high standards of news-related publishing, and the Crime and Courts Act 2013 supports that interest by sanctioning unregulated publishers and inappropriate internal compliance procedures.[254]

The third and fourth examples can be found in the High Speed Rail (London – West Midlands) Act 2017 and the High Speed Rail (West Midlands – Crewe) Act 2021, both of which empower the court to award 'exemplary damages … [if it is] appropriate to do so in the circumstances … whether or not another remedy is granted'.[255] The identically worded provisions of these two statutes sanction obligations, prohibitions or restrictions imposed by an environmental covenant which secures a non-correlative interest. In particular, the covenant is meant to secure public interests in local land change, with the overall objective to support the planned construction of a railway, ie, something for the benefit of the public at large. The non-correlative ground for such a punitive award is thus evident.

The fifth example comes from the Environment Act 2021, which empowers the courts to award punitive damages when enforcing an obligation under a conservation covenant pursuant to the Act. Subject to section 125(3) of the Act, damages for breach of the conservation covenant shall be assessed as traditional contract damages, except that '[i]n the case of breach of an obligation of the landowner under [the] covenant, a court may award exemplary damages in such circumstances as it thinks fit'.[256] It is without a doubt that the purpose of environmental covenants, which can be issued under the Act, is to protect and improve the natural environment and that this interest is intended to benefit our society and the public at large.[257] The non-correlative justification of the punitive award is thus evident here too.

Legislation does not only permit but sometimes also forbids punitive damages. These bans on punitive awards are not justified expressly in the

[253] ibid s 35(5) and s 36(4).
[254] See ibid s 35(3)(c) and s 35(4).
[255] High Speed Rail (London – West Midlands) Act 2017, s 51(10) and s 51(11), and High Speed Rail (West Midlands – Crewe) Act 2021, s 48(10) and s 48(11).
[256] Environment Act 2021, s 125(4).
[257] See, eg, the Preamble to the Environment Act 2021 and s 1(1)(b) of the Act.

sources, and so we can only speculate as to the real reasons behind the bans. For example, the Montreal Convention 1999[258] forbids punitive damages awards but does not explain why.[259] Possibly this can be explained by reference to the express need for 'compensation based on the principle of restitution',[260] ie, the need for all damages under the Montreal Convention to be justified by correlative reasons.[261] From the perspective of the normative realm of the Montreal Convention 1999, the punitive awards would thus be justified by non-correlative and therefore impermissible reasons. Another example is the Private International Law (Implementation of Agreements) Act 2020. This Act implements the 2005 Hague Convention into English law and thereby gives the courts the power not to recognise or enforce a foreign judgment in civil or commercial matters 'if, and to the extent that, the judgment awards damages, including exemplary or punitive damages, that do not compensate a party for actual loss or harm suffered'.[262] In other words, the courts may refuse to recognise or enforce a foreign judgment if it is not underpinned by correlative reasons, namely violations of the claimant's private interest. Two other statutes – the Competition Act 1988[263] and the Consumer Rights Act 2015[264] – explicitly prevent the courts from awarding punitive damages. The ban on punitive damage is not justified in these statutes, but the need to mention punitive damages expressly suggests that the circumstances in which damages are awarded according to these two statutes may give rise to punitive damages considerations. Indeed, it seems plausible to argue that both competition and collective consumer proceedings involve important non-correlative public interests, and because the violation of those interests could arguably invite the courts to punish the defendant's wrongdoing, it is helpful to make the ban on punitive damage express in the legislation.[265]

[258] Art 29 of the Convention for the Unification of Certain Rules for International Carriage by Air (the Montreal Convention) 1999. See also Carriage by Air Act 1961, s 1 and sch 1B, art 29 of this Act. See also Carriage by Air Acts (Implementation of the Montreal Convention 1999) Order 2002, SI 2002/263, sch 1, art 29; Carriage by Air Acts (Application of Provisions) Order 2004, SI 2004/1899, sch 1, pt 2, art 29, which all copy the text of art 29 of the Montreal Convention 1999.

[259] A similar ban on 'punitive or non-compensatory damages' can be found in Art 592 of the Trade and Cooperation Agreement (n 10) concerning liability for damage caused by unauthorised or incorrect personal data processing by Eurojust and the competent authorities of the United Kingdom in combatting serious crimes.

[260] Recital (5) of the Montreal Convention 1999.

[261] See also *Nelson v Deutsche Lufthansa AG* EU:C:2012:657 (n 26) para [20].

[262] Art 11(1) of the 2005 Hague Convention, implemented by the Private International Law (Implementation of Agreements) Act 2020.

[263] s 36.

[264] s 47C(1).

[265] *cf* also Art 3(3) of the European Parliament and Council Directive 2014/104/EU of 26 November 2014 on certain rules governing actions for damages under national law for infringements of the competition law provisions of the Member States and of the European Union [2014] OJ L349/1 (dissociating 'full compensation' under the Directive on the one hand from overcompensation and awards made in the non-compensatory measure on the other hand) and J Drexl, 'The Interaction Between Private and Public Enforcement in European Competition Law' in H Micklitz and A Wechsler (eds), *The Transformation of Enforcement: European Economic Law in Global Perspective* (Oxford, Hart Publishing, 2016) 139–46, 156–58 (discussing the objectives of the remedies under the directive).

At this point it is also worth looking at the ban on 'multiple damages' within the meaning of s 5(3) of the Protection of Trading Interests Act 1980. The Protection of Trading Interests Act 1980 states that no court in the United Kingdom

> shall entertain proceedings at common law for the recovery of any sum payable under … [a foreign] judgment for multiple damages … arrived at by doubling, trebling or otherwise multiplying a sum assessed as compensation.[266]

To reiterate the finding from section III in chapter one, the award under this section of the Act was expressly referred to as 'non-compensatory' by the High Court in *SAS Institute Inc v World Programming Ltd*.[267] In that case, the Court refused to enforce any part of an award in a US judgment requiring an English company to pay damages of $26 million. According to the High Court, the Act prevents the enforcement of 'causes of action which attract punitive or multiple damages such as those that are found under the [North Carolina Unfair and Deceptive Trade Practices Act]'[268] on which the damages claim in *SAS Institute Inc v World Programming Ltd* was based. This is because such awards effectively amount to enforcement of foreign trading interests and foreign market regulations. Arguably, the award of multiple damages thus gives effect to the foreign public interest. Indeed, according to *Service Temps Inc v MacLeod*, the purpose of section 5(3) of the Act is 'to prevent the enforcement … of legal measures and court judgments under United States antitrust legislation'.[269] And as Lord Hodge went on to clarify in *Service Temps Inc*, '[t]he rationale of that section is akin to the prohibition from the enforcement of foreign penal laws',[270] ie, the enforcement of foreign public interests.

Aside from the categories test, punitive damages are only available where (or to the extent in which) the defendant was not yet criminally penalised for the same misconduct. This limitation is not, strictly speaking, part of the *Rookes* test, but it can be derived from a significant body of case law that addresses the topic.[271] The rationale supporting this limitation is that if punitive damages were available next to, or in addition to, criminal sanctions, then the defendant would be penalised twice for the same misconduct. For obvious reasons, such double jeopardy is impermissible. Arguably, this limitation thus also supports the view that punitive damages protect non-correlative public interests, similarly to how criminal law protects these kinds of interests.

[266] Protection of Trading Interests Act 1980, s 5(1) and (3).

[267] *SAS Institute Inc v World Programming Ltd* (HC Comm) (n 22) [213], [234], [238], [239], [265], [269] and [271]. Similarly, see *SAS Institute Inc v World Programming Ltd* (CA) (n 22) [43].

[268] *SAS Institute Inc v World Programming Ltd* (HC Comm) (n 22) [244].

[269] *Service Temps Inc v MacLeod* [2013] CSOH 162, 2014 SLT 375 [32].

[270] ibid [35].

[271] See, eg, *Archer v Brown* [1985] QB 401 (QB) 421; *AB v South West Water Services Ltd* [1993] 2 WLR 507 (CA) 527, 531; *Borders* (n 249) [17] and [23]; *Devenish Nutrition Ltd v Sanofi-Aventis SA* (n 9) [20], [28] and [102]; *AT & Ors v Dulghieru & Anor* [2009] EWHC 225 (QB) [69] and [71]. *cf AXA Insurance UK Plc v Financial Claims Solutions Ltd* [2018] EWCA Civ 1330, [2019] RTR 1 [33], noted in E Katsampouka, 'Exemplary Damages and Insurance Fraud' (2019) 135 *LQR* 380, 382–83.

Finally, a reason why punitive damages can be defined as damages justified by non-correlative damage is the fact that the courts discuss punitive damages in terms of 'windfall' to the claimant. This label is explicable by the apparent lack of correlative damage on the claimant's side, ie, damage that would correspond to the award and that would be justified by the reciprocal freedom of the parties in dispute. In *Broome v Cassell & Co*, for instance, Lord Wilberforce expressly labelled punitive damages 'an unmerited windfall for the plaintiff'[272] on that basis. The same position was held in *Thompson*.[273] In fact, the language of 'a windfall' is used in case law more broadly when the judges criticise the claimant's prospect of obtaining double compensation – which again presents a situation where a part of the award lacks any correlative justification and is thus non-compensatory.[274] Scholars think alike. Cane, for instance, sees punitive damages as the claimant's 'windfall', for there is no correlativity between what is received in damages and what was suffered by the claimant.[275]

I think we can thus generally characterise punitive damages as damages the measure of which is justified by non-correlative reasons. In this sense, I agree with Weinrib that any meaningful justification of punitive damages (if it exists) is not organised by the idea of correlativity.[276]

II. Nominal Damages

Nominal damages are a symbolic award that gives the claimant 'no right to any real damages at all, yet … [it supports] a right to the verdict or judgment'[277] to affirm the violation of the claimant's right. The stated aim of nominal damages is declaration: a declaration of the defendant's wrong and, by implication, a declaration of the violated right. On the one hand, nominal damages differ from compensatory damages because, unlike compensatory damages (which also implicitly declare the violation of some rights by the defendant), nominal damages pursue declaration as their main goal. On the other hand, nominal damages also differ from the remedy of declaration, because while a declaratory relief is in principle available for all types of wrong, not every violation of protected interests attracts nominal damages. Only causes of action which are actionable per se, without the need to prove any

[272] *Broome v Cassell & Co Ltd (No 1)* (n 250) 1114.

[273] *Thompson v Commissioner of Police of the Metropolis* [1998] QB 498 (CA) 517.

[274] *Hussain v New Taplow Paper Mills* [1988] 1 AC 514 (HL) 523; *Smoker v London Fire Authority* [1991] 2 AC 502 (HL) 533.

[275] Cane (n 121) 118. *cf* Zipursky (n 58) 151–59 (proposing a theory according to which the claimant has a private right to be punitive, which includes subjective and objective punitiveness).

[276] E Weinrib, 'Punishment and Disgorgement as Contract Remedies' (2003) 78 *Chicago-Kent Law Review* 55, 84; Weinrib (n 60) ch 5. But *cf* PW Lee, 'Contract Damages, Corrective Justice and Punishment' (2007) 70 *MLR* 887.

[277] *Owners of the Steamship 'Mediana' v Owners of the Lightship 'Comet'* [1900] AC 113 (HL) 116 (Mediana case).

consequential damage to the claimant's interests, can be redressed by awards of nominal damages. The relevant causes of action are torts actionable per se, certain equitable wrongs, statutory wrongs and breaches of contractual rights.[278]

As Burrows points out, 'there is a strong argument that nominal damages are unnecessary given that one can always seek a declaration that one's rights have been infringed. However, under the present law, for better or worse, nominal damages do exist'[279] and, in contrast with declaration, that one's right was infringed, which can be applied across the board, nominal damages are only available in relation to certain wrongs. To retain nominal damages as a distinct remedy, we are thus bound to offer an account of these awards that explains their characteristic non-compensatory features. Accordingly, we should be able to explain: (i) why nominal damages are not awarded in addition to compensatory damages and (ii) why nominal damages can be obtained in relation to selected causes of action only.

The existing explanations usually avoid these questions and instead resort to all sorts of pragmatic or historical arguments, such as that it is unnecessary to award an additional nominal sum where compensation was already achieved, or that it is a matter of a historical fact that some torts are actionable per se and other torts are not. And indeed, historically, when the remedy of declaration was not available, nominal damages could have been interpreted as an award intended merely to facilitate recovery of costs for the successful claimant. Nowadays, however, nominal damages are no longer 'a mere peg on which to hang costs'[280] and we thus need a serious explanation that can account for them *qua* NCDs – unless we are, of course, willing to abandon the nominal remedy as a separate category.

To understand nominal damages, let us therefore look at some cases and analyse them under the framework introduced in chapter three. In *Constantine v Imperial Hotels Ltd*,[281] a well-known West Indian cricketer brought a claim against an innkeeper who wrongfully refused to check in the customer of colour and instead accommodated him in a neighbouring hotel.[282] Although the claimant did not suffer any material loss, the hotelier had groundlessly discriminated against the cricketer. Birkett J thought there was an important point of principle involved in this case to which prior authorities gave no clear answer.[283] It was ruled that, just like in *Ashby v White* (which was a case concerning wrongful denial of the right to vote),[284] nominal damages can be awarded where an absolute right is infringed,

[278] In more detail, see Edelman, Varuhas and Higgins (n 5) para 13-002.

[279] Burrows (n 1) 280 (referring to Lord Millett's obiter dicta in *Cullen v Chief Constable of the Royal Ulster Constabulary* [2003] UKHL 39, [2003] 1 WLR 1763 [81]). See also Burrows, *Remedies for Torts and Breach of Contract*, 2nd edn (n 34) 269–70.

[280] *Beaumont v Greathead* (1846) 2 CB 494 (Common Pleas) 499 (Maule J). The same view according to which nominal damages are a mere peg for costs can be found in, eg, *Joule v Taylor* (1851) 7 EX 58, 66, (1851) 155 ER 855, 858; *Kelly v Sherlock* (1865–66) LR 1 QB 686, 694.

[281] *Constantine v Imperial Hotels Ltd* [1944] KB 693 (KB).

[282] ibid 694.

[283] ibid 708.

[284] *Ashby v White* (n 159).

even if no loss or injury is sustained.[285] In this case, the nominal award worth £5.25[286] thus seems to have been justified by damage to the right as a category, ie, the objective (rather than subjective) side of the right in question. In other words, what appears to have been the key consideration is the defendant's interference with the relevant legal right seen as a legal institution that exists for the benefit of all members of the public, rather than interference with an individual stake in that right represented by the individual claim-right.[287]

To adapt what Chapman and Trebilcock write about punitive damages, we can say that what is worthy of the non-compensatory response is not the denial that the claimant had a right to accommodation, but 'a denial of rights in general (or, as Kant or Hegel would have it, … the infringement … of the category of Right)'.[288] This is why the interference in these cases, they go on to explain, is 'more than just the private affair of those (no matter how many) whose particular rights have been infringed'.[289] In this regard, it makes sense how the right to accommodation could have been transgressed as a category of right, provided that the defendant (as he arguably did) denied the importance of the right to accommodation cognitively, 'involving conscious or advertent indifference to the relevance of rights'.[290] This explains the public nature of the non-compensatory award, because it is the public who is the guardian of the relevant right as a category. In this regard, we can understand why the right to accommodation was seen as an absolute right and why it was thought important for the sake of the public that this right be vested equally in every individual.[291] On this interpretation, the reason for the award of nominal damages in *Constantine* is thus best interpreted as a non-correlative justifying reason.

To take a more recent example, we can look at *White v Withers LLP*.[292] In this case, the claimant's wife's solicitors gained possession of numerous copies and some originals of the claimant's private documents. They alleged to have obtained the document in accordance with the law for the purposes of proceedings for ancillary relief after divorce. But the husband sued them for, inter alia, 'wrongful interference with property by possessing, taking or intercepting the claimant's correspondence and documents including personal family letters, private and confidential letters concerning business opportunities and document containing financial information'.[293] The question on the appeal was whether it was correct to strike out the claim as not disclosing any viable cause of action. The situation was

[285] *Constantine v Imperial Hotels Ltd* (n 281) 703, 704.

[286] The actual award was five guineas (ibid 708).

[287] The notion of a right as a category is borrowed from B Chapman and M Trebilcock, 'Punitive Damages: Divergence in Search of a Rationale' (1989) 40 *Alabama Law Review* 741, 781–86 and will be further discussed in the text to n 590.

[288] ibid 781.

[289] ibid 781–82.

[290] ibid 782.

[291] *Constantine v Imperial Hotels Ltd* (n 281) 707.

[292] *White v Withers LLP* [2009] EWCA Civ 1122.

[293] ibid [1].

interesting because the husband had most likely pursued this claim maliciously, motivated by private vengeance, rather than by the desire to rectify the wrong. Note that there was no tort of malicious prosecution of civil proceedings at the time of the events in dispute.

The Court of Appeal held that the pleaded facts disclosed a viable cause of action and that the claim should thus not have been struck out, even though the claimant did not suffer any actual damage and the likely remedy would thus be only nominal damages. In his leading judgment, Ward LJ stated that if 'a trivial claim is brought, it is difficult to see anything more than nominal damages being suffered and I would encourage and expect such a claim to be struck out for being an abuse of the process'.[294] Sedley LJ concurred, stating that if there will be 'no appreciable damage … that is enough to allow the courts to call an early halt to any lawsuit in tort. The claim for a shilling in damages in order to prove a point and obtain an award of costs is history …, in contrast to when most of the leading cases were decided'.[295] That being said, it was ruled in *White v Withers LLP* that the claim should not be struck out because, despite the claimant's 'desire for vengeance on the lawyers acting for an estranged spouse …, the claimant's motive cannot shut the court's door'.[296] Further, the Court argued that 'it must always be remembered that solicitors are officers of the court and if they are shown to have done wrong they should face the judgment of the court'.[297] As put by Sedley LJ, '[i]t is in the public interest that the bounds of proper conduct be clarified'.[298] The Court thus recognised the need to vindicate the strength of the law and the public interest in clarification of the bounds of proper conduct as the ground for not striking out the claim and, possibly, for the award of nominal damages in this case.[299] These are clearly non-correlative reasons.

Other cases help to illustrate this non-correlative rationale of nominal damages as well. In *Lumba*,[300] nominal damages were awarded for a wrongful detention by the executive, purportedly pursuant to an unpublished policy, of foreign nationals convicted of criminal offences and subject to deportation orders who would have been detained even under the published policy. Although the violation of a public duty was considered only formal, the circumstances have justified the need to mark the wrong by a nominal award. The justification of nominal damages could not have been grounded in the claimants' private rights, because they did not (as a result of the wrong) suffer any actual harm.

Similarly, in *R (O) v Secretary of State for the Home Department*,[301] the Supreme Court confirmed (unanimously applying *Lumba*) that a failure to apply a valid

[294] ibid [65].
[295] ibid [72].
[296] ibid [74].
[297] ibid [67].
[298] ibid [67].
[299] See ibid [71], [74] and [92].
[300] *Lumba* (n 18).
[301] *R (O) v Secretary of State for the Home Department (Bail for Immigration Detainees)* [2016] UKSC 19, [2016] 1 WLR 1717.

policy when deciding whether to release the claimant would in all likelihood be considered unlawful and attract nominal damages for false imprisonment.[302] It was also confirmed in *R (O)* that since the judicial review (which the appellant was denied) would not bring the detainee any practical benefit – she would have remained in detention anyway – the purpose of the nominal award would accord with the purpose of the declaratory judgment that her detention was unlawful. But it would not remedy any private damage resulting from the wrong because the appellant had suffered none.[303] In *R (O)* the non-correlative interest at stake is probably best characterised as a public interest in upholding the relevant public duty to exercise the power to detain in line with the published requirements. This view well explains why even a slight formal violation of a public duty may be presumed to have caused adverse consequences on the right as a category.

Sometimes, a mere technical violation of a public duty could lead to an opposite outcome – ie, no award of nominal damages – if it is considered that no significant public interest was infringed by the defendant. Take, for example, the decision in *Cullen*.[304] In that case the appellant was detained by the police and briefly denied access to a solicitor. This was formally in breach of section 15 of the Prevention of Terrorism (Temporary Provisions) Act 1984, which gives the detainee a right of access to legal advice.[305] The question in that case was whether a statute which did not expressly confer a right to compensation on a person affected by a breach of statutory duty nevertheless conferred such a right impliedly and may thus be actionable per se.

It was made clear by Lord Millett in *Cullen* that access to legal advice is a 'cornerstone of a free society under the rule of law'.[306] This claim would suggest that access to legal advice is an important public interest, the violation of which could justify nominal damages. But according to Lord Millett, this right is 'of little intrinsic value … [Rather, the right's] importance lies in the potential seriousness of the consequences if [access to legal advice is not available]'.[307] And in this particular case, it was concluded that delayed provision of access to legal advice did not cause any damage and so should not attract even nominal damages.

The key to understanding Lord Millett's conclusion is the framing of his argument. As Lord Millett stated, it would be 'hopeless [if the appellant was …] entitled as of right as a matter of English law to damages (be they small or nominal) for a procedural irregularity made in good faith and which, though important, had no adverse consequences of any kind'.[308] Lord Millett thus seems to have believed that no damage – either correlative or non-correlative – results ipso facto from the breach of the right to access legal advice under section 15 of the Act. If this

[302] ibid [39]–[41] and [49]–[50].
[303] ibid [50]. *cf Lewis v Australian Capital Territory* (n 142) [170] and [174]–[176].
[304] *Cullen v Chief Constable of the Royal Ulster Constabulary* (n 279).
[305] ibid [3].
[306] ibid [50].
[307] ibid [50].
[308] ibid [59] and [61].

interpretation is correct, it helps to explain why nominal damages are not available in cases of all civil wrongs. The trivial breach of the relevant statutory duty did not, in this case, trigger any presumption of non-correlative damage that would justify the nominal award (although the minority had a different view and concluded that any breach of this specific statutory duty should be actionable per se).[309] Importantly for the present analysis, *Cullen* illustrates again that non-correlative reasons do play a critical role in relation to the availability of nominal damages.

Here is another argument to show the non-correlative rationale for nominal damages. In *Embrey v Owen*, it was held that '[a]ctual perceptible damage is not indispensable as the foundation of an action; it is sufficient to sh[o]w the violation of a right, in which case the law will presume damage; injuria sine damno is actionable, as was laid down in the case of *Ashby v. White* (2 Ld. Eaym. 938) by Lord Holt'.[310] Indeed, in *Mediana*, it was clarified that nominal damages are awarded for violation of your right when there is no real damage. As put by Earl of Halsbury LC, '"nominal damages" is a technical phrase which means that you have negatived anything like real damage, but that … there is an infraction of a legal right'.[311] Importantly, the term nominal damages 'does not mean small damages'[312] and 'the extent to which a person has a right to recover what is called by the compendious phrase damages … depends upon a variety of circumstances'.[313] Pursuing this line of thought, we can argue that what justifies the nominal measure of damages is some conventionally presumed damage that springs from the infraction of a relevant legal right. This presumed damage is not (and cannot be, ontologically speaking) the claimant's own damage because the law's own starting point is that there is no real damage. Damage, or put more precisely 'nominal' damage, is simply presumed and as such does not primarily reflect the individual's private stake in the infringed right. Put in other words, the presumed damage must be non-correlative. There is no express articulation in the law that would show us how exactly the judges (or the law) make this alleged presumption of damage in individual cases. But reasons of coherence dictate that what nominal damages respond to – when the 'compendious phrase damages' (as it was called in *Mediana*) is put to work – is some kind of damage. And if it is no real damage, then it must be presumed damage.

The idea that nominal damages respond to presumed damage aligns with the idea that all damages, as they are standardly defined, respond to some consequential damage, rather than just to the underlying civil wrong. This seems a rational reconstruction of the law governing the award of nominal damages – provided that we want to retain nominal damages as a remedy which is distinct from other

[309] ibid [21].
[310] See, eg, *Embrey v Owen* (1851) 6 Ex 353, 368, (1851) 155 ER 579, 585 (citing *Ashby v White* (n 159)).
[311] *Mediana* (n 277) 116.
[312] ibid 116.
[313] ibid 116.

types of damages (I will return to this point in a moment). Besides, if nominal damages respond to consequential (albeit nominal) damage, then it makes sense why nominal damages are not identical with the remedy of declaration.[314] It is not identical with a declaration because it does not directly respond to the liability establishing a civil wrong.

Unfortunately, the use of the nominal damages label is not entirely uniform, and so we might still find cases that use the label also as a shorthand for small damages or damages for inappreciable loss.[315] This complicates the analysis of the law because nominal damages in this sense would be but a liminal case of compensation, ie, a remedy for damage that is not nominally presumed but damage that is nominally small. For example, in a defamation case between Mr Grobbelaar and News Group Newspapers Ltd, the claimant obtained a nominal award of £1 because the value of his reputation was deemed to be only nominal.[316] This case will be analysed in more detail in section III, but the point here is that some nominal awards can be explained on a correlative basis.

Another example might be *Anglo-Cyprian Trade Agencies Ltd v Paphos Wine Industries Ltd.*[317] In this case, the claimants pleaded that they were sold valueless wines and claimed the full purchase price. It turned out that the defect in the goods (cork taint) can be fixed for a fraction of the full price, and the claimant was thus permitted to amend the statement of claim. Small damages, as requested in the amended statement of claim, were then awarded. According to the Court of Appeal, when interpreting this judgment, 'the plaintiff had claimed £2,000 for defects in wine, but ultimately what was recovered was the sum of £52 … which was in effect the award of nominal damages'.[318] Again, this usage of the phrase 'nominal damages' is more aptly described as a liminal case of compensation.

Indeed, several leading scholars believe that nominal damages are justified by correlative reasons, namely by a violation of the claimant's own claim-right. Stevens, for example, thinks nominal damages confirm that tort law is rights-based and that it perfectly fits the correlative structure of tort remedies.[319] Similarly, Goldberg and Zipursky understand nominal damages as evidence that violations of the claimant's rights are the distinctive reasons for tort law actions,[320] Hershovitz concurs that tort law 'does [corrective] justice … by saying, clearly and loudly, *this*

[314] See, eg, *R (Lauzikas) v Secretary of State for the Home Department* [2019] EWCA Civ 1168, [2019] WLR 6625 [33] (LJ Longmore): 'In the first place, the deputy judge has in my view conflated the concepts of liability and damages'.

[315] See, eg, *Roberts v Chief Constable of the Cheshire Constabulary* [1999] 1 WLR 662 (CA) 668: 'this infringement cannot be regarded as a purely nominal matter or a matter compensatable by entirely nominal damages' (Clarke LJ), which view was rejected by Lord Dyson in *Lumba* (n 18) [93].

[316] See *Grobbelaar v News Group Newspapers Ltd* [2002] 1 WLR 3024 (HL).

[317] *Anglo-Cyprian Trade Agencies Ltd v Paphos Wine Industries Ltd* [1951] 1 All ER 873 (KB).

[318] *Andrews Bros (Plastering) Ltd v Sherman* [1987] 5 WLUK (EWCA Civ).

[319] Stevens (n 60) 84.

[320] eg, JCP Goldberg and BC Zipursky, *Recognizing Wrongs* (Cambridge, MA, Harvard University Press 2020) 954–57.

defendant wronged that plaintiff,[321] and Gardner claims that nominal damages are 'nominally reparative' in that they mark the fact that there are reasons of corrective justice for this award, but there is nothing to repair (no actual loss).[322]

These correlative conceptions of nominal damages neither explain nor justify the nominal award entirely. First, these conceptions cannot explain why nominal damages belong to the category of 'damages' as defined in this book, because these conceptions do not analyse nominal damages as awards that rectify damage caused by a civil wrong. Rather, these conceptions understand nominal damages as an award for the civil wrong itself. Further, the correlative view does not explain why nominal damages are not available for all claim-right violations. Stevens argues, for example, that nominal damages 'should be awarded where the [claim-]right is infringed in an insignificant way, not where the infringement of the right causes no consequential loss'.[323] However, that view does not reflect the current law. As put by Lord Hutton in *Cullen*, we need to 'distinguish between a trivial breach for which no damages should be awarded and a breach of sufficient seriousness to call for an award of nominal or virtually nominal damages'.[324] Besides, Stevens's view would imply that nominal damages should in principle be available for all insignificant rights-infringements and that they should be in principle available also next to compensatory awards for consequential loss.[325] Neither of these implications is consistent with the existing law.

As the analysed cases show, nominal damages seem to respond to damage to only the most important interests when viewed from the perspective of the public. This observation could explain why they are not available for all claim-right violations. Indeed, in respect of torts actionable per se, nominal damages protect: 'liberty, corporeal integrity, and physical property in one's possession – and the tort of trespass protects them against direct invasion by positive interference even where no actual harm ensues … (libel is another, less happy, example)'.[326]

Similarly, in respect of contract law damages, it seems to be an important public interest that a person who voluntarily assumes an obligation by entering a contract does not breach that obligation. So, from the public's perspective, even the most harmless breach of the most insignificant contracts is still a breach of an

[321] S Hershovitz, 'Treating Wrongs as Wrongs: An Expressive Argument for Tort Law' (2017) 10 *Journal of Tort Law* 405, 443 (emphasis in original).

[322] J Gardner, 'Torts and Other Wrongs' (2011) 39 *Florida State University Law Review* 43, 56–58.

[323] ibid 84.

[324] *Cullen v Chief Constable of the Royal Ulster Constabulary* (n 279) [44] (Lord Hutton).

[325] A situation like this might occur when someone locks you in your house for a couple of hours but does not know that you have previously been held hostage by kidnappers and that this new – and clearly insignificant – violation of your right not to be falsely imprisoned can cause you enormous consequential harm in terms of mental health and possibly your ability to engage in social life. On Stevens's analysis, you should be entitled to obtain both damages for the consequential loss and nominal (substitutive) damages for the insignificant interference with your claim-right.

[326] T Weir, *A Casebook on Tort*, 10th edn (London, Sweet & Maxwell, 2004) 7. *cf Watkins v Home Office* [2006] UKHL 17, [2006] 2 AC 395 [24] and [25]; *Lachaux v Independent Print Ltd & Anor* [2019] UKSC 27, [2020] AC 612 [20].

important legal institution – a binding contract. As stated by Raz, the 'purpose of contract law *should* be … to protect both the practice of undertaking voluntary obligations and the individuals who rely on that practice'.[327] We could say that nominal damages are primarily concerned with the protection of the practice of contracting, and only secondarily with the protection of the individual who relies on it in a particular case. In this sense, contract law and its remedial toolkit 'recognizes and reinforces the social practice of undertaking voluntary obligations',[328] which is critical for the functioning of our society. We can support this view by an argument that if contractual promises were not binding regardless of consequential damage, commerce and markets would be significantly impaired, which would be detrimental to the society at large. Any breach of any contract thus results in 'institutional harm'[329] and such harm needs to be marked by the nominal monetary remedy to highlight its importance. It is not clear, so the interpretation would go, that a mere declaration or private compensation would be sufficient to achieve the same goal and that it would distinguish the publicly important from publicly less important interests.

The quantum of nominal damages supports the non-correlative interpretation of the law in this area as well. The quantum of nominal damages is highly standardised, typically in the region of £5. This suggests that the award is unconcerned with the claimant's interests but rather responds to some abstract conception of damage to non-correlative interests. Of course, the quantum of compensatory damages for pain, suffering and loss of amenity is also highly standardised, for instance in road traffic accident cases where the claimant suffers a whiplash injury that attracts a tariff award stipulated by the Whiplash Injury Regulations 2021.[330] That said, there is one important difference here. In the case of nominal damages, the award is standardised by nature because the damage to the protected interests is itself standard – it cannot be individualised because the nominal damage suffered is the same regardless of the claimant's individual circumstances. By contrast, the standardised quantum of compensation can be, in principle, individualised and the harm suffered could vary from one claimant to another, depending on their individual circumstances. The standardised compensation is not a matter of necessity but a matter of choice: on balance the legislature has decided to standardise these awards because it helps us to tackle, for instance, the otherwise disproportionate costs of whiplash claims caused by, inter alia, evidentiary difficulties and the starting uncertainty as to the monetary value of the damage suffered. In the case of nominal damages, the standardisation seems, however, baked into the nature

[327] J Raz, 'Promises in Morality and Law' (1982) 95 *Harvard Law Review* 916, 933 (emphasis in original).

[328] ibid 933.

[329] ibid 937.

[330] See also s 3 of the Civil Liability Act 2018 and *Hassam v Rabot* [2023] EWCA Civ 19; *Rabot v Hassam* [2024] UKSC 11. See also Judicial College, *Judicial College Guidelines for the Assessment of General Damages in Personal Injury Cases*, 16th edn (Oxford, OUP, 2022). In the literature, see Descheemaeker, 'Pecuniary and Non-pecuniary Loss: A Reinterpretation' (n 131) 90–95.

of the damage.[331] The nominal damage resulting from the wrong is probably best conceptualised as interference with the right as a category, ie, with the standard public interest in that right, rather than as interference with any individual private interest in that right.

We can conclude that the preceding analysis of nominal damages explains their specificities without the need to reach out for pragmatic or historical arguments. On the wrongs-based view advanced in this book, it becomes clear that the measure of damages is justified by the consequences of the wrong, not the wrong itself. And the insight that nominal damages are justified by consequential violations of publicly important interests explains why nominal damages are not available for all kinds of civil wrong (eg, negligence[332]). It also explains why it is important to permit their award even if the wrong does not cause the claimant to suffer any consequential damage. Moreover, we can say that if the claimant suffers consequential loss, then the public interest in marking the importance of a wrong will be effectively satisfied by the compensatory award. Hence, there is probably no public interest reason left to award nominal damages on top of compensatory damages, and there is no useful role for nominal damages if the claimant can show that they have suffered loss. This is because there is no apparent reason why the law should presume the right-violation would still cause the non-correlative damage. The presumed damage to important public interests is, in the case of nominal damages, premised on the assumption that the civil wrong would be left unnoticed. But if the claimant obtains compensation for the wrong, then this premise fails and the presumed damage does not occur. That is why, for example, it seems reasonable that nominal damages are not available for negligence.

III. Contemptuous Damages

Contemptuous damages are characterised as a separate type of NCDs by the literature, not primary sources. Primary legal sources, as was shown in section III of chapter one, do not use the term NCDs in relation to contemptuous damages. Still, given the presence of this category in the scholarly writings, it appears proper to analyse them at this point too, although, unlike nominal damages, contemptuous damages are extremely rare in the cases and have thus probably very little (if any) practical significance.

For the sake of the analysis, and in light of the conclusions in section III, chapter one, let us therefore accept that contemptuous damages are a distinct category of NCDs. As a separate category, contemptuous damages (sometimes also called

[331] *cf* Descheemaeker, 'The Standardisation of Tort Damages' (n 131) 17.

[332] However, as I will argue in sections III and IV of ch 5, the public interest analysis of NCDs supports the case for making nominal damages available for violations of all non-acquired private rights, including those protected by duties of care in negligence.

derisory or a farthing damages) are typically characterised as a minimal award that affirms the violation of the claimant's right, but which – unlike nominal damages – cannot be regarded as success in the claim.[333] In practice, however, it can be difficult to distinguish contemptuous damages from nominal damages, as will be shown.[334] Contemptuous damages are awarded to show the court's contempt for the damages claim. When awarded, they are typically a result of an unsuccessful claim for compensatory damages. In particular, their stated purpose is 'to indicate that while the claimant's legal rights have technically been infringed, the court has formed a very low opinion of the claimant's claim, or that his conduct was such that he deserved, at any rate morally, what the defendant did to him'.[335] In the literature, the phrase 'contemptuous damages' is typically associated with '"[g]old-digging" actions of defamation'.[336]

Indeed, it may be emphasised that the awards of contemptuous damages are not governed by the same rules as nominal damages and, regardless of some superficial similarities between the two categories, are therefore doctrinally distinct from nominal damages. For instance, there is no rule that would require the courts to award contemptuous damages only in cases of torts actionable per se and in cases of contract violations. And while the quantum of contemptuous damages is very small, just like in the case of nominal damages, the aim of the derisory award is a bit different. Evans LJ made this clear when he expressed that an award of nominal damages 'should not be taken to imply a contemptuous or derisory dismissal of the plaintiff's claim'.[337] In a different case, Goddard LJ made a comment to the same end, claiming that 'very often juries read in newspapers about a farthing damages; but that those were contemptuous damages, and not nominal damages'.[338]

The authority most often cited to illustrate the doctrines governing the award of contemptuous damages is *Grobbelaar v News Group Newspapers Ltd*, although the judgment itself unhelpfully refers to the award both as 'derisory' and 'nominal'.[339] The case concerned a dispute between Mr Grobbelaar – a famous professional footballer – and newspapers that allegedly defamed him by an 'accusation of match fixing … [which accusations were] completely destructive of his reputation as a professional footballer'.[340] In the first instance the jury found for the claimant and made an award of £85,000. The House of Lords held that the jury was right to hold

[333] *R (Collin) v Secretary of State for the Home Department* [2013] EWHC 4803 (Admin), [2013] 6 WLUK 144 [68].

[334] Which was the case even when Sir Frederick Pollock wrote his first treatise on the law of torts: *The Law of Torts: A Treatise on the Principles of Obligations Arising from Civil Wrongs in the Common Law* (London, Stevens & Sons, 1887) 121.

[335] Goudkamp and Nolan (n 29) para 23-007.

[336] Edelman, Varuhas and Higgins (n 5) para 13-009, fn 36.

[337] *Maurice Lubin and Prodev Ltd (formerly Property Developers Mortgage & Loan Company Ltd) v HTV Cymru (Wales) Ltd* [1992] 12 WLUK 38 (CA) [reported without pagination].

[338] *English and Scottish Co-Operative Properties Mortgage and Investment Society Ltd v Odhams Press Ltd* [1940] 1 KB 440 (CA) 461 (Goddard LJ).

[339] See *Grobbelaar v News Group Newspapers Ltd* (n 316).

[340] ibid [47] (Lord Hobhouse).

the newspapers liable in libel but that the claimant could not have been entitled to any substantial compensatory damages, because the evidence before the jury had completely destroyed the value of Mr Grobbelaar's reputation. The £85,000 award was thus reduced to merely a contemptuous award of £1.

Lord Bingham,[341] Lord Steyn,[342] Lord Hobhouse,[343] Lord Millett,[344] and Lord Scott[345] referred to the £1 substitute award as nominal in the sense of nominal compensation. The award, on this view, was justified by the nominal value of Mr Grobbelaar's 'reputation as a sportsman [which] has been destroyed by his corrupt dealings'.[346] On this reading, the nominal measure of compensation would be justified correlatively, even though the quantum of damages was reduced to £1. Indeed, Lord Hobhouse argued that while 'the sum of £85,000 was excessive and must be reduced … [a] much more modest, say a four figure [compensatory] sum, would … have been unappealable'.[347] If this is a correct interpretation of the court's approach, then damages in this case are but a liminal case of compensatory damages, thus distinct from non-compensatory nominal damages, but not much different from compensatory damages (except with the implication that the claimant would not be technically successful in their claim and this may have implications on costs). The conclusion here would be that contemptuous damages should not be characterised as non-compensatory.

A similar view was recently adopted in *Wright v McCormack*.[348] In this case, the defendant accused the claimant on Twitter of fraudulently claiming to be Satoshi Nakamoto – the inventor of Bitcoin. The claimant, a computer scientist, alleged that this libel had caused him serious harm to his reputation, including not being able to present at academic conferences. It turned out a few days before trial that the allegations regarding the serious harm were false. Chamberlain J thus ruled that 'the deliberately false case on serious harm advanced by Dr Wright … requires more than a mere reduction in the award of damages'.[349] The judge then went on to conclude that this fact alone 'makes it unconscionable that Dr Wright should receive any more than nominal damages'.[350] Similarly to *Grobbelaar*, the judge awarded a contemptuous sum (labelled as 'nominal') in order nominally to compensate the claimant for the harm to his otherwise worthless reputation. As was confirmed by the Court of Appeal in *Wright v McCormack*, in cases of defamation, it is permissible to have regard to the defendant's conduct up until the point of judgment because this conduct may affect the court's evaluation of the claimant's

[341] ibid [27].
[342] ibid [34].
[343] ibid [61].
[344] ibid [69].
[345] ibid [85] to [87].
[346] ibid [36] (Lord Steyn).
[347] ibid [61].
[348] *Wright v McCormack* [2022] EWHC 2068 (QB).
[349] ibid [144].
[350] ibid [144].

reputation and therefore the court's assessment of damages for the claimant's reputational harm.[351]

An alternative reading of these cases – a reading which would acknowledge a distinctive non-compensatory function of such damages – would focus on the reasons behind the court's contempt for the profit-seeking claim. On this reading, we might say that the House of Lords in *Grobbelaar* sought to halt Mr Grobbelaar's desire to profit from the legal dispute. It was clear that his claim was not motivated by his desire to rectify damage to his reputation. So while the claimant could have suffered damage to his low reputation (perhaps even worth the four-figure sum mentioned by Lord Hobhouse), the derisory sum was not intended to measure that damage. Instead, it was designed to replace (rather than reduce) any substantial award with an award expressing the court's contempt.

Indeed, the judges expressed their contempt for Mr Grobbelaar's litigation behaviour when referring to the award as 'derisory damages'.[352] More particularly, Lord Steyn argued that '[t]o award him anything more [than £1] would be an affront to sport, public justice and public policy'.[353] The position held by the House of Lords was that the system of justice cannot be abused and that the courts may use their powers to protect this non-correlative interest in the justice system by replacing the compensatory award with a derisory sum. In Lord Steyn's words, even to grant him an injunction would 'destroy the solemnity of an order of court'.[354] On this reading, the measure of the £1 award cannot be justified by any damage to the claimant's correlative interests. Instead, it could be analysed as an award justified by damage to the public interest in the solemnity of court orders.

A similar non-correlative justification can be found in other cases of contemptuous damages as well. For instance, in *Beevis v Dawson* the court awarded 'a farthing [in contemptuous] damages' to find for the claimant but stop this 'lamentable case'[355] and 'save the time of the court and save public expense'.[356] In *Dering v Uris*,[357] the court issued a verdict for the claimant but awarded him only a contemptuous halfpenny because the defendants had already offered Mr Dering fair compensation before the trial. Moreover, because the claimant was wasting the court's valuable time at the expense of other potential claimants, he was denied costs, and this denial was deemed to be in the interest of 'broad justice [and] policy'.[358] And in *Whittaker v Scarborough Post Newspaper Company*, Lord Esher ruled that '[i]f a libel were a trivial or ridiculous one, in respect of which the

[351] *Wright v McCormack* [2023] EWCA Civ 892 [57], [68], [69]. See also B Teng, 'Counterfactual Conundrum in Defamation' (2024) 140 *LQR* 182, 184 (commending the Court of Appeal for adopting a compensatory analysis of the case).
[352] ibid [28] and [36] (Lord Steyn) and [69] (Lord Millett).
[353] ibid [36] (Lord Steyn).
[354] ibid [40] (Lord Steyn).
[355] *Beevis v Dawson* [1957] 1 QB 195 (CA) 214.
[356] ibid 209.
[357] *Dering v Uris* [1964] 2 QB 669 (QB).
[358] ibid 672–73.

jury thought that an action ought not to have been brought, they would only give contemptuous damages, though many copies of the libel had been circulated'.[359] So, although the claimants could have suffered harm in these cases, the derisory sum did not reflect such harm. Instead, various non-correlative considerations prompted the courts to award contemptuous damages in place of any substantial sum.

Interestingly, this kind of reasoning is not dissimilar from situations when courts strike out vindictive claims for abuse of process – they do so on the basis of a public interest, and they are able to do so across the board, regardless of the nature of the defendant's wrong.[360] Similarly, section 57 of the Criminal Justice and Courts Act 2015 provides that in a case where a claim for damages in respect of personal injury (eg, in a road traffic accident[361]) has been exaggerated by a 'fundamentally dishonest' claimant, the court is to dismiss the claim altogether, including any unexaggerated part, unless satisfied that substantial injustice would thereby be done to him.[362] The rationale behind the statutory provision was 'to discourage fraudulent and exaggerated claims, which arise often in motor accident cases and so-called "trips and slips" claims … [which] cause substantial harm to society as a whole, not least in increasing the insurance premiums that motorists have to pay'.[363] So the court's powers to strike out abusive claims, as well as their powers to express their contempt for the claim, seem to be justified by very similar, if not the same, non-correlative reasons of public interest.[364]

There is one major issue with this analysis, though. The sanction imposed by way of contemptuous damages is a kind of penalty against the claimant and not against the defendant. The contemptuous measure, on this interpretation, would not be justified by the defendant's civil wrong or by wrongful consequences thereof. Thus, it would be questionable on this interpretation of the law whether contemptuous damages are 'damages' at all, given that the contemptuous aspect to the award is justified by the claimant's (not the defendant's) unacceptable conduct.

As a result, the non-correlative analysis would imply that contemptuous damages are not the farthing sum that the defendant pays to the claimant. Instead, the contemptuous measure would be better understood as something negative – a

[359] *Whittaker v Scarborough Post Newspaper Company* [1896] 2 QB 148 (CA) 149. See also *Grobbelaar v News Group Newspapers Ltd* (n 316).

[360] See CPR r 3.4(2)(b): 'The court may strike out a statement of case if it appears to the court that the statement of case is an abuse of the court's process or is otherwise likely to obstruct the just disposal of the proceedings.'

[361] *Woodger v Hallas* [2022] EWHC 1561 (QB).

[362] See *Versloot Dredging BV v HDI Gerling Industrie Versicherung AG* [2016] UKSC 45, [2017] AC 1 [95] (Lord Hughes);*Ivey v Genting Casinos UK Ltd* [2017] UKSC 67, [2018] AC 391 [74] (Lord Hughes).

[363] HL Deb 23 July 2014, vol 755, col 1267.

[364] *cf* N Sinanis, '"Damages, One Farthing": Under-compensation in Nineteenth-century Tort' in F Bettini and others (eds), *New Directions in Private Law* (London, UCL Press, 2023) 199 (arguing that contemptuous damages have historically been justified by non-correlative claimant-sided considerations only); *Iceland Foods Ltd v Birch* [2023] EWHC 3390 (KB) [20]–[21] (where the court confirms the public interest involved in deciding whether to permit the bringing of contempt proceedings under the CPR).

quantum of money subtracted from a substantial award that would otherwise have been made, had it not been for the claimant's contravention of the public interest in the administration of justice and in the limited court resources. On this interpretation, the derisory award would thus be understood as the reduction of the substantial award and not as the small award that is left.[365]

If that is correct (which I doubt), then contemptuous damages should not be labelled as 'damages'. If, by contrast, they are correctly labelled as 'damages' (and this I think is the better view), then we should probably admit that contemptuous damages – ie, the derisory sum that is left after the contemptuous reduction of the total sum – are in effect small damages that do not make for an independent NCDs category. They could be reinterpreted as either nominal damages *qua* liminal compensation, as was just shown, or as nominal damages *qua* non-correlatively justified awards.[366] For example, in *Lumba* (discussed above), the detainees obtained nominal damages because there was a public interest in marking the formal breach of the law by the officials – this was the declaratory function of nominal damages. Yet we can also say that the nominal award in *Lumba* was (at least partly) fulfilling a contemptuous function. The detained criminals did not suffer any real damage, and it would be objectionable as a matter of policy to allow them to profit from their claim.[367] Thus, on this interpretation of the case, the nominal award in *Lumba* can be said to have served a contemptuous function – the judges have made a small award to express their disapproval of the claim for damages.

In any event, it makes sense to exclude contemptuous damages from an interpretive theory of NCDs because they do not make for a distinct non-compensatory measure of damages. This conclusion is consistent with the primary sources. The literature that says otherwise, ie, the literature that regards contemptuous damages as a special type of remedy, should be viewed as incorrect. This claim advances (not contradicts) the findings made in Section 1.3 regarding the supposed scope of NCDs.

IV. Vindicatory Damages

Let us now turn to vindicatory damages. The stated purpose of vindicatory damages is to: (i) vindicate the claimant's rights which have been infringed, and (ii) 'to reflect the sense of public outrage, emphasise the importance of

[365] To this extent, the justification for the reductive effect of contemptuous damages resembles the justification behind the doctrine of illegality. Illegality is also grounded in public interests and, similarly to contemptuous awards, does not remedy a particular wrong. Instead, the doctrine of illegality prevents the claimant to bring a claim if it would be harmful to the integrity of the legal system. See *Patel v Mizra* [2016] UKSC 42, [2017] AC 467; *Stoffel & Co v Grondona* [2020] UKSC 42, [2021] AC 540 [23] and [46]; *Henderson v Dorset Healthcare University NHS Foundation Trust* [2020] UKSC 43, [2021] AC 563 [68], [72], [129] and [131].

[366] *cf* Edelman, Varuhas and Higgins (n 5) para 13-009 fn 36.

[367] See *Lumba* (n 18) [361] (Lord Brown (dissenting)).

the … [infringed] right and the gravity of the breach, and deter further breaches'.[368] As put by Lord Scott in *Ashley*, '[d]amages awarded for the purpose of vindication are essentially rights-centred, awarded in order to demonstrate that the right in question should not have been infringed at all'.[369] Such vindicatory considerations can be found in cases concerning abuse of state power,[370] invasion of privacy,[371] egregious violation of constitutional rights,[372] and unlawful detention.[373] True, compensatory damages may also have vindicatory effects,[374] but we are interested here in vindicatory damages as a category of NCDs.

The doctrinal category of vindicatory damages is perhaps best captured in *Ramanooop*[375] – a case concerning a vindicatory remedy under section 14 of the Constitution of Trinidad and Tobago (which is of course not part of English law, but in relation to which the vindicatory function of damages was helpfully discussed). The vindicatory award was made in respect of serious misbehaviour by a police officer towards the claimant, and it was made in addition to a compensatory remedy.[376] As noted by Lord Nicholls in *Ramanoop*, '[t]he fact that the right violated was a constitutional right adds an extra dimension to the wrong'.[377] This approach clearly separated the vindicatory effect of compensation from vindication as the main purpose of the award.[378]

Strictly speaking, however, vindicatory damages are not available under English law, or at least there is no express doctrine of vindicatory damages as such. The Supreme Court's decision in *Lumba*[379] is traditionally understood as a ban on vindicatory damages.[380] In *Lumba*, Lord Dyson saw 'no justification for letting such an unruly horse loose on our law'[381] and clearly stated that '[t]he implications of awarding vindicatory damages in the present case [of a battery and false imprisonment by an arm of the state] would be far reaching'.[382] And as was stated by the Court of Appeal, '[t]here is no principle in the law of England and Wales

[368] *AG of Trinidad and Tobago v Ramanoop* [2005] UKPC 15, [2006] 1 AC 328 [26] (Lord Nicholls). See also *Lumba* (n 18) [100] and *Ngumi v AG of the Bahamas* [2023] UKPC 12 [82].

[369] *Ashley v Chief Constable of Sussex* (n 19) [22].

[370] *Anam* (n 17).

[371] *Gulati v MGN Ltd* (n 18) [127]; *Gulati v MGN Ltd* [2015] EWCA Civ 1291, [2017] QB 149 [19]–[20], [42], [44] and [48].

[372] *AG of Trinidad and Tobago v Ramanoop* (n 368); *Lumba* (n 18) [99].

[373] See, eg, *Lumba* (n 18).

[374] *Sloutsker v Romanova* [2015] EWHC 2053 (QB) [77] (Warby J): 'Vindication is … an intrinsic part of compensation for [the tort of defamation] …, the gist of which is the effect on the claimant's reputation and standing in the eyes of others'.

[375] *AG of Trinidad and Tobago v Ramanoop* (n 368).

[376] ibid [19].

[377] ibid [19].

[378] For the same interpretation, see *Lumba* (n 18) [224].

[379] ibid (n 18).

[380] Such an interpretation can be derived from, eg, *Weller v Associated Newspapers Ltd* [2014] EWHC 1163 (QB), [2014] EMLR 24 [189]–[191]; *Gulati v MGN Ltd* (n 18) [128]; *Gulati v MGN Ltd* (n 371) [19]; *Shaw v Kovac & Anor* [2017] EWCA Civ 1028, [2017] 1 WLR 4773 [50]–[54] and [84]; *Lloyd v Google LLC* [2018] EWHC 2599 (QB), [2019] 1 WLR 1265 [68].

[381] *Lumba* (n 18) [101] (Lord Dyson).

[382] ibid [101] (Lord Dyson). Similarly, ibid [237] (Lord Collins).

of "vindicatory" damages'.[383] In a recent Australian decision (which might be seen as persuasive in its interpretation of several English authorities on the matter), the High Court of Australia also held that substantial damages cannot be awarded 'simply for the infringement of the plaintiff's rights'[384] and that '[t]here is no place for a separate species of vindicatory damages'.[385]

You may thus object that the entire discussion of vindicatory damages is irrelevant. But since both the courts and the literature clearly engage with the *idea* of vindicatory damages[386] (regardless of whether a corresponding *doctrinal category* exists in English law), it is worth exploring whether this *idea* captures a distinctive function of damages, what reasons justify this function and whether it can be clearly contrasted with compensation. Finally, if it is possible to identify a distinctive *idea* of vindicatory damages, it is worth asking whether there are at least some hidden awards of vindicatory damages in English law, ie, awards which in reality pursue vindication as their main aim although the courts do not expressly mark them as a distinct category of vindicatory damages.

This section shows that the idea of vindicatory damages can be defensibly understood as a remedy justified by violations of non-correlative interests. It also shows that there is at least one award of damages in English law that fits the idea of vindicatory damages (although it is not expressly labelled as such) and can therefore be meaningfully characterised as a hidden award of vindicatory damages.

Besides, the decision in *Lumba* itself contains a number of conflicting views on the matter, which supports the conclusion that the 'cases which have used the language of vindication [are] in need of rationalisation'.[387] Only three Justices in *Lumba* (Lords Dyson, Collins and Phillips) dismissed the idea of vindicatory damages as a separate doctrinal category, arguing that any formal introduction of such a category into English law would be redundant given the existence of other non-compensatory remedies and given the vindicatory effects of other awards.[388] These three Justices also argued that it would be dangerous to draw an analogy between the constitutional law case of *Ramanooop* and the English law of tort in that it could, in the absence of a written constitution, cause a lot of uncertainty about if and when such vindicatory damages are available under common law more broadly.[389]

[383] *Lee Bostridge v Oxleas NHS Foundation Trust* [2015] EWCA Civ 79 [5].

[384] *Lewis v Australian Capital Territory* (n 142) [159].

[385] ibid [172]. Although this judgment was not accepted without criticism: see, eg, S Frauenfelder, 'Rewriting History: Lewis v ACT and Counterfactual Analysis in Unlawful Imprisonment' (2024) 55 *Australian Bar Review* 92, 101: 'A view that nominal damages – ordinarily an award of $1 – is sufficient vindication of the right to liberty is difficult to accept. … For someone who has been imprisoned against the law, nominal damages might justifiably be seen as derisory rather than vindicatory.'

[386] See ch 1, section III and the literature in n 31.

[387] Edelman, Varuhas and Higgins (n 5) para 18-029.

[388] *Lumba* (n 18) ibid [100] and [101] (Lord Dyson), [228], [233], [236] and [237] (Lord Collins), [335] (Lord Phillips).

[389] ibid [100] (Lord Dyson), [224] (Lord Collins) and [335] (Lord Phillips). But cf ibid [217] (Baroness Hale).

Four other Justices in *Lumba* did not reject the idea that, in English law, substantial damages could be justified by the need to mark the wrong and the gravity of its breach, by the need to highlight the public importance of the violated duty and by the need to express the sense of public outrage against the defendant's deplorable conduct (all of which are arguably non-correlative considerations).[390] In particular, three of these four Justices (Lords Hope and Walker and Lady Hale) would have made some kind of vindicatory award. One of these four Justices (Lord Kerr) thought that vindication is a legitimate aim of remedies, but he was of the opinion that an award of nominal damages and the court's finding of false imprisonment already fulfilled this vindicatory function.[391] Seen in this perspective, the view that vindicatory damages cannot be awarded under English law was thus in the minority in *Lumba*.

Two other Justices – out of the nine in total – (Lords Brown and Roger) made no specific remarks on the matter because they would not have awarded any damages to the detainees, ie, not even nominal damages. Their conclusion had nothing to do with the (un)availability of vindicatory damages under English law, and so we cannot infer whether their position supports or denies the proposition that vindicatory damages should or should not be available under English law. Instead, they thought the application of an unpublished detainment policy was not the 'but for' cause of the detainment of the appellants, and so the appellants' claim should fail on this ground. The detainees would have been rightly detained anyway, and so, argued Lords Brown and Roger, the correct counterfactual reasoning is that no freedom of movement was infringed by the state officers in the present case.[392]

In a later case, *Gulati*, we also find judicial pronouncements that are more nuanced and that do not straightforwardly ban vindicatory damages. Thus, the Court of Appeal in *Gulati* stated that 'vindicatory awards *of the kind* … the Supreme Court held in [*Lumba*] could not be awarded',[393] not that vindicatory damages cannot be made altogether. Similarly, in *Shaw v Kovac*, for example, the Court of Appeal acknowledged that it 'may be debated whether actions framed in breach of privacy have possibly something of a special status in this regard'.[394] This is aligned with Lord Dyson's pronouncement in *Lumba* that vindicatory damages must be dismissed for 'the purpose of vindicating a *claimant's* common

[390] ibid [176], [178] and [179] (Lord Hope), [181] and [195] (Lord Walker), [196], [213], [214] and [217] (Baroness Hale), [252] and [256] (Lord Kerr), [343], [344] and [361] (Lord Brown with whom Lord Rodger agreed).

[391] ibid [256].

[392] ibid [360] and [361].

[393] *Gulati v MGN Ltd* (n 371) [44] (emphasis added).

[394] See, eg, *Shaw v Kovac & Anor* (n 380) [53]. *cf Alexander Aristides Reid v Katie Price* [2020] EWHC 594 (QB) [51]: '[A]lthough vindicatory damages are not recoverable in this context, in misuse of private information and data protection claims, damages may be awarded for loss of autonomy or loss of control' (Warby J). *Cf* also Edelman, Varuhas and Higgins (n 5) para 18-023 to 18-028 and S Fulham-McQuillan, 'Infringement of Autonomy as Damage in Medical Negligence' (2023) 139 *LQR* 126.

law rights'[395] infringed by a false imprisonment or battery. It can thus be argued that the ban only concerned violation of correlative private interests of the claimant, established under common law. Effectively, this would mean that vindicatory damages can be awarded for non-correlative damage, or under statute, or in equity. As Lord Dyson made clear, the justificatory reasons for vindicatory damages cannot, in English law, be conceived in terms of 'constitutional rights',[396] given the absence of a codified constitution.[397] Thus, if it can be shown that some damages awards in English law pursue in reality vindication as their main aim – and I will try to demonstrate below that at least one such award exists – this does not need to be in conflict with the authority in *Lumba*.

To be clear, I am not suggesting that we should necessarily regard vindicatory damages as a separate doctrinal category of NCDs, especially if it turns out that the reasons that justify the vindicatory award are the same reasons that justify other types of NCDs. In *Lumba* itself, Lord Collins doubted 'that the concept of vindicatory damages should be introduced into the law of tort. In truth, despite the [express] suggestions to the contrary in the Privy Council in *Ramanoop* … vindicatory damages are akin to punitive or exemplary damages'.[398] Lord Collins thought that compensatory, nominal damages, and punitive damages already cover the arena of vindicatory effects, and there is thus no need 'for the creation of a head of vindicatory damages at common law'.[399] This would mean that the *idea* of vindicatory damages was probably thought of by Lord Collins as one that can be justified by both correlative and non-correlative reasons.

Indeed, scholars also sometimes regard vindicatory damages as 'functionally superfluous'.[400] Barker, for instance, argues that they are 'a parasite upon … purposes that already flow through the veins of existing private law remedies',[401] namely compensatory, nominal and punitive damages. Barker does not argue that vindicatory damages necessarily fulfil the functions of all these three measures at once, but that all vindicatory awards are reducible to one or more of these three measures. This reasoning clearly suggests that, in situations where vindicatory awards can be distinguished from compensatory damages, such awards may give

[395] *Lumba* (n 18) [101] (emphasis added).

[396] eg, ibid [100]. See also *Weller v Associated Newspapers Ltd* (n 380) [189]; *Gulati v MGN Ltd* (n 371) [48].

[397] See also *Watkins* (n 326) [26].

[398] *Lumba* (n 18) [233] (referring also to *Merson v Cartwrights* [2005] UKPC 38 and *Attorney General of St Christopher, Nevis and Anguilla v Reynolds* [1980] AC 637 (HL)).

[399] *Lumba* (n 18) [237]. Similarly, eg, *R (DN (Rwanda)) v Secretary of State for the Home Department* [2018] EWCA Civ 273, [2019] QB 71 [42]. By contrast, in *Lloyd v Google LLC* (n 380) [68], Warby J argued that vindicatory damages are not merely intended 'to mark the commission of the wrong' and are thus distinct from nominal awards.

[400] K Barker, 'Private and Public: The Mixed Concept of Vindication in Torts and Private Law' in SGA Pitel, JW Neyers and E Chamberlain (eds), *Tort Law: Challenging Orthodoxy* (Oxford, Hart Publishing, 2013) 86.

[401] ibid 90. Similarly Stevens (n 31) 568; Pearce and Halson (n 31) 86; Ventose (n 31) 245; Varuhas (n 176) 290–92.

effect to the same justificatory reasons as either nominal or punitive damages, ie, to non-correlative reasons.

The key question then is whether there are any awards distinct from compensatory damages which would also pursue a distinct vindicatory function, but which are not labelled as nominal or punitive in the cases. If that were the case, we could say that such awards in reality fulfil the function of vindicatory damages. Baroness Hale took a similar approach in *Lumba* when she contended that '[i]n reality, this [practice of awarding vindicatory damages] may well be what was happening in the older cases of false imprisonment, before the assessment of damages became such a refined science'.[402]

In line with this thinking, let us now focus on *Rees v Darlington Memorial Hospital NHS Trust*[403] which 'in reality' well conforms with the idea of vindicatory damages (although the relevant award was not labelled as such). This example will allow us to answer whether such hidden award of vindicatory damages is justified by non-correlative reasons, just like other NCDs.

In *Rees*[404] the claimant gave birth to a healthy child after a negligently performed sterilisation operation carried out by the defendant, the Darlington Memorial Hospital. Ms Rees suffered from a genetic condition that caused her a severe visual handicap, thus making it much riskier that she may not have a healthy child and much more difficult to bring up any child given her own handicap. The claimant obtained compensation for the stress, trauma and costs associated with the unwanted pregnancy and birth. In addition, the judges awarded her a conventional sum of £15,000 to 'mark the injury and [the non-pecuniary] loss [caused by the negligent violation of] the freedom to limit the size of one's family',[405] and also to mark the violation of 'the opportunity to live her life in the way that she wished and planned'.[406]

Some authors interpret the conventional award in *Rees* as compensation 'for non-pecuniary loss, namely a mother's mental distress consequent on having her lifestyle plans disrupted'.[407] I am not convinced by this correlative justification of the award. The straightforward method to quantify the damage to her correlative interest in reproductive autonomy and autonomy over her life would be to focus on the supposed factual consequences linked with this abstract harm, ie, to assess her damage by reference to the cost of upbringing the child (future losses). This was rejected on the basis of *McFarlane* (where neither the child nor the parent was disabled).[408] *McFarlane* had closed the door to any compensation for the cost of

[402] *Lumba* (n 18) [217].
[403] *Rees v Darlington Memorial Hospital NHS Trust* [2004] 1 AC 309 (HL).
[404] ibid.
[405] ibid [8].
[406] ibid [8].
[407] Burrows (n 62) 251. See also Descheemaeker, 'Pecuniary and Non-Pecuniary Loss: A Reinterpretation' (n 131) 91. This kind of interpretation was also advanced in *Lewis v Australian Capital Territory* (n 142) [169].
[408] *McFarlane v Tayside Health Board* [2000] 2 AC 59 (HL).

upbringing the child because it would be contrary to the public policy to award the claimant damages as if the child should not have lived had the wrong not been committed.[409] In accordance with this policy, the majority in *Rees* thought it inappropriate for the law to engage in such appalling counterfactual exercise.

But since the mother in *Rees* was disabled, the House of Lords distinguished this case from *McFarlane* and argued that, in this context, the claimant's damage could in principle be assessed by reference to the extra costs of childcare caused by her disability.[410] After all, in *Parkinson*[411] (which was also a variant of the factual scenario in *McFarlane*), the Court of Appeal already allowed for compensation for the extra costs of childcare caused by the child's disability. In that case, the analysis 'treat[ed] a disabled child as having exactly the same worth as a non-disabled child. It afford[ed] him the same dignity and status. It simply acknowledge[d] that he costs more'.[412]

Very surprisingly, for me at least, this individualised assessment on the basis of 'extra costs' was not relied on in *Rees*. Instead of compensating the claimant's own correlative damage, a conventional sum to 'compensate them for the [abstract] injury to their autonomy'[413] and for the serious wrong 'having a far-reaching effect on the lives of the parent and any family she may already have'[414] was granted, as if the claimant's damage was not susceptible to assessment in money and as if the claimant's future losses (the eventual extra costs) were irrelevant. This interpretation looks more like an attempt to justify the vindicatory sum by the need to mark the wrong against reproductive autonomy as a category, not by the need to offset correlative damage to the claimant's private interests.

One may try to explain *Rees* as a case of general damages (ie, damages that are 'not susceptible to measurement in money'[415]) which are intended to compensate the claimant for their abstract loss. The difficulty with this explanation is that general damages are sometimes awarded to serve non-compensatory goals too, and it is difficult to know whether general damages are sometimes masquerading as another type of damages.[416] This explanation could thus not falsify that *Rees* was concerned about a non-compensatory award. And the decision itself suggests that the award was not intended to compensate any individual loss.[417] Indeed, the award was referred to in the judgment as neither compensatory, nor purely

[409] In more detail on this decision, see C Auckland and I Goold, 'Offsetting Damages in Wrongful Conception and Birth Cases: A Way Through the Post-McFarlane Mire' (2022) 138 *LQR* 407.

[410] See, eg, *Rees v Darlington Memorial Hospital NHS Trust* (n 403) [39], [63].

[411] *Parkinson v St James and Seacroft University Hospital NHS Trust* [2001] EWCA Civ 530, [2002] QB 266.

[412] ibid [90] (Hale LJ).

[413] *Rees v Darlington Memorial Hospital NHS Trust* (n 403) [70].

[414] ibid [17].

[415] *Wright v British Railways Board* [1983] 2 AC 773 (HL) 777 (Lord Diplock) (emphasis removed).

[416] See more in J Goudkamp and E Katsampouka, 'Punitive Damages and the Place of Punishment in Private Law' (2021) 84 *MLR* 1257, 1282–85.

[417] *cf Rees v Darlington Memorial Hospital NHS Trust* (n 403) [40]–[41] (Lord Steyn), explaining in his dissenting opinion why the global sum may not be justified in these circumstances.

penal, nominal, 'let alone a derisory' sum.[418] Instead, it was intended to 'afford some measure of recognition of the wrong done [and] … a more ample measure of justice'.[419] This is, as we saw earlier, a characteristic description of vindicatory functions of damages.

The conventional global sum (£15,000) awarded in response to the wrong itself can thus hardly be justified on a correlative basis. It looks as though the House of Lords in *Rees* made the award to mark the wrong against the right to autonomy, not as a concrete correlative interest of the claimant, but as a general category that should be protected for the benefit of the wider public. The House of Lords did not say anything express in the judgment to support this interpretation, but it seems to me that this interpretation offers a convincing and justified explanation of what the court in reality did. In this light, I think it is defensible to analyse *Rees* as a case in which non-correlative reasons, namely violations of public interests in the protection of reproductive autonomy, underpinned the need to mark the wrong and vindicate the right. As later confirmed by the Court of Appeal in *Shaw v Kovac*, the damages award in *Rees* cannot be explained solely by the claimant's individual damage,[420] and so although the Court of Appeal sought to follow the supposed ban on vindicatory damages from *Lumba*,[421] it implicitly acknowledged that the measure of damages can be at least partly justified on a non-correlative basis.

As we have seen, *Rees* can be at least partly explained as a case of hidden award of vindicatory damages, regardless of the stated ban on vindicatory damages in English law. It appears clear that the *idea* of vindicatory damages can help us make sense of the awards and, importantly, that the idea is linked with non-correlative justifying reasons.

Other cases concerning vindicatory functions of damages seem to support the non-correlative analysis of this function too, although it would probably be misleading to characterise those awards as actual or hidden awards of vindicatory damages. For example, the vindicatory considerations discussed in *Ashley*[422] are hardly explicable by reference to correlative damage of the injured party. In Lord Scott's words, the relatives of the deceased victim sought 'to obtain a public admission or finding that the deceased Mr Ashley was unlawfully killed by PC Sherwood'.[423] They wanted to obtain 'a public vindication of the deceased's right not to have been subjected to a deadly assault [by the police]'.[424] Indeed, Lord Rodger approved of claimants advancing their claim 'in order to try to establish

[418] ibid [8] and [74]. It should be noted though that three of out seven judges dissented on the point of the conventional award.

[419] ibid [8] (Lord Bingham). This majority position was expressly criticised by Lord Hope (dissenting) at [74] (see also Lord Hope in *Lumba* (n 18) [179]). *cf* D Nolan, 'New Forms of Damage in Negligence' (2007) 70 *MLR* 59, 79–80 and A Mulligan, 'A Vindicatory Approach to Tortious Liability for Mistakes in Assisted Human Reproduction' (2020) 40 *Legal Studies* 55.

[420] *Shaw v Kovac & Anor* (n 380) [78]–[84].

[421] See ibid [50]–[54] and [84].

[422] *Ashley v Chief Constable of Sussex* (n 19).

[423] ibid [23].

[424] ibid [23].

a point of law which would help others in a similar plight'.[425] And even Lord Neuberger (dissenting) stated that 'it is reasonable for Mr Ashley's estate to wish to establish that his death was unlawfully caused and because there is a public interest element in proceeding'.[426] As noted by Arden LJ in the Court of Appeal's decision (which was affirmed by the House of Lords), '[t]he public has high expectations of the police … [and] the claimants seek in these proceedings … an explanation … of the fatal wounding of James Ashley and it subsequent disclosure to the public'.[427] It may thus be argued that the award of damages marking the wrong must have had a non-correlative justificatory ground, most likely some public interest.[428]

With Varuhas, who has written extensively on the topic of vindicatory damages, we can thus interpret the vindicatory measure of damages as a signal that the judiciary sends to our society about the public importance of underlying rights and interests in the legal system.[429] Similarly, Steel argues that vindicatory awards protect 'the value of the rule of law',[430] which would also suggest that they protect non-correlative interests and that these interests can be characterised as public interests. Overall, short of claiming that vindicatory damages do exist as a matter of legal doctrine, we can say that there are clearly some vindicatory awards and vindicatory aspects of damages that are unconcerned with correlative consideration and that thus fit the definition of NCDs as damages justified by non-correlative reasons. It is not entirely clear, however, whether these vindicatory awards are sufficiently distinct from other types of NCDs.

V. Gain-Based Damages: Restitutionary Damages

The following two sections will look at gain-based damages. Gain-based damages are typically contrasted with compensatory damages since they are measured by the defendant's gain and not by the claimant's loss.[431] In line with the current developments in the law of restitution, we can separate gain-based *damages* from other gain-based remedies. What triggers liability in damages is a wrong, as opposed to other types of causative event which trigger other gain-based remedies such as restitution of unjust enrichment.[432] In this sense, '[a] remedy in unjust

[425] ibid [70].
[426] ibid [110].
[427] *Ashley v Chief Constable of Sussex* [2006] EWCA Civ 1085, [2007] 1 WLR 398 [189].
[428] Similarly, see Priel (n 59).
[429] Varuhas (n 34) 17–18.
[430] S Steel, 'False Imprisonment and the Fetch of Hypothetical Warrant' (2011) 127 *LQR* 527, 528.
[431] See, eg, Pearce and Halson (n 31); Virgo (n 94) 4.
[432] See, eg, *One Step (Support) Ltd v Morris-Garner* (n 15) [114] (Lord Sumption). See also P Birks, 'Rights, Wrongs, and Remedies' (2000) 20 *OJLS* 1, 27–36; Edelman (n 70) 33ff; C Webb, *Reason and Restitution: A Theory of Unjust Enrichment*, 1st edn (Oxford, OUP, 2016) ch 2; J Edelman and E Bant, *Unjust Enrichment*, 2nd edn (Oxford, Hart Publishing, 2016) 19–24; C Rotherham, 'Restitution for Wrongs' in E Bant, K Barker and S Degeling (eds), *Research Handbook on Unjust Enrichment and Restitution* (Cheltenham, Edward Elgar, 2020); Stevens (n 94) Part VI.

enrichment is not a claim of damages'.[433] Let us therefore focus on wrongs-based awards measured by the defendant's gain.

It should be clarified from the beginning that there is no universally accepted classification of the different sub-types of gain-based damages, let alone their labelling. For example, the Law Commission's 1997 report on *Aggravated, Exemplary and Restitutionary Damages* uses the phrase 'restitutionary damages' for several different remedies: an action for 'money had and received'; an 'account of profits'; and (restitutionary) 'damages',[434] acknowledging that the law in this area is ripe for rationalisation. As was already recognised by the Law Commission in that report, what further complicates the analysis of such gain-based awards is the fact that, 'there are cases (sometimes analysed as awarding restitution) where one can realistically argue that the plaintiff has suffered a loss, in the extended sense that the plaintiff has not been paid what he or she would have charged for permitting the defendant's conduct'.[435]

The book's scoping overview of the current usage of the term NCDs in section III of chapter one does not ascertain (and for reasons of brevity of the textual evidence found for the purposes of that section even cannot ascertain) in what sense the phrases gain-based, restitutionary or disgorgement damages are used when these are referred to as NCDs. What is only clear is that they are all gain-based in the sense that their measure is made with reference to the defendant's gain. This complexity, which springs from the sources, has no easy solution. But if we are to analyse whether any such gain-based awards (however they are labelled) have a common rationale with other NCDs, we need to adopt one framing according to which we will organise them internally, without changing the meaning of the labels associated with that framing during the argument. The 'fit' of any such framing with the existing usage of the labels will never be perfect, given the unstable usage of the terms in the sources.

What follows is thus by no means a universally accepted classification of the different sub-types of gain-based awards. Rather, it is a convenient classification for the present purposes, as it is consistent with the dividing line drawn between compensatory and non-compensatory *functions* of damages as set out in section II of chapter two and further elaborated in section V of chapter four. It was argued in those sections that compensatory functions of damages can be defined by reference to compensable harm and that compensable harm is explicable in terms of correlative damage to the claimant's interests, because the protection of those interests is underpinned by the norms of corrective justice. Conveniently, a similar association between the norms of corrective justice and one group of gain-based damages is made in the literature, which is why it will be relied on for the present purposes. It is convenient because it allows us to distinguish gain-based damages, which can be analysed on a correlative basis as a remedy that pursues restitution of correlative gain as the main aim (and which damages can thus be alternatively

[433] *Sempra Metals Ltd v Revenue & Anor* [2007] UKHL 34, [2008] 1 AC 561 (HL) [31] (Lord Hope).
[434] Law Commission (n 42) 4 (para 1.10).
[435] ibid 28 (para 1.4).

analysed as damages the purpose of which is to compensate the claimant's normative loss that corresponds to the defendant's actual gain), from gain-based damages that do not aim to rectify the claimant's correlative damage.

In this sense, it is sometimes said that while all gain-based damages are measured by reference to gain, they pursue either restitution (restitutionary damages) or deterrence (disgorgement damages) as their main objectives.[436] These two sub-types of gain-based remedy – and the present book will adopt this classification – thus serve different functions and are available in different situations, although they might often be grouped under a single heading of gain-based awards. Restitutionary damages are said to be available in cases where a wrong results in a benefit to the wrongdoer which exceeds the loss to the victim, who suffers a lesser loss or, frequently, no actual loss at all.[437] Disgorgement damages are available if the claimant cannot show loss resulting from a breach of contract and if it is necessary to disgorge any profit gained from the defendant's breach of the contract.[438] Disgorgement damages can also be awarded 'for cynical commission of torts as diverse as trespass, conversion, libel, inducing breach of contract, intimidation, fraud and deceit'[439] as well as for some equitable wrongs where compensatory damages are not sufficient to deter the defendant.[440]

As put by Edelman, who is one of the strongest advocates of the distinction between restitutionary and disgorgement gain-based damages:

> Whilst … restitutionary damages are primarily concerned with corrective justice and reversing transfers between parties, disgorgement damages are concerned with broader notions of deterrence. Restitutionary damages therefore should generally be available but disgorgement damages should only be available where there is an additional interest … [and] a need for additional deterrence of wrongdoing and historically this interest has been recognised in relationships of close trust and confidence and in instances of wrongs committed cynically, that is, deliberately or recklessly with a view to gain.[441]

[436] See, eg, Edelman (n 70) ch 3; Virgo (n 94) 4–6; Edelman, Varuhas and Higgins (n 5) chs 15 and 16. For a critique of the 'restitutionary' label in this context, see *Devenish Nutrition Ltd v Sanofi-Aventis SA* (n 9) [144] (Longmore LJ).

[437] Edelman, Varuhas and Higgins (n 5) paras 15-001 to 15-003 and 16-001 to 16-004. *cf* Edelman, Varuhas and Colton (n 37) ch 14 which refers to these 'licence fee damages' as 'restitutionary damages'.

[438] *Blue Monkey Gaming Ltd v Hudson* [2014] All ER (D) 222 (Ch) [605], referring to *Blake* (n 8) 285. See also *Blue Sky One Ltd v Mahan Air* [2009] EWHC 3314 (Comm) [320].

[439] Edelman (n 70) 136.

[440] ibid 191 and 212ff. The relevant awards are, however, more commonly labelled 'account of profits' than 'disgorgement damages' in these cases. If we accept that account of profit is merely an equitable remedy, then the Senior Courts Act 1981, s 49(1) states that 'wherever there is any conflict or variance between the rules of equity and the rules of the common law with reference to the same matter, the rules of equity shall prevail'.

[441] Edelman (n 70) 86. See also C Rotherham, 'The Conceptual Structure of Restitution for Wrongs' (2007) 66 *CLJ* 172; F Giglio, 'Pseudo-Restitutionary Damages: Some Thoughts on the Dual Theory of Restitution for Wrongs' (2009) 22 *Canadian Journal of Law and Jurisprudence* 49 (both of them critically examining Edelman's dual theory of restitution for wrongs). See also *One Step (Support) Ltd v Morris-Garner* (n 15) [114].

Under the framework introduced in chapter three, restitutionary damages are thus justifiable by wrongdoing against the claimant's interests (we say 'at the claimant's expense'). Take, for example, restitutionary awards for intellectual property wrongs. These awards reflect a reasonable or notional royalty fee for the wrongful conduct.[442] Similarly, 'wherever an abstraction or invasion of property has occurred … the law ought to yield a recompense under the category or principle … of price or of hire'.[443] A situation like this might occur, for example, '[i]f A, being a liveryman, keeps his horse standing idle in the stable, and B, against his wish or without his knowledge, rides or drives it out'.[444] As a matter of law, the defaulter will be required to pay a fair price for the interference with the claimant's property rights. We might label these awards as user, negotiating, Wrotham park, or restitutionary damages,[445] but the label is immaterial for the purposes of our analysis.

Importantly, they cannot be awarded in conjunction with compensatory damages[446] because the reasons that justify the loss-based compensation do not materially differ from the reasons that justify this kind of gain-based remedy – both of these types of award are intended to redress damage to the claimant's private interests by putting him in a position he would have been in had the wrong not occurred. In other words, they are intended to restore the value of the claimant's protected interests (if one wishes to use that language).[447]

A similar point was already made in chapter one, section III and chapter two, section II and it was concluded there that restitutionary damages do not stand in any stark opposition to compensatory damages because they both give effect to individual rights and are based on the *restitutio in integrum* principle, just like compensatory damages. Both of these types of award are justified correlatively since they respond to interferences with the claimant's private interests. 'Compensation and restitution for wrongs have a similar, albeit inverse, function', as Giglio argues.[448] Or, as persuasively put by Bastarache J in a Canadian Supreme Court decision in *Kingstreet*, '[r]estitution [here] is a tool of corrective justice. When a transfer of value between two parties is normatively defective, restitution functions to correct that transfer by restoring parties to their pre-transfer positions'.[449]

[442] eg, *Catnic Components Ltd v Hill & Smith Ltd* [1983] FSR 512 (Ch); *Blayney (t/a Aardvark Jewellery) v Clogau St Davids Gold Mines Ltd* [2002] EWCA Civ 1007, [2003] FSR 19; *Irvine v Talksport Ltd* [2003] EWCA Civ 423, [2003] 2 All ER 881.

[443] *Watson, Laidlaw & Co Ltd v Pott, Cassels & Williamson* (n 125) 31 (Lord Shaw).

[444] ibid 31.

[445] See, especially, *Devenish Nutrition Ltd v Sanofi-Aventis SA* (n 9) [37] (Arden LJ); *One Step (Support) Ltd v Morris-Garner* (n 15) [3], [25]–[30] (Lord Reed).

[446] See *Tang Man Sit (Deceased) v Capacious Investments Ltd* (n 145) 521.

[447] See, eg, *Devenish Nutrition Ltd v Sanofi-Aventis SA* [2007] EWHC 2394 (Ch), [2008] 2 WLR 637 [114]; *One Step (Support) Ltd v Morris-Garner* (n 15) [30], [58]–[60], [63], [90], [92].

[448] Giglio (n 441) 6. See also R Cunnington, 'Gain-based Damages for Breach of Contract' in D Saidov and R Cunnington (eds), *Contract Damages: Domestic and International Perspectives* (Oxford, Hart Publishing, 2008) 217–19.

[449] *Kingstreet Investments Ltd v New Brunswick (Finance)* [2007] 1 SCR 3 (SCC) [32] (Bastarache J). On the same note, Weinrib wrote, that '[i]n sum, both kinds of rectification – the compensation of loss and the restitution of gain – are available to every kind of private law relationship. … Kinds of rectification therefore play no role in the juridical classification of obligation' (Weinrib (n 82) 51).

On this account, the main difference between restitutionary and compensatory damages is in how we quantify their measure, not in how we justify the measure.

This analysis is also consistent with how English judges tend to think about these awards. Consider, for example, what Keyser J said about the distinction between punitive and compensatory damages. In *AXA Insurance UK Plc v Financial Claims Solutions Ltd & Ors*, he stated that punitive damages 'are (at least so far as the second category is concerned) available for the case where compensatory damages are inadequate to remove the wrongful gain achieved by the tort where paying compensation in accordance with normal principle would leave the tortfeasor "up on the deal".'[450] Clearly, Keyser J thought that compensatory damages can, when contrasted with NCDs, include loss-based as well as gain-based compensation. An extreme illustration of the similarity between the two types of award can be found in *Swindle v Harrison*,[451] where Evans LJ characterised restitutionary damages simply as 'damages' and 'compensation'.[452] As observed by Cunnington, '[h]istorically, the courts have drawn a clear distinction between compensatory relief and restitution … [recently, however, we see] the courts exhibiting an increasing willingness to construe compensation as incorporating both loss-based and gain based awards'.[453]

Restitutionary damages – in the sense of damages measured by reference to the defendant's wrongful act made at the claimant's expense (where this 'expense' can be represented as a normative loss that is a logical corollary of the defendant's actual gain) – are therefore not justified by non-correlative reasons and, as a matter of their rationale, are not intended to rectify violations of public or societal interests. In other words, restitutionary damages do not share the justificatory rationale that is common to all other NCDs awards. The similarity between compensatory and restitutionary damages (on this account) is why Giglio calls this kind of restitutionary damages 'pseudo-restitutionary damages'[454] and it might have also been a reason why Burrows devoted a separate chapter to restitutionary damages next to a chapter on NCDs in his first edition of *Remedies for Torts and Breach of Contract*.[455]

If my analysis is correct, we should regard restitutionary damages not as NCDs – which is how they are traditionally seen – but simply as one way to compensate the claimant for damage to his private interests in line with the *restitutio in integrum* principle. By way of conclusion, it is thus submitted here that restitutionary damages are not normatively unified with other NCDs and it is probably even misleading to label them as NCDs because it wrongly suggests that they are based

[450] *AXA Insurance UK Plc v Financial Claims Solutions Ltd & Ors* [2017] EWHC 3803 (QB) [17].

[451] *Swindle v Harrison* [1997] 4 All ER 705 (CA).

[452] A similar critique of this judgment is presented in, eg, SB Elliott, 'Restitutionary Compensatory Damages for Breach of Fiduciary Duty?' (1998) *Restitution Law Review* 135.

[453] R Cunnington, 'Changing Conceptions of Compensation' (2007) 66 *CLJ* 507, 507–08.

[454] Giglio (n 441).

[455] Burrows, *Remedies for Torts and Breach of Contract* (1st edn) (n 34). Note that chapters are organised differently in later editions of this book.

on a completely different basis from compensatory damages. This is consistent with the fact that primary sources do not, strictly speaking, characterise such restitutionary damages as non-compensatory. My conclusion here is thus an important advancement (not a denial) of the findings made in section III of chapter one regarding the supposed scope of NCDs.

Of course, one may doubt the divide between restitutionary and disgorgement damages, as indeed many scholars do,[456] because the law does not fully reflect this sharp theoretical distinction (the labels restitutionary and disgorgement damages are sometimes used as alternatives[457]). This division springs not from how the labels are used in cases, but from how we analyse the justificatory rationales for the awards made in those cases. As such, we may see the categories of restitutionary and disgorgement damages as interpretive (rather than descriptive) categories, which would appear to be a problem for the book's methodology. One could argue that the book aims to provide an interpretive theory of interpretive categories, which makes the interpretive theory itself immune to falsification. But that would be a misunderstanding. The book engages with the descriptive (not interpretive) category of gain-based awards. The interpretive sub-types of gain-based are used to organise the analysis and to make sense of the unstable (as a matter of labelling) area of the law of damages, not to claim that such sub-types exist as distinct doctrinal categories. Yet if we are to analyse 'damages' measured by reference to gain next to other NCDs and if we want to make some general claims about their justifications (rather than claims about a handful of isolated awards that can be found in the cases), it makes sense to try to classify their sub-types according to the two fundamental justifications presented in section V of chapter three, especially since a cognate classification comprising restitutionary and disgorgement damages is already recognised by the literature. For the purposes of this book, the supposed divide between the two sub-types of gain-based damages thus represents a sound and acceptable basis.

VI. Gain-Based Damages: Disgorgement Damages

In the light of the preceding analysis, it would seem clear that disgorgement damages must be justified by non-correlative damage, as otherwise they would be indistinguishable from restitutionary awards. And they are distinguishable from each other. As Virgo puts it, unlike restitutionary damages, 'disgorgement remedies have a deterrent or distributive function'.[458] In this sense, disgorgement damages

[456] The division is contested by several scholars. See, eg, Rotherham (n 441); Giglio (n 441); A Burrows, *The Law of Restitution*, 3rd edn (Oxford, OUP, 2011) 633–35; Barnett (n 68) ch 6; S Watterson, 'Gain-Based Remedies for Civil Wrongs in England and Wales' in E Hondius and A Janssen (eds), *Disgorgement of Profits: Gain-Based Remedies throughout the World* (Cham, Springer, 2015) 31, 42–44.

[457] eg, *Phonographic Performance Ltd v Ellis* (n 244) [36].

[458] Virgo (n 94) 6 (footnote omitted).

have the same goals as punitive or vindicatory damages. Just like in the case of punitive or vindicatory damages, the disgorgement awards are designed to deter, prevent, mark and penalise the exceptional gravity of a wrong that was committed by the defendant. But unlike in the case of punitive or vindicatory damages, the disgorgement awards are quantified by reference to the defendant's wrongful gain.

Disgorgement awards are said to strip the wrongdoer of gains regardless of whether those gains are acquired at the claimant's expense.[459] Disgorgement damages, in contrast with restitutionary damages, demand some 'exceptional circumstances … [or] a legitimate interest in preventing the [d]efendant's profit-making activity and, hence, in depriving him of his profit'.[460] Accordingly, Cane believes that disgorgement damages express public disapproval of the defendant's wrongful conduct and that they should not belong to private law.[461] Other commentators also notice the social importance of the interests at stake in relation to disgorgement damages.[462] Disgorgement damages thus seem to discourage wrongs-based profit-seeking activities that impair public interests.

In *AG v Blake*, for example, the defendant's invasion of the interest in the integrity of national security and intelligence services was thought to be sufficient to warrant all Mr Blake's profits being disgorged, which profits he, as a former member of those services, gained by disclosing state secrets. The damage to the overarching interest in every intelligence officer's lifelong duty of non-disclosure in respect of secret and confidential information (including formerly confidential information) was seen as an exceptional justifying reason for the award that stripped Mr Blake of *all* his profits.[463] According to commentators, the award in *Blake* was justified by the violation of the public interest in maintaining the confidentiality of the official information he was not entitled to disclose, and this public interest should be regarded as an exceptional type of reason.[464] We can therefore argue that '[w]hat makes the tortfeasor's [successful profit-seeking] conduct especially worthy of sanction is not its impact on the interests of the plaintiff … but its impact on … a social institution',[465] ie, a non-correlative public interest.

You may object that the court in *Blake* also relied on the claimant's 'legitimate interest'[466] in depriving the defendant of his profit. This might at first glance

[459] Cane (n 41) 321; Watterson (n 456) 33.

[460] *Blue Monkey Gaming Ltd v Hudson* (n 438) [605].

[461] Cane (n 41) 322–23.

[462] eg, H Dagan, *Unjust Enrichment: A Study of Private Law and Public Values* (Cambridge, CUP, 1997) 12–31; C Rotherham, 'Deterrence as a Justification for Awarding Accounts of Profits' (2012) 32 *OJLS* 537, 544–45.

[463] *Blake* (n 8) 285F. The exceptionality of was resolutely confirmed in *One Step (Support) Ltd v Morris-Garner* (n 15) [35].

[464] See, eg, M Halliwell, 'Profits from Wrongdoing: Private and Public Law Perspectives' (1999) 62 *MLR* 271, 279–80; T Aplin, 'The Future of Breach of Confidence and the Protection of Privacy' (2007) 7 *Oxford University Commonwealth Law Journal* 137, 147.

[465] Cane (n 275) 117. See also P Cane, *Responsibility in Law and Morality* (Oxford, Hart Publishing, 2002) 222.

[466] *Blake* (n 8) 285H.

suggest that the award was, after all, justified by the claimant's private interests. Yet we need to keep in mind that the claim in *Blake* was advanced by the Attorney General (AG) as a representative of the public interest. Thus, the legitimate interest was still a public interest. The duty was not owed to the specific claimant (ie, to the specific AG), and its breach did not cause damage to the AG's (and only the AG's) private interests.

However, the terminology here is difficult again. As we can see, the gain-based award in *Blake* fits the interpretive category of 'disgorgement damages', rather than 'restitutionary damages', although the adjective 'restitutionary' is used throughout the judgment (Lord Nicholls himself 'prefer[ed] to avoid the unhappy expression "restitutionary damages"'[467] to describe the gain-based award in *Blake*).

Another case that can help us understand the justificatory reasons for disgorgement awards is *AG v Observer Ltd, AG v Guardian Newspapers Ltd (No 2), AG v Times Newspapers Ltd (No 2)*.[468] Similarly to the situation in *Blake*, the House of Lords took account of '[t]he damage to the public interest' when ordering the defendant to disgorge gains obtained by the misuse of confidential information in this case. Of course, breach of confidence (which was at the heart of this case) is an equitable wrong. As such, it falls outside the purview of this book. Yet their Lordships' reference to the damage to the public interest is instructive here because, as *Devenish*[469] and the Senior Courts Act 1981[470] make clear, the same kind of remedies should be available in the same circumstances, even if the cause of action is different, and common law remedies should follow the logic of equitable remedies in such situations in order to avoid incoherence in the law. And so if disgorgement of profits is motivated by public interests in equity, there is a good reason to apply the same non-correlative rationale to common law damages. A full exploration of account of profits for breach of trust, breach of fiduciary duty, accessory liability for breach of trust and fiduciary duty, and breach of confidence (including trade secrets) is beyond the scope of this book. Yet it is good to keep in mind that the no-profit rule exists in relationships where trust (rather than a reciprocal commercial relationship) is central.

As observed in *AG v Observer Ltd*,[471] justice may sometimes require that the courts have the power to disgorge the wrongdoer's benefits and to teach him that no one should be permitted to take advantage of his own wrongdoing, even if that profit does not additionally impair private interests of the victim. The principle according to which the law should not allow 'a man to make profit by a wrong',[472]

[467] ibid 284. See also A Gray, 'Disgorgement damages' (2013) 7 *Journal of Business Law* 657, 657–59.

[468] *AG v Observer Ltd, AG v Guardian Newspapers Ltd (No 2), AG v Times Newspapers Ltd (No2)* [1990] 1 AC 109 (HL) 259, 262.

[469] *Devenish Nutrition Ltd v Sanofi-Aventis SA* (n 9) [4].

[470] Senior Courts Act 1981, s 49(1): 'wherever there is any conflict or variance between the rules of equity and the rules of the common law with reference to the same matter, the rules of equity shall prevail'.

[471] *AG v Observer Ltd* (n 468) passim.

[472] *Jegon v Vivian* (1870–71) LR 6 Ch App 742 (CA Ch) 761 (Lord Hatherley).

thus also supports the conclusion that the award of disgorgement damages can be justified by non-correlative reasons. In cases where the courts disgorge *all* profits of the defendant even though not all of it was achieved at the expense of the claimant, there needs to be another reason why *all* the profit is considered unjust and wrongful. For example, this may be when one acts in bad faith and thus breaches his fiduciary duty – such breach is a breach of trust as a category, rather than breach of a concrete reciprocal commercial obligation, as discussed earlier.[473] Supposedly, where the law seeks to protect trust as an institution (not just individual obligations) and posits some restrictive rules to do that, a breach of those rules does not generate profit at the claimant's expense. Instead, it can be said that the gain was achieved at the expense of the publicly valuable institution of trust at large. In this sense, disgorgement damages would rectify violations of public interests and can be analysed as awards justified by non-correlative reasons.

Non-correlative reasons seem also to underpin disgorgement awards against fiduciaries and dishonest assistants (which again are relevant by virtue of the relationship between common law and equitable remedies, as stated above). 'There is now a body of modern case law at first instance which recognises that the court has the power to order an account of profits against a dishonest assistant, even where no corresponding loss has been suffered by the beneficiary.'[474] More generally, the disgorgement rule against trustees or fiduciaries (requiring them to account for any profits they derive from their office or position) 'ensures that trustees and fiduciaries are financially disinterested in carrying out their duties.'[475] Although it is unclear from the latest Supreme Court case law whether the rule to account for profits is a primary duty or secondary (wrongs-based) liability,[476] it appears clear that the rule allows the claimant to demand disgorgement damages against the trustee or fiduciary regardless of whether he has any legitimate private interest in the profit being disgorged (ie, the profit does not need to be gained at his expense). It is the very institution of trust – the existence of which is undoubtedly beneficial to the functioning of our society – that is protected by those disgorgement awards.[477] These awards should be distinguished from account of profits 'which ought to have been made'[478] for the claimant as part of the fiduciary duties and which would thus be based on correlative reasons. Also, these awards should be distinguished from account of profits that is not wrongs-based.

[473] *Murad & Anor v Al-Saraj & Anor* [2005] EWCA Civ 959, [2005] WTLR 1573 [108] and [122] (Parker LJ).

[474] *Novoship (UK) Ltd v Mikhaylyuk* [2014] EWCA Civ 908, [2015] QB 499 [71] (further cases are listed in that paragraph).

[475] *Blake* (n 8) 280G.

[476] *Rukhadze v Recovery Partners GP Ltd* [2025] UKSC 10 [2], [20], [209]–[220], [258].

[477] Similarly, in *HRH Prince of Wales v Associated Newspapers Ltd*, for example, the Court of Appeal held that there is an 'important public interest in the observance of duties of confidence'. See *HRH Prince of Wales v Associated Newspapers Ltd* [2006] EWCA Civ 1776, [2008] Ch 57 [67].

[478] *Novoship (UK) Ltd v Mikhaylyuk* (n 474) [124].

The gain-based award in *Hendrix* can shed light on disgorgement damages too. This is because the inspiration for the claim in *Hendrix* was the exceptional disgorgement remedy in *Blake*.[479] Both the claim in *Hendrix* and the claim in *Blake* were based on breach of a negative contractual obligation – an obligation not to do something. The ruling in *Hendrix* was, however, distinguished from *Blake*. The circumstances of the dispute in *Hendrix* were not considered exceptional, and the defendant was thus not required to give up on all their profits from their use of Hendrix's recordings in breach of the agreement. Accordingly, the defendant was ordered to pay only a reasonable sum (user fee) for that use. The essence of the award in *Hendrix* was justified correlatively (see section II of chapter two) because the claimant was deemed to have a legitimate *private* interest in depriving the defendant of their unjust profit. In *Hendrix*, not all profits of the defendant were deemed unjust because not all profits were wrongfully gained at the expense of the claimant. Such a correlative, rights-based justification for the account of profits has been recently confirmed by the Supreme Court's decision in *Lifestyle Equities CV*, for example.[480] This contrast between *Hendrix* and *Blake* further highlights the distinct non-correlative nature of disgorgement damages.

Only in exceptional circumstances, affecting important interests beyond the claimant-defendant reciprocal relationship, are the courts prepared to state that 'there is a very great public interest in seeking to discourage' others from similar wrongdoing.[481] On this ground, for example, a claim for disgorgement damages was advanced in *Devenish*, but the court struggled to identify any exceptional circumstances to justify the disgorgement and therefore did not grant the remedy. It was thought by the court that, without an exceptional justification, 'an account of profits of the kind advanced would give Devenish a windfall. … [T]he law is not in the business of transferring monetary gains from one undeserving recipient to another'.[482] By contrast, had there been some non-correlative damage, the court seemed prepared to disgorge the profits and divert them into the claimant's pocket.

Finally, by way of supporting the previous analysis, it can also be argued that disgorgement damages are justified by violations of public interests to the extent to which disgorgement of a wrongful profit overlaps with Category 2 punitive damages. Some authors would go as far as to claim that punitive damages awarded in Category 2 cases are in fact disgorgement damages.[483] Indeed, disgorgement damages and punitive damages for profit-seeking wrongful activities become almost indistinguishable

[479] *Experience Hendrix LLC v PPX Enterprises Inc* (n 143) [16]. See also M Graham, 'Restitutionary Damages: The Anvil Struck' (2004) 120 *LQR* 26 and *One Step (Support) Ltd v Morris-Garner* (n 15) [89] and [90].

[480] *Lifestyle Equities CV & Anor v Ahmed & Anor* [2024] UKSC 17, [2025] AC 1 [155] ('The reason for redirecting the profits to the owner of the right is not to punish or deter wrongdoing. It is to achieve the goals which the right exists to further.') and [156] ('Whereas an award of damages may make the infringer worse off than if the infringement had not occurred, an account of profits does not have this effect.').

[481] *AG v Observer Ltd* (n 468) 197.

[482] *Devenish Nutrition Ltd v Sanofi-Aventis SA* (n 9) [158] (Tuckey LJ).

[483] See, especially, Weinrib (n 276).

from each other in cases where the profit-seeking intention results in some real gain, but which gain cannot be disgorged in full (eg, because part of the gain had already been confiscated in criminal proceedings). In *AT & Ors v Dulghieru & Anor* – a case concerning young women who were trafficked into the UK from Moldova for the purposes of sexual exploitation and prostitution – the award of £60,000 in punitive damages was made not only to 'mark the court's disapproval of … [the] outrageous conduct',[484] but also to prevent the defendants' wrongful enrichment. The defendants' illegal gains totalled approximately £786,000 (as exemplified by confiscation orders)[485] and the court made it clear that 'the rationale behind an award of [Category 2] exemplary damages is primarily one of preventing unjust enrichment'.[486] Likewise, in *PJS v News Group Newspapers Ltd*, for example, the Supreme Court entertained the thought (without deciding) that an account of profits might sometimes serve the same function as exemplary damages and could in theory be used where there is a doctrinal ban on exemplary damages, such as in the case of damages for misuse of private information at common law.[487] This strongly suggests that the reasons for disgorgement damages and punitive damages overlap and therefore that disgorgement awards can be analysed as remedies justified by violations of non-correlative interests. In this light, disgorgement damages do not give effect to individual rights based on reciprocal freedom, and this remedy is thus rightfully labelled as non-compensatory.

VII. Conclusion

This chapter showed that most NCDs (as they are discussed in the primary and secondary sources) do not give effect to considerations based on individual rights. With the exception of contemptuous damages, restitutionary damages and nominally compensatory awards, the categories discussed in this section turned out to be non-rights-based. In particular, we saw that the measure of such NCDs is justified by non-correlative reasons, meaning that the distinction between the two fundamental justifications for measures of damages, as introduced in section V of chapter three, is real. This presses on us the need to work out the concrete implications of this distinction, which will be done in Part II. Here, it can be concluded, in a descriptive mode, that most types of NCDs stand in contrast with (rather than next to) compensatory damages.

I hope to have persuaded the reader that the awards of punitive, nominal, vindicatory and disgorgement damages do not seek to rectify damage to individual rights or damage to private interests of the claimant. Instead, a better interpretation of the law in relation to these measures is that they are justified by non-correlative

[484] *AT & Ors v Dulghieru & Anor* (n 271) [73].
[485] ibid [69].
[486] ibid [71].
[487] *PJS v News Group Newspapers Ltd* [2016] UKSC 26, [2016] AC 1081 [42]. Similarly, see *Salt Ship Design AS v Prysmian Powerlink SRL* [2021] EWHC 2633 (Comm) [462] and [463].

damage. This justificatory rationale distinguishes them clearly from compensatory awards. That said, we saw that small awards of compensation are occasionally, and unhelpfully, labelled as nominal damages. It was argued that these small awards should be distinguished from nominal damages stricto sensu.

These findings support the conclusion that NCDs are normatively unified, despite being statedly separate remedies. This conclusion fits fully with the way in which primary legal sources use the term NCDs. However, it should be noted that restitutionary and contemptuous damages are sometimes discussed in the literature as NCDs, which is confusing. In fact, the analysis has revealed that the category of contemptuous damages either compensates the liminal loss that the claimant has suffered (typically because of the very low value of his reputation) or that they are not 'damages' (because their measure is not justified by the defendant's wrong or to wrongful consequences thereof). On this analysis, it is internally inconsistent to hold that contemptuous damages are both 'non-compensatory' and 'damages'. Thus, it should pose no difficulty to stop referring to contemptuous damages as a separate kind of NCDs. In relation to restitutionary damages, then, we already saw in sections III of chapter one and II of chapter two that many (if not all) of the awards associated with this label are seen as compensatory after the Supreme Court decision in *One Step*.[488] Here too it should thus not be too controversial to stop referring to such awards as NCDs, even though they are sometimes explained as gain-based awards with their distinctive function.

As a result, if we want to understand what NCDs have in common and what unites them, we should revise the scope of the inquiry as first tentatively set out in section III of chapter one. We should exclude restitutionary and contemptuous damages from the definiendum of NCDs. If we do so, we can say that all NCDs are justified by non-correlative reasons. Given the possible doctrinal implications of the fundamental distinction between the rights-based and non-rights-based measures of damages, we should not take the findings of the present chapter lightly.

Alternatively, if we want to retain the existing (albeit somewhat inconsistent) usage of the term NCDs in both the primary sources and the literature, it seems sensible to come up with a new label that would highlight the common features of punitive, nominal, vindicatory and disgorgement damages. We saw that these four types of non-compensatory remedy promote various non-correlative public interests, rather than any other type of non-correlative interest. We can thus collectively call them 'public interest damages'. This claim needs to be made with caution, because the cases only sometimes discuss these non-correlative considerations explicitly as considerations of 'public interest'.[489] Whether or not we can say that all non-correlative reasons that justify NCDs amount to violations of public interests is something that will be explored in the following chapter.

[488] See *One Step (Support) Ltd v Morris-Garner* (n 15); Edelman, Varuhas and Higgins (n 5) ch 15.

[489] eg, the 'public interest' in: (i) reckless defamatory publications, (ii) gains obtained by deliberate misuse of confidential information, (iii) explanations of fatal actions by police officers, or (iv) bounds of proper conduct of solicitors as officers of the court.

PART II

Public Interest Damages

5

Non-Compensatory Damages and Public Interests

So far, it has been demonstrated that punitive, nominal, vindicatory and disgorgement remedial measures stand in contrast with compensatory measures in that they are not justified by damage to the claimant's private interests. As such, they do not give effect to individual rights of the claimant and to reciprocal freedom between the parties. Instead, these non-compensatory measures are justified by non-correlative damage and give effect to what is – at least in certain cases – expressly characterised as public interest.

Public interest was briefly discussed in chapter three as an example of a non-correlative justifying reason, ie, reasons not giving effect to individual rights and not grounded wholly or predominantly in the reciprocal freedom between the parties. What remains unclear, however, is whether all the non-correlative reasons that justify NCDs are reducible to violations of public interests and, relatedly, whether we can thus say that the reasons behind such NCDs can positively be described as considerations of public interest.

The chief aim of this chapter is thus to explore whether 'non-correlative damage' and 'damage to public interests'[490] are coterminous and, relatedly, whether all non-correlatively justified NCDs can be defined as damages justified by damage to public interests, or as 'public interest damages' for short. The answer to both of these questions will be in the affirmative. It will be argued that if we want to understand what damages stand in contrast with compensatory awards, then the 'public interest damages' category should be the focal point of our attention. This chapter suggests that the unstable term (and the supposed doctrinal category of) NCDs should be dispensed with and the idea of damages standing in contrast with compensation on the *restitutio in integrum* principle should be reinterpreted in terms of 'public interest damages'. A clear advantage of the 'public interest damages' category is that it informs us about the nature of these awards independently of our understanding of compensatory damages, ie, it tells us what the non-correlative justifying reasons are, as opposed to what they are not. This, in turn, helps us to focus on the questions concerning when such public interest damages are justified, as opposed to when they are not justified.

[490] For the sake of clarity, let us recall that it was accepted in ch 3 that any violation of protected interests amounts to damage to those interests. Thus, damage to public interests is just another way to describe various violations of those interests.

Before we begin, a short methodological observation is in order. To answer the central question of this chapter, the following text seeks to pin down the 'publicness' (ie, the public nature) of our interest in the disputed matters, not the 'publicness' of the disputed matters themselves. After all, the claim in this chapter is not that all NCDs are justified by violations of the same matters – for example, non-arbitrary exercise of investigatory powers by officials, the liberty of men, fundamental principles of the constitution, the interest in housing, fair competition, or promotion of high standards of news-related publishing.[491] Instead, the claim is that NCDs are justified by damage to various matters which are all protected primarily in the public (as opposed to private) interest. However, we must not confuse the question of whether some matters are generally protected by the law as a public interest with the question of whether some matters are protected by the law *qua* public interest in a specific dispute. What we are concerned with here is the specific protection of the disputed matters *qua* public interests, ie, the latter question, not the former. It will be argued in this chapter as well as in chapter six that what can be generally ascertained are the ethical reasons based on which specific matters in dispute can be protected in the public interest, not the general categories of matters or ex ante lists of specific matters that will always be protected in the public interest. By pinning down the 'publicness' and a method to identify whether the specific matters in dispute are likely to be regarded as matters of public interest, this chapter then works out whether cases concerning interferences with matters of public interest overlap with cases concerning non-correlatively justified NCDs.

The chapter proceeds as follows. Section I thus surveys relevant legal and academic sources that attempt to define the notion of public interest. We will see that the concept of public interest is not well-defined, but that the use of the concept is well-established.

Section II thus defines the concept by reference to the well-established use. It is argued that the notion of public interest should not be understood as an objective statement of fact about whether something is a matter of public interest. As the book makes clear elsewhere,[492] it would be a mistake to expect that we can provide a list of things regarded as being protected either in the public interest or in the private interest. The same matters can be of both private and public concern. The key to the conclusion that matters in dispute amount to damage to some public interest is whether the law is ready to protect the matters in dispute without regard to whether a private interest in these matters supports or opposes this conclusion. In this regard, the notion of public interest should be understood as a token of the special level of protection that the law is ready to assign to matters in dispute, namely that the law is ready to protect these matters by way of damages regardless of whether individual interests in the disputed matters might conflict

[491] For more examples, see ch 4 and n 489.
[492] See especially sections II in ch 5, II in ch 6 and II in ch 7.

with the public interest. This is because these matters are deemed to be significant for the functioning of our society and should therefore not be open to control by any private individual, as that might, in light of the specific circumstances of the dispute, compromise their supposed public significance. This is illustrated in section II by the well-known case of *R v Brown*.[493]

Section III argues that we should not seek to determine this 'publicness' of protected interests by way of an empirical inquiry. In practice, such an inquiry is not open to the courts.

By proposing a method to determine whether the infringed interests are likely to be regarded as matters of public interest in a given dispute – I call it a 'hypothetical waiver' method – section IV seeks to provide the courts as well as parties with a better tool to operationalise the public interest analysis.

Sections V and VI test the hypothetical waiver method against the leading damages cases. The testing aims to establish whether the hypothetical waiver method is accurate, ie, whether it would produce the same outcomes as regards both availability and unavailability of non-compensatory awards in comparison with the outcomes reached according to the existing doctrines. It is demonstrated in section V and VI – admittedly by way of a non-falsifiable thought experiment concerning how the courts could have decided the disputes in front of them had they relied on the hypothetical waiver method – that the method is sufficiently accurate, meaning that we have a strong reason to believe that all non-correlatively justified NCDs are indeed justified by damage to public interest in various matters[494] as opposed to private interest in the same or other matters. Given its accuracy, the hypothetical waiver method is thus also suggested as a convenient way to test whether NCDs *qua* public interest damages should be available in specific situations. The analysis will also suggest that, normatively, public interest damages should be available more broadly than the existing law permits. For example, it is argued in sections III and IV that a relevant interference with *any* right not acquired as a result of the claimant's choice should be seen as a good justification for an award of NCDs.

Section VII concludes that we can collectively reinterpret all non-correlatively justified NCDs as 'public interest damages'. To be sure, my claim is not that correlative reasons have no justificatory role in relation to NCDs awards. My claim is that they do not play a key role in justifying their non-compensatory *measure*, as opposed to the defendant's remedial liability.[495] The analysis so far showed that NCDs are obtained by the claimant if and only if the defendant's wrongdoing concurrently amounts to a violation of: (i) the claimant's protected private interests – this violation justifies the defendant's liability to the claimant and the possibility to award *some* damages – and (ii) the relevant non-correlative interests – this violation justifies the non-compensatory measure of the damages

[493] *R v Brown (Anthony Joseph)* [1994] 1 AC 212 (HL).
[494] See, eg, the examples provided in n 514, the text to n 491 and the text following n 550.
[495] In more detail, see section I of ch 3.

award. This concurrent existence of the two justifying reasons well explains why the claimant (rather than someone else) obtains the NCDs award.

I. The Public Interest: An Undefined Concept[496]

To see whether the non-correlative considerations which justify NCDs are public interest considerations, it is first necessary to pin down the concept of public interest. Only then can we start testing whether the relevant awards give effect to the supposed public interest in the disputed matters. This section argues that one of the key obstacles to our defining the public interest properly is the general lack of distinctions between: (i) the concept of public interest, (ii) methods of determining which matters are in the public interest, and (iii) specific matters which are protected in the public interest. These distinctions will be relied on in this book.

Familiar as it is, the notion of 'public interest' is almost universally accepted as being devoid of any stable and clear meaning.[497] For example, English courts do not ever define the notion of public interest and yet interchangeably use it to refer to 'public interest in matters X',[498] 'a public interest in matters X'[499] and 'matters X that are in the public interest'.[500] Such uses of the notion are confusing because they elide claims about the 'publicness' of interest in matters X, with claims about the general public who are interested in matters X and which therefore determines whether that interest is a public interest, and also with claims about matters X which are in the public interest.

[496] Sections I and II are based on V Janeček, 'Three Problematic Assumptions About Public Interests in Law' in L Tichý and M Potacs (eds), *Public Interest in Law* (Cambridge, Intersentia, 2021).

[497] eg, V Held, *The Public Interest and Individual Interests* (New York, Basic Books, 1970); P Häberle, *Öffentliches Interesse als juristisches Problem: Eine Analyse von Gesetzgebung und Rechtsprechung* (Athenäum Verlag 1970); J Bell, 'Public Interest: Policy or Principle?' in R Brownsword (ed), *Law and the Public Interest* (Stuttgart, Franz Steiner Verlag, 1993); A Bělohlávek, 'Public Policy and Public Interest in International Law and EU Law' (2012) 3 *Czech Yearbook of International Law* 117; M Lee, 'The Public Interest in Private Nuisance: Collectives and Communities in Tort' (2015) 74 *CLJ* 329, 331–34, 343; A Sanchez-Graells, 'The Procurement Act 2023's Kaleidoscopic View of the Public Interest' [2025] *Legal Studies* (FirstView).

[498] Recently, see, eg, *Maugham v Uber London Ltd* [2019] EWHC 391 (Ch), [2019] Costs LR 521 [56]: 'because there is public interest in issues illustrated by and surrounding this case does not mean that the issues actually raised in these proceedings are themselves of general public importance'; *Bates v Post Office Ltd (No 3)* [2019] EWHC 606 (QB) [586]: 'Post Office understands that there is public interest in promoting the transparency and understanding of matters which are of interest to the public.'

[499] See, eg, *Discover Land Co LLC v Jirehouse* [2019] EWHC 2249 (Ch) [90]: 'There is a public interest in ensuring that proceedings to enforce orders and undertakings are not brought unless they pass a threshold of seriousness.'; *Moher v Moher* [2019] EWCA Civ 1482 [45]: 'There is a public interest in the proper maintenance of the wife by her former husband.'

[500] See, eg, *R (Kuzmin) v General Medical Council* [2019] EWHC 2129 (Admin) [19]: 'it was in the public interest for doctors to provide a response (including oral evidence) to serious allegations made against them'; *Health and Care Professions Council v Selvaraj* [2019] EWHC 2195 (Admin) [10]: 'the interim order is necessary for the protection of members of the public and is in the public interest.'

Similarly, the UK legislature employs the notion of 'public interest' in a vague sense without ever defining it. Sometimes, 'public interest' is referred to as a key consideration for the application of a statutory provision, but the 'public interest' itself remains unspecified.[501] Sometimes, statutes identify considerations according to which some matters should be protected in the public interest, for example, the number of people affected in the given case or whether some constitutional values are at stake.[502] But again, the notion of 'public interest' remains unclear. Sometimes, the courts are required to 'promote the [specific] public interest [already] recognised by the [statute]', such as in the case of tax laws.[503] But again, the statutory law does not explain the concept or what implications the 'publicness' of the relevant interest has for the courts' decisions.

From a scholarly perspective, this vagueness is inexcusable. From a practical viewpoint, it also matters that we maintain distinctions between different types of claim, because statements about the nature of our interest in some matters, about the methods to determine public interest (such as by reference to what members of the public are interested in) and about matters which are deemed to be in the public interest cannot be justified by the same reasons. The arguments and evidence put forth in defence of each of these claims would be different. A claim about the members of the public would probably require some empirical grounding; a claim about the interest in X would require some theoretical, legal and conceptual argumentation; and a claim about X would require a combination of the two methods. The point made here is that when scholars, lawyers and courts discuss 'public interest' or 'public interests', it is highly desirable that they be transparent about the type of claim that they have in mind. This is equally true if we are to rely on public interest considerations as the reasons to justify NCDs.

Rare attempts have been made to explain, on a general level, what individual instances of public interest have in common, yet these explanations are not very helpful either. For example, in *Flood v Times Newspapers Ltd*, which concerned the law of defamation, Lord Phillips observed that 'it will not always be in the public interest to publish matters which are of public interest'.[504] He then went on

[501] See, eg, s 84 of the Law of Property Act 1925; s 213(2) of the Enterprise Act 2002; s 4 of the Defamation Act 2013; s 84 of the Criminal Justice and Courts Act 2015; sch 1, para 4, s 31(2) of the Claims in respect of Loss or Damage arising from Competition Infringements (Competition Act 1998 and Other Enactments (Amendment)) Regulations 2017/385.

[502] See, eg, s 84 of the Fair Trading Act 1973 (no longer in force); s 88(6)–(8) of the Criminal Justice and Courts Act 2015; s 26(2)–(6) of the Data Protection Act 2018.

[503] *R (Whistl UK Ltd (formerly TNT Post UK Ltd)) v Revenue and Customs Commissioners* [2014] EWHC 3480 (Admin), [2015] STC 1077 [59]. See also, eg, Investigatory Powers Act 2016 (identifying, protecting and promoting numerous specific public interests); ss 117A and 117B of the Nationality, Immigration and Asylum Act 2002 (determining public interest in relation to decision made under the Immigration Acts); sch 1, para 1, ss 21(4) and 52(6) of the Digital Economy Act 2017 (identifying and promoting 'the public interest in access to a choice of high quality electronic communications services').

[504] *Flood v Times Newspapers Ltd* [2002] UKSC 11, [2012] 2 AC 273 [33] (affirming Lord Hobhouse's position in *Reynolds v Times Newspapers Ltd & Others* [2001] 2 AC 127 (HL)).

to employ Lord Bingham's definition of matters which are of public interest to the community:

> [By matters of public interest] we mean matters relating to the public life of the community and those who take part in it, including within the expression 'public life' activities such as the conduct of government and political life, elections … and public administration, but we use the expression more widely than that, to embrace matters such as (for instance) the governance of public bodies, institutions and companies which give rise to a public interest in disclosure, but excluding matters which are personal and private, such that there is no public interest in their disclosure.[505]

This general definition of matters of public interest is vague and does not elucidate the public nature (ie, the 'publicness') of our interests in those matters. Lord Mance, in a different context, has recently criticised the possibility that the

> [c]ourts would be required to make a value judgment, by reference to a widely spread mélange of ingredients, about the overall 'merits' or strengths, in a highly unspecific non-legal sense, of the respective claims of the public interest and of each of the parties.[506]

In scholarship, the position is not much different. Two notable intellectual traditions teach us about public interest(s) (note that it is not entirely clear in which of the senses identified above the notion of public interest is used in these two traditions). They are associated with Bentham and Rousseau.[507] The Benthamite tradition, also labelled as 'aggregative', sees public interests as sums of individual interests. The second tradition, sometimes labelled as 'unitarian', claims that public interests consist of universally shared private interests.[508] Yet such definitions do not convey much information beyond the observation that public and private interests somehow overlap.

The English-language literature sometimes addresses the so-called 'public interest law', ie, law relating to group or public interest litigation.[509] This typically concerns environmental issues, social issues, product liability issues, competition law cases and other matters of public interest. Yet the literature does not define the concept of public interest or how to identify relevant public interests in those cases.

[505] *Reynolds v Times Newspapers Ltd & Others* [1998] 3 WLR 862 (CA) 909 (Lord Bingham).

[506] *Patel v Mizra* (n 365) [206] (Lord Mance).

[507] For an overview, see TM Benditt, 'The Public Interest' (1973) 2 *Philosophy & Public Affairs* 291.

[508] S Peter, *Public Interest and Common Good in International Law* (Stuttgart, Helbing Lichtenhahn Verlag, 2012) 10. *cf* C Bezemek and T Dumbrovský, 'The Concept of Public Interest' in L Tichý and M Potacs (eds), *Public Interest in Law* (Cambridge, Intersentia, 2021) who list five standards (not definitions) of public interest: (i) Individualistic standard (Bentham's aggregation of individual interests), (ii) Ideal communitarian standard (Rosseau's general will), (iii) Deliberative communitarian standard (Habermas's or Ackerman's public interest as constitutional politics), (iv) Unitary conception (Platonist objective alignment of individual and public interest), (v) Rawlsian necessities in a Burkean perspective (objectifying the actual interest).

[509] See, eg, A Homburger, 'Private Suits in the Public Interest in the United States of America' in A Homburger and H Kötz, *Klagen Privater im öffentlichen Interesse* (Neuwied, Alfred Metzner Verlag, 1975); BA Weisbrod, JF Handler and NK Komesar (eds), *Public Interest Law: An Economic and Institutional Analysis* (Oakland, University of California Press, 1978); HW Micklitz and N Reich (eds), *Public Interest Litigation before European Courts* (Baden-Baden, Nomos, 1996).

One would hope that the concept of public interest would be defined at least in the writings on the so-called interest theory of law.[510] For example, in a relatively marginal part of his work, Roscoe Pound[511] offered a theory of social interests, the process of their origination and their role in the law.[512] Pound regarded public interests as 'claims or demands or desires asserted by individuals involved in or looked at from the standpoint of political life – life in politically organized society'.[513] 'They are the claims which are involved in the maintenance, the activity and the functioning of society',[514] he added. But beyond these words, Pound did not attempt to define the concept of public interest as a distinct category.[515] Similarly, Philipp Heck, the founding father of the so-called jurisprudence of interests (*Interessenjurisprudenz*), did not define the concept of public interest[516] and neither did his eminent followers.[517]

A possible explanation regarding why the proponents of the jurisprudence of interest failed to define public interest is that the 'concept of interest [on which they relied … was] being inflated to such proportions'[518] that it conflated various perspectives. Pound, for example, stipulated that an interest is 'a demand or desire or expectation which human beings, either individually or in groups or associations or relations, seek to satisfy'.[519] However, this explanation would miss the key point, namely that the 'publicness' of protected interests need not be determined by the specific matters (ie, interests) which are protected in the public interest.

[510] The jurisprudence of interests was influential especially in the first half of the 20th century and had its proponents across the common law and civil law world. An English reader may find helpful a translated collection of some of the core texts in J Hall and others (eds), *The Jurisprudence of Interests: Selected Writings of Max Rümelin, Philipp Heck, Paul Oertmann, Heinrich Stoll, Julius Binder, and Hermann Isay* (Cambridge, MA, MM Schoch tr, Harvard University Press, 1948).

[511] The issues of social and public interests occupied only 1 out of 34 chapters (or 8 out of 151 sections) of Pound's *Jurisprudence*, vols 1–5 (St. Paul, West Publishing, 1959).

[512] ibid, vol 3. See also R Pound, 'A Theory of Social Interests' (1921) 15 *Papers and Proceedings of the American Sociological Society* 16; R Pound, 'A Survey of Social Interests' (1943) 57 *Harvard Law Review* 1; R Pound, 'A Survey of Public Interests' (1945) 58 *Harvard Law Review* 909. See also EW Patterson, 'Pound's Theory of Social Interests' in P Sayre (ed), *Interpretations of Modern Legal Philosophies: Essays in Honour of Roscoe Pound* (Oxford, OUP, 1947).

[513] Pound (n 175) 23.

[514] ibid 23–24.

[515] *cf* ibid 16, 23–24, 337, 342–43.

[516] *cf*, eg, P Heck, 'Gesetzauslegung und Interessenjurisprudenz' (1914) 112 *AcP* 1; P Heck, *Begriffsbildung und Interessenjurisprudenz* (Tubingen, Mohr Siebeck, 1932) (most of this text is available in English in Hall and others (n 510); P Heck, *Interessenjurisprudenz* (Tubingen, Mohr Siebeck, 1933).

[517] *cf*, eg, Hall and others (n 510); G Ellscheid and W Hassemer (eds), *Interessenjurisprudenz* (Darmstadt, Wissenschaftliche Buchgesellschaft, 1974).

[518] H Isay, 'The Method of the Jurisprudence of Interests: A Critical Study' in Hall and others (n 510) 316. Similarly, eg, P Oertmann, 'Interests and Concepts in Legal Science' in Hall and others (n 510) 75; G Colm, 'The Public Interest: Essential Key to Public Policy' in CJ Friedrich (ed), *Nomos V: The Public Interest* (New York, Atherton Press, 1962) 115; FJ Sorauf, 'The Conceptual Muddle' in CJ Friedrich (ed), *Nomos V: The Public Interest* (New York, Atherton Press, 1962) 183–90; M Feintuck, 'The Public Interest' in *Regulation* (Oxford, OUP, 2004) 1–34.

[519] Pound (n 175) 16.

In any event, it is clear that the concept of public interest is not properly defined, although judges, legislatures and academics seem often to rely on some implicit idea of public interest. Feintuck, for example, argues that any attempt to define the concept is destined to fail because 'what is meant and understood by the term "the public interest" is extremely fluid; the term itself remains persistently part of political, legal and regulatory discourse'.[520] I disagree. The key issue that prevents us from finding any definition of the concept is, I think, that the relevant sources (many of which were discussed above)[521] frequently confuse, or at least do not pay attention to, the said distinctions between:

(i) the concept of public interest,
(ii) the methods of determining that some matters are in the public interest, and
(iii) the specific matters that are deemed to be in the public interest.

The point here is not to explore when exactly and why the existing literature does not distinguish between the three issues,[522] but that these need to be distinguished if we are to define the concept properly and use it to analyse NCDs.

Had it not been for the confused cases, laws and writings, it would be clear that we first need to know: (i) how the concept of public interest is to be defined before we can tell, (ii) how public interests are determined and before we can tell, (iii) which specific matters are in the public interest. Although the third question is central to delivering a particular judgment, we need to acknowledge that the third question can only be answered by reference to the second question, and the second question by reference to the first question. As Benditt convincingly argues, the concept of public interest dictates the adequate methods of determining public interests, and not vice versa.[523] This is crucial because otherwise we would find ourselves defining the concept of public interest by the process that leads to its determination.[524] If that were the case, then whoever has the relevant procedural powers and authority would be able to stipulate which matters are in the public interest, and this would introduce circularity and arbitrariness into decision-making.

Given that the courts and legislatures evidently consider specific matters to be in the public interest, it thus seems inevitable that there must be at least an implicit definition of the concept of 'public interest' in those instances. In fact, legislatures do 'not attempt to define what is meant by "*the public interest*" … [because they

[520] Feintuck (n 518) 34.

[521] See also, eg, CJ Friedrich (ed), *Nomos V: The Public Interest* (New York, Atherton Press, 1962); RE Flathman, *The Public Interest: An Essay Concerning the Normative Discourse of Politics* (New York, Wiley, 1966); Held (n 497); R Brownsword (ed), *Law and the Public Interest* (Stuttgart, Franz Steiner Verlag, 1993); L Tichý and M Potacs (eds), *Public Interest in Law* (Cambridge, Intersentia, 2021) and the sources mentioned therein.

[522] Benditt and Held give illustrations of writers failing to distinguish between stages (i), (ii) and (iii) in order to demonstrate that the confusion is real and a problem (although they do not exactly use my language and my specific three-fold distinction). See Benditt (n 507) 292–97; Held (n 497) 12–13.

[523] Similarly, see Benditt (n 507) 293.

[524] The 'public interest as process' is further discussed, eg, in Bell (n 497) 29.

believe] this is a concept which is well-established in the English common law'.[525] But as this section demonstrated, no agreed definition of the concept exists. One may accept that it is well-established that some matters are in the public interest, for example, national security[526] or standards of commercial morality.[527] Further, one may accept that there are well-established legislative processes that determine the relevant public interests in statutes. And one may even accept that the use of public interests is well established, for example, that public interests are used as overriding considerations in legal arguments. As famously put by Judge Felix Frankfurter, the concept of public interest is often used as a 'vague, impalpable but all-controlling consideration' in delivering justice.[528] But I think it is hard to accept that there is a well-established definition of the concept.

To fill this gap, the following section will seek to define the concept of public interest by reference to the well-established use and function of that concept in disputes over interpersonal matters (ie, by its being typically used as the overriding consideration in delivering justice). To be sure, I will focus only on interpersonal matters because, as the cases discussed in chapter four demonstrate, no award of NCDs was made unless the claimant had his concrete stake in the disputed matters. As we know, a court cannot protect any matter of public interest by way of damages unless: (i) a private person commences legal proceedings, and (ii) the private person can establish a cause of action, ie, a private wrong committed against him. Without (i) and (ii) being satisfied, there is nothing that the court can do to protect the public interest. Besides, if the claimant had no actual stake in the disputed matters, what reason would he have to defend those matters against interferences by other private individuals? To adapt the words of Paoli, who drafted one of the first eighteenth-century constitutions, any matter of public interest would be 'but a laughable fiction'[529] for the individual member of the public unless he had some concrete (liberty) rights associated with the public interest in question.

Thus, when discussing public interests in this book, we will only look at the 'publicness' of our interest in matters the violation of which can result in an interpersonal wrong. This is not to say that every legally protected interest – interpersonal or not – is not protected for the benefit of the public. In this sense, however, the concept of public interest would be very close to the abstract idea of rule of law[530] and the claim that something is in the public interest would not

[525] Explanatory Note to the Defamation Act 2013, para [30] (emphasis in original).

[526] *R (Mohamed) v Secretary of State for Foreign and Commonwealth Affairs* [2009] EWHC 152 (Admin), [2009] 1 WLR 2653 [34] (discussing various means of protection of 'the identified public interest' of national security).

[527] *Abacrombie & Co, Re* [2008] EWHC 2520 (Ch) [5] (ruling that activities of a company are contrary to 'a clearly identified public interest' if they do not meet 'a minimum standard of commercial morality').

[528] F Frankfurter in HB Phillips (ed), *Felix Frankfurter Reminisces* (New York, Reynal, 1960) 72.

[529] AM Graziani, *Pascal Paoli: Père de la partie corse* (Paris, Tallandier, 2002) 139.

[530] For such an absolute approach to the concept, see, eg, L Tichý, 'Public Interest and its Importance in Law' in L Tichý and M Potacs (eds), *Public Interest in Law* (Cambridge, Intersentia, 2021) 28–29 and 36.

add anything to the claim that such interest is legally protected, as we explained in the methodological note in the opening text to this chapter. Luckily, it is in the nature of interpersonal disputes that they are (or at least should be) limited to disputes over interpersonal matters in which the parties have some interest, and so the restricted meaning of 'public interests' should be no objection to the present argument. Terminologically, some authors might prefer to call such interpersonal matters 'social' interests and to distinguish them from more abstract matters that are protected in the 'public' interest.[531] But since this divide between social and public interests is not a widely accepted terminological complexity,[532] the following text will proceed with the adjective 'public' when exploring the supposed non-correlative interest in interpersonal matters.

II. The Public Interest: A Well-Established Use

How should the concept of public interest be understood for the purposes of our analysis? Let us begin with a specific example concerning public interest protection. In *R v Brown*,[533] a group of sado-masochists, willingly and enthusiastically participated in the commission of acts of violence against each other for sexual pleasure. It was held by the House of Lords that despite the consent of the participants, 'it would not be in the public interest that deliberate infliction of actual bodily harm during the course of homosexual sado-masochistic activities should be held to be lawful'.[534] Accordingly, it was ruled that Mr Brown's own private interests – as demonstrated by his consent to engage in these sexual activities – were not the key to deciding whether the law would consider the conduct contrary to public interests and hence illegal. This public (ie, criminal) law case is one of the clearest illustrations of how public interest considerations operate when it comes to the impermissibility of certain types of interpersonal harm. I will thus use this illustration, although it cannot, as the law stands, be regarded as authority for damages disputes.

The 'publicness' of our interest in the disputed matters signalled to Mr Brown and to others that certain aspects of one's sexual life could be damaging to the functioning of our society. It was argued in that case that 'injuries to which consent would be irrelevant were those which resulted in actual expense to the public by reason, for example, of the expenses of hospital or other medical treatment, or payment of some benefit'.[535] Lord Jauncey added that 'the free flow of blood from a [wounded] person who is H.I.V. positive … can infect another and an inflicter

[531] See Pound (n 175) 23.
[532] See, eg, CM Sharkey, 'Punitive Damages as Societal Damages' (2003) 113 *Yale Law Journal* 347.
[533] *R v Brown (Anthony Joseph)* (n 493).
[534] ibid 246 (Lord Jauncey).
[535] ibid 238 (Lord Jauncey).

who is carried away … by drink or drugs could very easily inflict pain and injury beyond the level to which the receiver had consented'.[536] According to the House of Lords, citizens should therefore be forbidden to cause each other serious bodily harm under the excuse of their private sexual preferences.

I do not mean to suggest that the decision in *R v Brown* was right, but that the decision is typical of how the 'publicness' of interests manifests itself. The judgment in *R v Brown* made it clear that courts are prepared to limit private control over matters that are important for the functioning of our society because sometimes such control would clash with the public interest in those matters. In other words, the 'publicness' of the matters in dispute signalled to citizens that courts are ready to prioritise the public interest in those matters over anyone's private interest in those matters. As argued by Potacs, for example, 'it is a common feature of "public interests" that they constitute reasonable arguments in a rational discourse about the functioning of a society'.[537] There may be various ethical and political reasons why some matters are in the public interest (and therefore why they can be, in specific interpersonal disputes, protected *qua* public interests, ie, regardless of whether individual interests in the disputed matters might conflict with the public interest in those matters). We will look at those ethical reasons in chapter six, but here we can already see that the 'publicness' of certain interests need not always be universally accepted by all members of the public.

It is important to highlight that the 'publicness' of our interest in the disputed matters, once identified, serves as a token of a strong protection that the law is ready (but not necessarily bound) to exercise in relation to the matters in dispute. If there is an identified public interest in the disputed matters, then it makes sense to limit one's private control over those matters, because no individual should be allowed freely, let alone fully, to control matters which are in the public interest. The lack of free control is thus justified by the significance of the relevant matters for the functioning of our society. In other words, it follows from the well-established use of the concept of public interest that the notion, when deployed, indicates to the members of the public *qua* participants in the legal system that the law is ready to provide the disputed matters with an enhanced degree of protection in comparison with the protection of private interests in those matters.[538] Individual NCDs cases, as explored in chapter four, confirm the diminished significance of private interests in those disputes, because the violations of one's private interests in the disputed matters did not justify the non-compensatory measure. And the express labelling of specific interests as 'public' in some of those cases was probably intended to add some gravity to those matters and to highlight that the disputed

[536] ibid 246 (Lord Jauncey).

[537] M Potacs, 'Public Interest in Legal Interpretation' in L Tichý and M Potacs (eds), *Public Interest in Law* (Cambridge, Intersentia, 2021) 51.

[538] A similar observation was made in A Erh-Soon Tay and E Kamenka, 'Public Law – Private Law' in SI Benn and GF Gaus (eds), *Public and Private in Social Life* (London, Croom Helm, 1983) 83.

matters are not solely a private concern and that the courts are ready to protect such matters in a slightly different way to how they would protect private interests by way of damages.

In this regard, it makes sense to define the concept of public interest by this well-established use. This means that the meaning of the concept needs to be understood from an internal viewpoint of the participants in the legal system (eg, judges, lawyers, parties, etc) who are actually interested in the disputed matters.[539] By contrast, it does not seem very helpful to define the concept of public interest from an external viewpoint of the observers of the system. The notion of public interest is not determined by an *ex ante* classification of legally protected interests, ie, whether certain matters belong to the private or public class. For example, the Digital Economy Act 2017 promotes 'the public interest in access to a choice of high quality electronic communications services',[540] but this fact does not imply why and how the interest will be protected and what it means from the internal viewpoint of a participant in the legal system. It is not clear, for example, whether private consent or private interest in this 'access to a choice of high quality … services'[541] can justify interferences with such access.

To summarise, from the internal viewpoint, the notion of public interest can be plausibly defined as a message to the parties and to the public more generally that certain matters are critical for the functioning of our society[542] and that private interferences with those interests may be sanctioned as such, ie, as being critical for our society and thus not open to control by individuals (on the justification behind this protection, see more in chapter six). The compound phrase 'public interest', when deployed in a judgment, can thus be understood as a token of this special type of protection that the law is ready to provide with respect to matters that private individuals should not be allowed freely to control because individuals should not be allowed to determine what is in the public interest in the first place.

Any relevant interference with such public interest(s) thus justifies a court to protect those matters without specific regard for anyone's private interest in those matters, because individuals should not be allowed to decide what is good for the public and how it can be interfered with (the justification behind this limitation of private control over the disputed matters will be discussed in chapter six as well). As was ruled in *R v Coney*, for example, while the claimant 'may compromise his own civil rights [and interests, he] cannot compromise the public interests'.[543] The 'publicness' of our interest in the disputed matters thus dictates that private

[539] The internal viewpoint has been most famously presented by Hart (see, eg, HLA Hart, *The Concept of Law*, 3rd edn (Oxford, OUP, 2012) ch 5. See also SJ Shapiro, 'What Is the Internal Point of View?' (2006) 75 *Fordham Law Review* 1157; CL Barzun, 'Inside-Out: Beyond the Internal/External Distinction in Legal Scholarship' (2015) 101 *Virginia Law Review* 1203, 1221, 1245–53.

[540] Sch 1, para 1, ss 21(4) and 52(6) of the Digital Economy Act 2017. Further examples are mentioned in nn 503–501 above.

[541] ibid.

[542] See, eg, J Raz, 'Reasons for Action, Decisions and Norms' (1975) 84 *Mind* 481.

[543] *R v Coney* (1882) 8 QB 534, 554 (Hawkins J).

individuals do not and should not freely (and certainly not fully) control those interests. After all, the typical purpose of the proclamation that there is sufficient public interest in some matters is that the protection of those matters will be given a priority over the parties' private interests.

Of course, when public and private interests collide, such as in private nuisance cases when the court decides whether to award damages instead of an injunction, the public interest in question is balanced against the private interest and does not always need to trump the latter. For example, in *Fearn*, the Supreme Court clarified that 'the public interest may sometimes justify awarding damages rather than granting an injunction to restrain the defendant's harmful activity'[544] and guided the Chancery Division (without deciding) that they may therefore want to consider 'whether there is a public interest in maintaining the gallery with a 360-degree view capable of overriding the claimants' prima facie remedy of an injunction'.[545] But even if the private interest (in this case the property rights of Fearn and others) will be ultimately given legal protection, this does not undermine the fact that the function of the supposed proclamation that there is a public interest in maintaining the view (should the Chancery Division decide that there is one) is to signal that the law is ready to rely on such interest in order to override the private interests of the claimants. As such, we can see that the 'publicness' is clearly non-correlative because it is not concerned with giving effect to individual rights.

III. How to Determine which Matters are of Public Interest?

If the concept of public interest is to be defined in line with section II, how is it to be determined that something is in the public interest? Before we turn to the 'hypothetical waiver' in section IV, it is necessary to dismiss one misleading assumption that can be found in the literature,[546] namely the belief that certain matters are protected *qua* public interests because the members of the public have actual common concern for them. For example, under the Benthamite view, public interests are sums of individual interests, and under Rosseau's view, public interests consist of universally shared private interests, as was explained above. This would mean that public interests are constituted by actual interests of members of the public. Some thinkers go as far as to claim that 'something is in the public interest if, and only if, it is in the interest of each and every member of the public'.[547]

This is a problematic assumption. The fact that some interests are legally protected as public interests does not imply that those interests are common to all

[544] *Fearn & Ors v Board of Trustees of the Tate Gallery* [2023] UKSC 4, [2023] 2 WLR 339 [122].
[545] ibid [132].
[546] See, eg, the literature listed in n 497.
[547] Benditt (n 507) 295 (interpreting B Barry, *Political Argument* (New York, Humanities, 1967)).

members of the public. Privacy protection, for example, is in the public interest even if some people do not want to hide anything or share anything with others. Likewise, it is a problematic assumption because even if all members of the public would sometimes like to disobey legal rules (think of speeding or taxation) or even if all members of the public had a prudential interest in doing something which is contrary to the public interest (think of the interest in travelling to see and care for your loved ones during a pandemic, despite clear governmental restrictions on the movement of individuals that are designed to prevent the spread of a disease such as Covid-19), it is clearly not in the public interest that they do so. And as we saw in relation to *R v Brown*,[548] private and public interests in the relevant matters may collide, in which case the 'publicness' typically takes precedence. It is thus difficult to believe there is any necessary link between the idea of legally protected public interests and interests common to all members of the public.

Moreover, even if we accepted that matters of public interest can be identified by asking what is of actual concern to members of the public, it would be difficult to define those members. Does it only include national citizens? Does it also include foreign workers, or foreign visitors who may be viewed as (temporary) members of the public? How about minors? Do children and their parents have an equally strong title to have their interests protected? And how about the interests of members of future generations who will pay the debt for the decisions our society makes nowadays? Should 'the public interest' be determined by reference to interests of our ancestors? These are difficult questions that have not yet been satisfactorily answered in the literature.

As a result, we can see how unhelpful it is to view legally protected public interests as matters which are in the interest *of* the public or *of* all the members of the public. Such an empirical approach to determining which matters are to be protected *qua* public interests is misleading because it aims to make a claim about the members of the public, when in fact we should be making claims about the 'publicness' of our interest in the disputed matters. So when scholars claim that various public wrongs 'infringe the values and interests that the community have a shared and mutual concern for',[549] we should refrain from interpreting such claims as empirical claims about the public.

A better way of testing whether something is in the public interest is to ask whether that interest is (or is suitable for being) legally protected *for* all members of the public, because such a claim does not require empirical proof. Freedom of religion or freedom of speech, for example, are in the public interest even if some individuals do not believe in God or currently have nothing to say. The key idea here is that everyone can choose to exercise these freedoms, and all those who consider themselves members of the public can claim to be legally entitled to do so. It is in this sense that matters of public interest are shared by members of the

[548] n 533.
[549] Wall (n 54) 177 (footnote omitted).

public. These interests are (or are suitable for being) protected for the benefit of all members of the public. By contrast, my own pecuniary loss stemming from the defendant's negligence is not (and is not suitable for being) protected for the benefit of the public.

Thus, regardless of whether any individual claimant believes it is in the public interest that, for example, state officials do not abuse their power, he can hold the state officials liable for such conduct under the doctrine of punitive damages (oppressive, arbitrary and unconstitutional acts by the servants of the government[550]). Similarly, everyone may benefit from the public interests in privacy protection, the public interest in environmental protection, the public interest in the practice of contracting and so on and so forth. The public interest in these matters is akin to a public interest in fundamental institutions that form the backbone of our society and that provide a fundamental infrastructure without which the society would arguably not function well (whereby 'well' can be defined with regards to the type of political organisation that the society wishes to maintain, such as is the case in relation to different forms of democracy).

Similarly, there is a sense in which all non-acquired private rights and protected interests belong to this fundamental societal infrastructure because they are vested in every individual regardless of their wishes and because such rights exist for the benefit of all members of the public. We may even argue that some of these rights and interests are a condition precedent for the existence of other rights, thus being more fundamental than others and thereby more significant for the functioning of our society (I elaborate on this argument in more detail in section IV and chapter seven, section I[551]). In this sense, any wrongs-based violation of such fundamental non-acquired rights and interests could arguably justify an award of NCDs *qua* public interest damages, which is a point to which I will return in the following.

Now, you may think that all the past cases which resulted in NCDs awards will serve as a strong indication of the current 'publicness' of the relevant matters.[552] You may think that if the disputed matters were already protected for the benefit of the public, then they will be again so protected in the future. This line of reasoning could be dangerous, in my view. Each dispute is different, and, as was explained in section I, the specific matters which are in the public interest must be determined by a method which, in turn, must be determined by the concept of public interest; not vice versa. And so if the meaning of 'publicness' of our interest in specific matters in dispute is a message to the parties and to the public that those matters are critical for the functioning of our society and that private interferences may be sanctioned as being critical for the functioning of our society as well (after all, we saw that it is integral to the notion of 'public interest' that individuals should not be allowed freely to control matters of public interest), then it would be wrong to believe that we can determine public interests by simply looking at the catalogue

[550] *Rookes* (n 97) 1226.
[551] See the text to nn 784–790.
[552] *cf*, eg, the interests identified in ch 4.

of matters previously protected by awards of NCDs. Various interferences with the same or similar matters may justify very different conclusions about the significance of such conduct for the functioning of our society. So, to reiterate, the claim in this book is not that NCDs are all justified by violations of the same matters, but that the non-correlatively justified NCDs are all justified by damage to matters which are protected primarily for the public benefit.

IV. The 'Hypothetical Waiver' Method

A person can in principle freely and fully control the protection of his interests insofar as that control is grounded in his individual right, because it is his private choice to determine how the individual right will be exercised and what matters he wants to protect on the basis of that right. And if this control is unlawfully taken from him or if it is somehow limited, we can say that the person suffers compensable damage to his private interests.[553] In accordance with the norms of corrective justice, we can thus say that the 'privateness' of protected interests implies that the protection of such matters is legitimately controlled by the private right-holder. Importantly, when it comes to private interests, the claimant can also decide to waive their rights and therefore to waive the protection of such interests.

This section argues that no such waiver can be exercised in relation to public interests, and neither should it be possible to do so. When determining whether the events in dispute cause damage to public interests, it is thus convenient to rely on what I call a 'hypothetical waiver' method. The gist of the 'hypothetical waiver' is that whenever we would conclude that, at the time of the events in dispute, the claimant was not or should not have been allowed to waive the protection of the relevant matters, then we may say that those matters are deemed to be in the public interest and may be protected as such. Building on the concrete definition of the 'public interest' concept from section II, this method allows us directly to determine whether we are willing to protect these matters *qua* public interests. Throughout this section, I will clarify the 'hypothetical waiver' method and why it is suited to determining whether something is in the public interest.

At the outset, it is necessary to explain what 'waiver' means. According to *Stroud's Judicial Dictionary*, for example, there are at least 13 senses in which 'waiver' is used.[554] As observed by Goudkamp, '[t]he courts have often remarked that the myriad uses that the law finds for the doctrine of waiver has rendered it

[553] *cf* E Voyiakis, *Private Law and the Value of Choice* (Oxford, Hart Publishing, 2017).

[554] This was pointed out in *Banning v Wright (Inspector of Taxes)* [1972] 1 WLR 972 (HL) 979 (Lord Hailsham), referring to *Ross T Smyth & Co Ltd v TD Bailey, Son & Co* [1940] 3 All ER 60, (1940) 164 LT 102 (HL) 106. See also S Wilken and K Ghaly, *The Law of Waiver, Variation, and Estoppels*, 3rd edn (Oxford, OUP, 2012).

incapable of concrete definition'.[555] And while the word is 'not a term of art',[556] it always 'involves the idea of giving up or abandoning some right or rule'.[557] According to Goudkamp and Nolan, '[w]hen lawyers speak of "waiver" they may mean to refer to conduct by the claimant which signifies an intention to relinquish a right of action for a legal wrong'.[558] Indeed, in his *Treatise on the Law of Waiver*, Bowers defines waiver as 'the voluntary abandonment or surrender, by a capable person, of a right known by him to exist, with the intent that such right shall be surrendered and such person forever deprived of its benefit'.[559] Similarly, the *Oxford Dictionary of Law* defines waiver as '[t]he act of abandoning or refraining from asserting a legal right'.[560]

Based on this general definition of waiver, it is clear that the claimant cannot abandon or refrain from asserting a legal right to NCDs, because, as we already know, non-correlatively justified NCDs are not – by definition – grounded in the claimant's correlative right. In this sense, the claimant cannot waive the right to NCDs, because he does not have it. Or to be more precise, he does not have it prior to the court decision which bestows on him the right to obtain the non-compensatory remedy.

You may argue that the court has a public duty to award NCDs in some circumstances and that the claimant has therefore a corresponding subjective public right to obtain the award. But he would still not be able to waive the protection of the interests that underpin the public duty, because the duty would not be grounded in the subjective right. For example, the right to an impartial tribunal exists 'principally for the purpose of upholding public confidence in the administration of justice'.[561] And while the courts tend to conceive this right as a subjective right held against the judiciary, the duty of impartiality protects the public interest. As put by Kirby J (a minority position) in the Australian case *Gotkas*, the public interest 'belongs not to the litigant alone but to the public at large and to the legal system of which the Judge is a member'.[562] The subjective right is merely a liberty derived from the public duty and from the public benefit. 'Private litigants should [therefore] not be able to sacrifice the public interest in maintaining the reality and appearance of justice because they find it expedient to do so', argues Goudkamp.[563]

You may further object that, according to the overall definition of damages in this book (chapter two, section I), no damages rights can be waived prior to

[555] J Goudkamp, 'The Rule Against Bias and the Doctrine of Waiver' (2007) 26 *Civil Justice Quarterly* 310, 315.

[556] *Banning v Wright* (n 554) 981 (Lord Reid).

[557] ibid 979 (Lord Reid), cited with approval, eg, in *Armia Ltd v Daejan Developments Ltd* [1979] SC 56, [1979] SLT 147 (HL) 72.

[558] Goudkamp and Nolan (n 29) para 26-075.

[559] RD Bowers, *A Treatise on the Law of Waiver* (Denver, WH Courtright Publishing, 1914) 19.

[560] Law (n 81), entry 'waiver'.

[561] Goudkamp (n 555) 310.

[562] *Goktas v Government Insurance Office of New South Wales* (1993) 31 NSWLR 684, 687 (cited according to Goudkamp (n 555) 325 fn 79).

[563] Goudkamp (n 555) 327.

the court decision because damages are rights that arise from the judgment. But this objection would be misplaced. The protection of correlative private interests is owed to the parties as of right and thus regardless of the court decision.[564] The protection of those interests can thus be waived. By contrast, in the case of NCDs – insofar as they are not justified by correlative reasons – the remedial right against the defendant and the remedial duty owed to the claimant need to be distributed by the court first. Accordingly, prior to the decision, the claimant cannot waive the non-compensatory remedial right or the right to the protection of the relevant interest.

To be clear, the claimant can consent to certain interferences with his own interests, but he cannot waive the precondition of the breach, ie, the legal protection of the relevant interest and the law's constant readiness to protect the disputed matters as something critical for the functioning of our society. To give an example, private individuals may consent to the processing of their personal data, but they cannot surrender their right to consent to such processing. Indeed, according to the UK GDPR, the right to consent to the processing of personal data and the right to withdraw such consent at any time cannot be waived.[565] Similarly, in relation to trespassory torts such as false imprisonment, the claimant can consent to his detention, but it would not make sense if he could waive his liberty to deny such consent. In other words, it would make no sense if the private stake in the public interest against unlawful detention could be entirely abandoned. In these situations, the public interest in the protection of the underlying matters is considered more important than unrestricted freedom of choice and more important than the private claimant-defendant considerations. So while a claimant can privately consent to the violation of his liberties (recall *R v Brown*), he cannot waive the public interest protection of those liberties. The protection of those liberties remains rooted in the public interest.

This raises a more fundamental question concerning which rights are waiverable in the relevant sense. Does the tort of negligence involve a waivable duty, for example? It is true that *volenti* is (almost always) a defence in negligence. But if we ask whether one can waive a right not to be treated in a certain way without one's consent, it is unlikely that negligence is 'waiverable' in the relevant sense – one cannot give up entirely one's right not to be treated negligently without one's permission. If consent is built into the specification of the right, it is arguably the case that *all* non-acquired private law rights (ie, rights not acquired as a result of the claimant's choice) are not waiverable in this sense and that the claimant's consent to their violation is thus no defence in respect of the 'public' wrongfulness of that interference. If so, that would entail, on the hypothetical waiver method,

[564] See Gardner (n 106) and Steel and Stevens (n 106).

[565] Article 7(3) of the Regulation (EU) 2016/679 of the European Parliament and of the Council of 27 April 2016 on the protection of natural persons with regard to the processing of personal data and on the free movement of such data, and repealing Directive 95/46/EC (General Data Protection Regulation) as retained by the United Kingdom (the UK GDPR).

that whenever a non-acquired private right is violated, NCDs should, in principle, be available. This would be a significant departure from the existing law, which draws no such line when it comes to the availability of NCDs, but it appears to be a logical corollary of the waiver method. It would also help strengthen the idealist view of duties in the law of negligence, as opposed to the cynical view according to which there are in fact no legal duties of care and the law of negligence merely imposes compensatory liability for carelessly caused harms.[566]

There also appear to be some good reasons that justify the conclusion concerning the waiverability of non-acquired private rights. In contract law, for example, the claimant will typically be entitled to waive all the various acquired contractual rights and hence control their protection, but he would not be able to waive the rights that underline the whole practice of contracting, ie, the publicly important legal infrastructure that makes contracting possible. Similarly, the private claimant will not be allowed to waive the protection of rights that stem from mandatory statutory provisions (eg, provisions concerning consumer protection). Contractual duties stemming from these statutory provisions will apply to the parties and cannot be waived. In this sense, they are not acquired, and their protection is not dependent on one's private consent. Likewise, the conditions of liability in tort law will typically be based on non-acquired private rights which are arguably non-waiverable in the relevant sense because their existence (and therefore their protection) is not dependent on the claimant's specific consent or other manifestations of the claimant's free choice.

However, we should not overstate the importance of liability establishing breaches of rights for measures of damages. As was explained in chapter three, section I, it is not the civil wrong (seen as interference with the claimant's right) which justifies the specific measure of damages, but the consequential damage that springs from that wrong. Such damage can amount to consequential violation of various rights or, more generally, to consequential violation of various protected interests. And the question of non-waiverability needs to be asked with respect to this consequential damage, not with respect to the liability establishing harm. Thus, while all non-acquired private rights might arguably be suitable for nominal damages awards (where the consequential damage to the public interest can generally be presumed on the basis of the liability-establishing wrong), it is unlikely that a mere liability-establishing infringement of these non-acquired private rights would be sufficient to justify any other form of NCDs. What we would need to search for is some consequential violation of non-acquired rights and legally protected interests which arguably exist for the benefit of the public, rather than for the benefit of any particular individual.

This modified claim, namely that whenever there is a consequential violation of non-acquired private rights, NCDs should, in principle, be available, therefore does not look like such a significant departure from the existing law (as will be

[566] See NJ McBride, 'Duties of Care – Do They Really Exist?' (2004) 24 *OJLS* 417.

demonstrated in sections V and VI), save perhaps in relation to nominal damages. In relation to nominal damages, the modified claim would still imply that where the breached duty (including the duty of care in negligence) is regarded as significant for the functioning of our society, it could arguably justify an award of NCDs. However, given that negligence is not actionable without proof of resulting harm, it is clear that there will always be an award of compensation that will discharge the function of nominal damages, and the NCDs award would thus no longer be an appropriate response to the events in dispute, as was discussed in section II of chapter four. The only conceivable scenario where nominal damages would be an appropriate response is when the claimant would seek them expressly (instead of compensation) in order to prove the point of law and that the defendant had acted negligently. It is unclear, however, whether the court would not strike out this claim as an abuse of process.[567]

Now, we may ask if the non-waiverability of public interests is justified. As was discussed in section II, there are good reasons why we should not let the private individuals waive the protection of matters of public interest. The claimant should not abandon or refrain from asserting a protection of matters of public interest because if that waiver was effective, it would imply that an individual can determine what is and what is not important for the functioning of our society. As per the relevant jurisprudence of the European Court of Human Rights in *Håkansson*, 'a waiver … must not run counter to any important public interest'[568] and if the waiver of a liberty right could effectively, and forever, surrender the protection of the underlying public interest, then the waiver would clearly run contrary to that public interest. Note that this is not a circular argument. We can argue that it is in the public interest that private individuals are not allowed to waive the protection of matters of public interest. For example, the right not to be subjected to arbitrary and unconstitutional exercise of public power (Category 1 punitive damages) can be said to be derived from the public duty that the officials have and that this duty protects the public interest in lawful and non-arbitrary exercise of those official powers. In this sense, any alleged waiver of the subjective liberty right by the claimant should not be capable of actually abandoning the protection of the public interest from which the liberty right is derived.

Of course, 'waiver' has a broader meaning than just abandonment of a right or abandonment of the protection of the underlying interest that justifies the claimant's liberty rights. Accordingly, you may object that the hypothetical waiver method is not sufficiently specific to allow us to distinguish between situations where 'waiver' means abandonment and when 'waiver' means something else. Indeed, one significant alternative usage of the word 'waiver' is concerned with election. 'Waiver' is sometimes used in the sense of election between alternative

[567] For more detail on this point, see ch 7, section I.B.
[568] *Håkansson and Sturesson v Sweden* (1990) 13 EHRR 1 [66], cited with approval in *Millar v Dickson* [2001] UKPC D4, [2002] 1 WLR 1615 [20].

rights inconsistent with one another.[569] In such circumstances, the waiver is a way to describe the consequences of one's election – a consequence which 'may be inferred from the facts and circumstances of the case',[570] a consequence that implicitly results from the election.

In the case of NCDs, however, the election can have no bearing on whether an interference with the relevant interests is wrongful or not. This is so because the public interest analysis reveals that non-correlatively justified NCDs are incompatible with each other only to the extent they protect the same public interest. And so if the claimant elects a particular type of NCDs, this does not necessarily imply that the protection of the interests sanctionable by other NCDs would be waived. Furthermore, since compensatory and non-compensatory damages are generally compatible with each other, their relationship does not even give rise to the implicit waiver discussion.

Setting this argument aside, one may still assert that the claimant has some liberty rights (not claim-rights) to benefit from the public interest[571] and this liberty right may, or may not, be exercised by the claimant – she may always elect to sue or not to sue the defendant and thereby implicitly waive the relevant public interest protection. Further, these days, '[i]n most litigious situations the expression "waiver" is used to describe a voluntary, informed and unequivocal election by a party not to claim a right or raise an objection which it is open to that party to claim or raise'.[572] On this pragmatic view, we could say that by having this choice, the claimant is, in effect, in control over the protection of the underlying interests.

It may be tempting to accept this position but I think it would be wrong to view any surrender of liberty rights – even by way of choosing not to sue the defendant – as a waiver of the public interest protection. The claimant can always decide not to sue the wrongdoer, but this non-exercise of the subjective right is different from a waiver of rights. As Liau convincingly argues, the claimant's standing in private law (the power to sue) is separate from the underlying substantive rights.[573] As such, this 'election' could hardly ever amount to an unequivocal waiver, and it cannot have any bearing on the law's readiness to protect the underlying interests, because the claimant can always change his mind and bring the defendant to court at a later date. The election not to sue thus cannot be expressly linked with relinquishment of rights, except perhaps in settlement agreements.

Further, although the claimant's choice not to sue the defendant may resemble a waiver of the protection of the public interests in question, it would

[569] eg, *Kammins Ballrooms Co Ltd v Zenith Investments (Torquay) Ltd* [1971] AC 850 (HL) 882; *China National Foreign Trade Transportation Corp v Evlogia Shipping Co SA of Panama* [1979] 1 WLR 1018 (HL) 1034.

[570] *Armia Ltd v Daejan Developments Ltd* (n 557) 72 (Lord Keith).

[571] On the notion of 'liberty rights', see WN Hohfeld, 'Some Fundamental Legal Conceptions as Applied in Judicial Reasoning' (1913) 23 *Yale Law Journal* 16.

[572] *Millar v Dickson* (n 568) [31] (Lord Bingham).

[573] T Liau, *Standing in Private Law: Powers of Enforcement in the Law of Obligations and Trusts* (Oxford, OUP, 2023) 1–12.

be a mistake to interpret that choice as an implicit waiver of that public interest protection. This is so because it is difficult to see how a waiver of the protection of public interests can ever be: (i) voluntary, (ii) informed, and (iii) unequivocal – all of which are legal requirements for an effective waiver of rights.[574] For example, if the election not to sue the defendant were to be regarded as an informed and unequivocal waiver of the public interest protection, the claimant would need to know (be informed) that the interest is unequivocally public and therefore outside his control. So he would be informed that he cannot waive the protection, which is why we would not be able to regard the election as a valid waiver. Alternatively, the claimant would need to accept that the interest in dispute can be viewed as something unequivocally private (ie, something which can be controlled), in which case the election would only amount to a waiver of the private interest protection and would have no bearing on the protection of the underlying public interests in the disputed matters.

We should therefore accept the conclusion that, voluntarily or not, the claimant cannot exercise any waiver in relation to public interests. The paradox here is that prior to the court's decision the waiver cannot be voluntary, informed and unequivocal, and after the court's decision the waiver cannot have any effect on the protection of the relevant public interests. A waiver made post-decision would at best relinquish the claimant's remedial rights.

All this suggests that the hypothetical waiver method is a good way to determine the 'publicness' of protected interests in the law of damages: if we would conclude that, at the time of the events in dispute, the claimant was not allowed or should not have been allowed to waive the protection of the interests in dispute, then those interests may only be protected for the public benefit.

I do not want to claim that the hypothetical waiver method is the only way to determine 'publicness' of interests in the law of damages. But I think that this method is reliable because the adequacy of this method is dictated by the definition of the concept of public interest, and not vice versa. That concept was defined in section II where it was stated that the 'publicness' of protected interests is a token of the level of protection that stems from a public interest in those matters. In particular, it was stated that the 'publicness' explains and justifies why the courts are and should be willing to protect certain matters regardless of anyone's private interest in the disputed matters. As shall thus be clear, the hypothetical waiver method stems directly from this definition.

To be sure, the waiver method only determines *whether* we are willing to protect something *qua* public interest in a given dispute, not whether courts actually should make NCDs awards or whether the matters in dispute are to be generally protected as public interests with which individuals can never interfere. It allows the courts and the parties to tackle issues of public importance without entering

[574] eg, *Watson v Sadiq* [2013] EWCA Civ 822 [62]; *JSC BTA Bank v Ablyazov & Ors* [2013] EWCA Civ 1551, [2013] 1 WLR 1845 [79].

the difficult ethical and political argumentation regarding what is generally – ie outside of a particular dispute – good for the functioning of our society.

V. Testing the Method: Cases Concerning Damage to Public Interests

Chapter four demonstrated that interferences with various non-correlatively protected matters justified the courts awarding NCDs. Chapter five has shown, so far, that public interests are protected by virtue of non-correlative reasons and that the 'publicness' of interests in dispute can be in principle determined by the 'hypothetical waiver' method. In order to complete the argument and substantiate the claim that all non-correlatively justified NCDs are to be defined as damages justified by damage to public interests, it needs to be demonstrated that the waiver method is sufficiently accurate. In other words, it needs to be demonstrated that the courts would have been able to award NCDs in all the cases in which they did in fact award NCDs had they expressly identified the justifying reasons as reasons of public interest and, vice versa, that they would not have been in a position to award NCDs in all the cases in which they did not in fact award NCDs had they expressly failed to identify the 'publicness' of the justifying reasons. The purpose of sections V and VI is thus to test the hypothetical waiver method's accuracy and to ascertain whether all non-correlatively justified NCDs can be positively defined as public interest damages.

Before we begin testing the hypothetical waiver method, three methodological clarifications are in order. First, let me stress that the 'testing' of the method that follows is simply a thought experiment. Whether or not the courts would have approached the cases in the way suggested below is something that can never be ascertained. As such, this part of my argument is not falsifiable. The purpose of sections V and VI is merely to test whether the hypothetical waiver could work accurately in concrete cases. These two sections demonstrate how the courts could have identified the 'publicness' of the interests in disputes presented to them had they asked whether the claimant was not or should not have been allowed to waive the protection of those interests at the time of the events in dispute. One may therefore disagree with my application of the hypothetical waiver method to the relevant cases, ie, with the specific conclusion regarding the 'publicness' of the relevant matters, but such disagreement is not an argument against the method itself.

Second, I test the accuracy of the waiver method against the leading cases only. In principle, the hypothetical waiver method should be applicable to any case, but it would be impracticable to focus on every outlier or insignificant decision. If it turns out that the method is sufficiently accurate in relation to the leading cases, then there is a compelling reason to believe in the overall accuracy of the method. The word 'leading' is, of course, merely an approximation, as there are no doubt different views on how to determine a 'leading' case. But it is still a useful approximation. To identify the leading cases, I surveyed recent editions of the relevant books and supplemented this survey with an online search of the most frequently cited judgments concerning NCDs and awards that are not easily explicable in compensatory terms.[575] I do not look at the leading compensatory damages cases because it has already been demonstrated in earlier chapters of this book that compensatory measures are not justified by damage to public interests.

Third, when assessing the accuracy, I am not concerned with the question of what particular remedy (let alone in what particular quantum) the court could have awarded had they used the waiver method. The aim is to test whether the courts would have been able legitimately to make their awards in *a non-compensatory measure*. For this purpose, this part of the book is organised according to whether the examined cases concerned damage to public interests (section V) or not (section VI). After I have analysed the leading cases, I decided to present them to you under this organising scheme to make the analysis easier to follow. For my reader's convenience, the leading cases are grouped within those sections according to the specific types of NCDs addressed in those cases, but you will see that on the public interest analysis, the stated doctrinal distinctions between individual types of NCDs are probably not as clear as they are typically thought to be.

A. Punitive Damages Cases

Rookes[576] is undoubtedly the leading judgment on punitive damages, albeit no punitive award was in fact made in that case. The relevant wrongdoing discussed in *Rookes* was the tort of intimidation, namely intimidation by means of an unlawful strike. The defendants, who were Mr Rookes's workplace colleagues, wanted Mr Rookes to be dismissed from his employment. To achieve that goal, they abused their role as officials of the employer's union and threatened the employer in that they wanted deliberately to engineer an unofficial wildcat strike unless their demands were met. Mr Rookes was dismissed, but since he thought the dismissal unfair, aggravating, and instigated by his colleagues, he sued them and not the employer. Interestingly, the events in dispute were primarily in violation of the employer's interests. The claimant was harmed by the defendants' conduct only indirectly.

[575] I used the following materials: SF Deakin and Z Adams, *Markesinis and Deakin's Tort Law*, 8th edn (Oxford, OUP, 2019); Burrows (n 62); J Beatson, A Burrows and J Cartwright, *Anson's Law of Contract*, 31st edn (Oxford, OUP, 2020); A Burrows, *A Casebook on Contract*, 7th edn (Oxford, Hart Publishing, 2020); Goudkamp and Nolan (n 29); J Steele, *Tort Law: Text, Cases, and Materials*, 5th edn (Oxford, OUP, 2022); Chen-Wishart (n 29); Witting (n 6); Giliker (n 29); M Lunney and K Oliphant, *Lunney & Oliphant's Tort Law: Text and Materials*, 7th edn (Oxford, OUP, 2023); H Beale, *Chitty on Contracts*, 35th edn (incorporating 1st supplement, London, Sweet & Maxwell, 2024) ch 30; E McKendrick, *Contract Law: Text, Cases, and Materials*, 11th edn (Oxford, OUP, 2024); O'Sullivan (n 29); McBride and Bagshaw (n 29); WE Peel, *Treitel on the Law of Contract*, 16th edn (London, Sweet & Maxwell, 2025); Edelman, Varuhas and Higgins (n 5).

[576] *Rookes* (n 97).

In general terms, Lord Devlin concluded in *Rookes* that 'the tort of intimidation is always punishable [by punitive damages]',[577] but that the facts in this case do not 'bring the case within either of the [first] two categories' of punitive damages awards.[578] It is not entirely clear from the judgment why Lord Devlin thought the requirements for punitive damages were not satisfied, but the most plausible interpretation is that his Lordship relied on the general requirement set out earlier in the judgment, namely that the claimant 'cannot recover exemplary damages unless he is the victim of the punishable behaviour'.[579] Indeed, Mr Rookes was not the direct victim of the defendants' wrongdoing. Instead, we can argue that the (potentially) punishable behaviour was directed against the employer, although it was Mr Rookes who suffered the consequences.

Hypothetically, had the employer – as a direct victim – brought an action against the employees, a question arises as to whether the employees could have been justly ordered to pay damages in the punitive measure. Was the employer in a position to waive their right not to be subjected to an unlawful strike? When put this way, it is clear that the employer could not have influenced whether or not the strike would have been lawful. It was not their claim-right.

You may think that if an employer waives (consents to) breach of contract, then it might be argued that the conduct is no longer a breach, but that would miss the point. First, if the employer consented to breach of contract (ie, to the employees' withdrawal of work), then the withdrawal would no longer amount to a 'strike' in the sense of a justified withdrawal of work that is in breach of the duty to work. Second, the nature of the unlawfulness of the threatened strike in question was primarily based on its being contrary to the agreement between the trade union (of which the defendants were representatives) and the employer, not on its being contrary to the general duty to work. In particular, there was a 'special term deemed to be incorporated in each union man's service contract'[580] which provided that 'in the event of any relevant trade dispute there should not be a strike or a lock-out but that the dispute should be resolved in the manner therein indicated'.[581] Thus, the union members of which the defendants were representatives have voluntarily limited their right to strike up front, and the threat of inducing others to withdraw their labour contrary to the agreement between the union and the employer was thus unlawful. Third, their intimidation was brought about by means of an unlawful strike as well as by means of other tortious conduct.[582] It was held by Lord Reid that the relevant statutory provision that generally protects the striking workers from liability does not provide immunity with respect to 'inducement of breach of contract where that is brought about by intimidation or other illegal means

[577] ibid 1232.
[578] ibid 1232.
[579] ibid 1227.
[580] ibid 1182 (Lord Evershed).
[581] ibid 1181 (Lord Evershed).
[582] ibid 1194 (Lord Evershed).

and the section must be given a similar construction with regard to interference with trade, business or employment'.[583] As shall be clear here as well, it was not up for the employer to decide (by way of waiver or otherwise) what the extent of the statutory immunity from liability is. And since the employer's consent to the breach of individual contracts of employment is not built into the specification of the right not to be subjected to an unlawful strike, the protection of the matters in dispute was thus non-waiverable.[584]

Therefore, it seems likely that the infringement of the employer's interest not to be subjected to an unlawful strike would have constituted damage to a public interest. This, I think, may have been the reason why the jury and the judges were willing to entertain the thought that the employees' intimidation could have attracted the non-compensatory remedy. A similar line of reasoning would apply to Mr Rookes. He too could not have affected whether or not the defendant's strike and the specific methods of inducing others to breach their contract (used as part of the overall strategy to intimidate the employer by the risk of strike) would amount to wrongdoing or not. It was not his call to make because Mr Rookes did not control the protection of the public interest against unlawful strike. This may be another reason why the jury and the judges entertained the thought about punitive damages when discussing Mr Rookes's claim. In this sense, we may thus say that the waiver method would be accurate.

Another leading case is *Rowlands v Chief Constable of Merseyside Police*, where it was held that a chief officer of police can be vicariously liable for torts committed by his officers because he 'bear[s] public responsibility for the conduct of the officers concerned'.[585] Mrs Rowlands was a vigilant citizen. She made a telephone complaint about her neighbour's noisy behaviour. A police patrol arrived in response to the call. Yet they arrested Mrs Rowlands (and not her neighbour) and did so unlawfully and in front of her children.[586] Here it seems clear that Mrs Rowlands was not in a position to waive her liberty right not to be subjected to the unlawful arrest. Such a waiver, if effective, would have a drastic impact on the public trust in police officers. She could have chosen not to sue them. And she also could have chosen not to claim punitive damages. But it was not open to her to waive the lawfulness requirement in relation to the arrest, let alone her right to protest the arrest. Such a waiver would conflict with an important public interest concerning trust in police forces. The court would thus have been right to make the non-compensatory award if it applied the waiver method. That conforms with the actual award made by the court in this case under Category 1 punitive damages.

[583] ibid 1178 (Lord Reid).

[584] Note that this is different to the situation where the employer would agree to an amendment to the terms of the (framework) agreement with the trade union. Such an agreement could possibly re-define the conditions under which the threat of strike would be unlawful. It would not, however, re-define the non-waiverability of the right not to be subjected to an unlawful strike.

[585] *Rowlands v Chief Constable of Merseyside Police* [2006] EWCA Civ 1773, [2007] 1 WLR 1065 [47] (Moore-Bick LJ).

[586] ibid [2].

The hypothetical waiver method seems accurate also in relation to another leading punitive damages case – *2 Travel Group Plc (in liq) v Cardiff City Transport Services Ltd*.[587] The wrongdoing in this case was caused by anti-competitive behaviour by the defendant. We can thus ask: Would the anti-competitive behaviour not have been wrongful had the claimants waived the protection of their interests in the competition? No, it would not, because even if the claimants had waived their liberty right, accepted an apology, or expressed consent with the interference with the relevant interests, this would not be material for the court's assessment of the wrongfulness of the action – none of these reasons is sufficient to conclude that the violation of a legally protected interest in a fair market competition is not wrongful. The claimant could have decided not to sue the wrongdoer, they could have settled the proceedings, or they could have simply withdrawn the claim, but none of this would have made the wrongdoer's conduct lawful.

It is true that competition law protects both individual and collective interests in the right to fair competition, but in *2 Travel Group* it was discussed at length that the wrongdoer's behaviour was worthy of punishment because it showed cynical disregard for the right to fair competition *qua* category (ie, as a category important for the functioning of the legal system) and not because of the disregard shown in respect of the specific claimant's private interest in that right.[588] The attack on the right was considered outrageous and intolerably unjust because the wrongdoer knew that they were doing something illegal and reckless, irrespective of whether the private claimant was aware of the wrongdoing.[589] Arguably, then, the relevant infringement could have been regarded as wrongful by the court regardless of the claimant's private interests, and the claimant's waiver would not have changed this. In relation to the public interest in fair market competition, the claimant was not and should not have been able to waive its protection. Had the public interest in the disputed matters been identified in this way in *2 Travel Group*, the court would have been in a position legitimately to award damages in a non-compensatory measure. Indeed, the court awarded NCDs in that case, which speaks in favour of the waiver method's accuracy.

Interestingly, when writing about punitive damages, Chapman and Trebilcock also argue that an important justifying reason is not primarily a violation of some private interests, but 'a denial of the relevance of rights altogether'.[590] As was already discussed in section II of chapter four, for Chapman and Trebilcock, the right as a category (not the individual interest that is derived from that category) is what is wrongfully violated in such cases.[591] And so if the remedy protects the right *qua* category, it also explains why the law does not even require the victim's direct

[587] n 242.

[588] ibid [468]–[477].

[589] ibid [586], [593], [598]. But *cf A v Bottrill* [2002] UKPC 44, [2003] 1 AC 449 in which the Privy Council (New Zealand) held that punitive damages may be awarded even in exceptional and rare cases of inadvertently negligent conduct (ibid [37], [50], [63], [64]).

[590] Chapman and M Trebilcock (n 287) 781.

[591] ibid 782.

knowledge of the violation of the right *qua* category. Chapman and Trebilcock then go on to compare punitive damages with criminal law sanctions and argue that violation of the right *qua* category also well explains why the law requires the wrongdoer's subjective knowledge of the wrongdoing, because '[a]nything less, such as mere negligence or mistake, cannot explain why the state, as guardian of the category of Right, is a party to the action [in criminal law]. That is, anything less cannot explain the public law nature of the criminal law.'[592] For the wrongdoer 'to deny the category of Right, he must engage that category *as a category*, that is, conceptually. This means that his denial … must be cognitive, involving conscious or advertent indifference to the relevance of rights'.[593]

As a matter of law there is no explicit requirement that NCDs would only be available for culpable wrongdoing, but if a violation of the right *qua* category requires (conceptually) a cognitive denial of that right, it is generally to be anticipated that culpability will be present in such NCDs cases. This is an interesting implication which might help us to argue against the availability of NCDs in cases of inadvertent wrongdoing. While this is by no means conclusive, it is telling that none of the NCDs cases discussed in this book so far can be easily characterised as a case of inadvertent wrongdoing.

A similar line of thought concerning the interference with the right as a category can be applied to the leading case of *Wilkes v Wood*.[594] In that case, the defendant unlawfully issued a general search warrant against the claimant. The warrant was issued based on a mere suspicion that the claimant might have published a libel against the King. This exercise of the state power by the defendant was found to be in violation of the right to liberty of every man, not just in violation of the sphere of protection of a particular right-holder, ie, the violation of the private liberty of Wilkes, who was a member of Parliament at the time of the events in dispute.[595] Thus, we can argue that the warrant and its execution damaged the right to liberty as a category and thus as a manifestation of the public interest in liberty. By applying the hypothetical waiver method, we can argue that the right not to be detained and searched could not have been waived by the private claimant. The waiver of the claimant's private interests would not have made the violation lawful, because the warrant would still have been in violation of the right as a category, and the protection of that right should not have been controlled by private individuals. At best, the hypothetical waiver of Wilkes's own liberty right would have made the act not unlawful in relation to the particular claimant, thus depriving Wilkes of any right to compensation. But the claimant's hypothetical waiver would not have affected the wrongfulness of the search warrant or the interference with Wilkes's liberty as such. It follows that the court would have probably made a non-compensatory

[592] ibid 782.
[593] ibid 782 (emphasis in original).
[594] *Wilkes v Wood* (n 220).
[595] ibid 490, 498, 499. That such arbitrary warrants are against the public interest was subsequently made clear in, eg, *Huckle v Money* (n 223) and *Entick v Carrington & Ors* (n 223).

award in this case even if it used the hypothetical waiver method. This is consistent with the decision actually reached in that case. The jury found for the claimant in *Wilkes v Wood* and awarded him 'a thousand pounds [in non-compensatory] damages'.[596]

The final leading case concerning punitive damages is *Drane v Evangelou*.[597] This case concerned unlawful eviction. In this particular case, punitive damages were awarded in response to the defendant's conduct that was contrary to the right to housing as protected by the Rent Act 1965. In fact, the defendant could have even been prosecuted for an offence under section 30 of the Act.[598] It seems clear that, given the relevance of criminal law and the interference with the housing rights as a category, the hypothetical waiver method would have also substantiated the non-compensatory award in this case. Besides, Lord Denning argued in this case that punitive damages could in principle have been awarded for '[m]onstrous behaviour'[599] even if punitive damages were not claimed by the unlawfully evicted claimant.[600] This statement, albeit contentious and clearly contrary to the current procedural rules,[601] shows that the interests the violation of which justified the punitive award were thought of by Lord Denning as public interests. If the court can make a wrongs-based award which the claimant did not plead, it means that the court can deem an infringement of the relevant interests wrongful regardless of what the claimant argued in his claim and regardless of whether the claimant would have waived the protection of those interests.

B. Nominal Damages Cases

In *Stoke-on-Trent City Council v W&J Wass Ltd*,[602] the defendant held markets on locations controlled by the Stoke-on-Trent City Council, the claimant. By doing so, the defendant disturbed the claimant's market rights, which are traditionally seen as 'a legal *monopoly* in respect of the holding of a market within a certain area'.[603] The sole issue in the appeal case was the 'award of damages for the period extending between the commencement of the council's [own] market and [the] grant of the permanent injunction at trial'.[604] The damages in question were not in lieu of an injunction, but merely a remedy for the unlawful rival market which infringed the interests of the rightful owner of the market right – the council. No

[596] *Wilkes v Wood* (n 220) 499.
[597] *Drane v Evangelou* (n 240).
[598] ibid 461F (Lawton LJ).
[599] ibid 457 (Lord Denning MR).
[600] ibid 458, 459 (Lord Denning MR), referring to the County Court Rules. See also *Broome v Cassell & Co* [1971] 2 QB 354 (QB) 378G–378H, 382, 399H.
[601] In more detail on this point, see the text to n 820.
[602] *Stoke-on-Trent City Council v W & J Wass Ltd* [1988] 1 WLR 1406 (CA).
[603] ibid 1418D (Nicholls LJ) (emphasis added).
[604] ibid 1409H (Nourse LJ).

loss was proven in this case, but the council wanted to obtain compensation on the user principle, assessed as a hypothetical fee for what could have been demanded by way of permitting the rival market to be held. No compensation was awarded. Instead, the council only obtained nominal damages for the nuisance.

The levying of an unlawful rival market is a nuisance, rather than a trespass, ruled Nourse LJ.[605] It was confirmed by the Court of Appeal that the law protects the right-holder only 'against being disturbed in the enjoyment of his right'.[606] Thus, if an unauthorised market is held without disturbing the lawful market, the owner of the lawful market has no remedy, either for damages or otherwise. What is more, it was ruled that in the absence of consequential loss, the claimant has a valid cause of action only against a 'same day market',[607] because the law presumes that when a competing market is held on the same day, the right-holder's enjoyment is ipso facto disturbed.[608] It was ruled that in the case of a same-day rival market, the owner of the market right can thus be awarded nominal damages.[609]

The starting question is whether this nominal award, for such presumed disturbance of the right, is aptly characterised as non-compensatory. I will not repeat the argumentation made in section II in chapter four to this effect. Instead, I will simply try to apply the hypothetical waiver method onto the facts and legal rights engaged in this case. The market right confers a monopoly. We may thus ask if the right-owner should be allowed to waive the protection of the monopoly in relation to rival markets held on different days or the same days as the days during which the monopoly is exercised. In the ordinary course of affairs, it is natural to assume that the monopoly is violated whenever the same-day market is held without authorisation. A same-day market always violates the monopoly. The claimant may decide not to exercise or enforce the monopoly right against the defendant, but they cannot waive the protection of the monopoly itself. Only one entity can have the monopoly at a time. Thus, if the purpose of the award was to protect the monopoly (in contrast with any other types of control right with respect to the market), then the private claimant could not have waived the protection of this interest. If the protection of the monopoly *qua* category were up to an individual waiver, it would cease to be a monopoly at all. Thus, the waiver method would probably also justify a non-compensatory remedy in this case. If, by contrast, the purpose of the award was different – perhaps to protect the private right of enjoyment of the monopoly rights in question – then the claimant was probably in a position to exercise the waiver, and the nominal award would be but a case of liminal compensation. Either way, the hypothetical waiver method would be accurate.

Another leading case concerning nominal damages is *Alexander v Home Office*. This case concerned unlawful direct racial discrimination of the claimant

[605] ibid 1410G (Nourse LJ).
[606] ibid 1418G (Nicholls LJ).
[607] ibid 1418H (Nicholls LJ).
[608] The relevant authorities are cited by Nourse LJ at ibid 1410E-F and by Nicholls LJ at ibid 1419D-E.
[609] ibid 1419G (Nicholls LJ).

by a prison officer that had resulted in the claimant being treated in the prison 'not as an individual but as a racial stereotype'.[610] This case well illustrates the distinction between public and private interests when it comes to violations of highly abstract values and interests such as the right to dignity and the right to equal treatment, both of which rights are protected by the law against unlawful discrimination. It was clarified in *Alexander* that we should distinguish between subjective and objective unlawful discrimination. A single incidence of discrimination has an objective aspect which amounts to a statutory wrong[611] and a subjective aspect which is consequent on such wrongful treatment and which amounts to compensable damage.[612] It was stated in *Alexander* that such compensable damage may include non-material harm such as injured feelings.[613]

The appellate court in *Alexander* stated that what should be sanctioned is both the fact that the defendant had discriminated against the claimant (the objective aspect) and that the claimant had been discriminated against (the subjective aspect). The first instance court vindicated the anti-discrimination right by finding unlawful racial discrimination and, accordingly, reduced the measure of damages to reflect the fact that part of the wrong was already remedied by this finding itself. Yet the Court of Appeal ruled that a successful vindication of the right cannot mitigate the compensatory award.[614] It appears sensible to understand this decision as implying that the rationales for the objective and subjective aspects of the discriminatory conduct must have differed from each other. And so the moderated award of £500 in general damages (the first instance court ordered only £50)[615] must have given effect to some non-rights-based considerations. According to the appellate court, the award should not be small because that would 'trivialise or diminish respect for the public policy to which the [Race Relations Act 1976] gives effect'.[616]

As regards the subjective aspect, it is clear that one should be able individually to determine if one feels hurt. Yet in relation to the objective aspect of unlawful discrimination, we may argue that the claimant was not in a position to pardon the wrongfulness of a discriminatory act, even if that act had discriminated against the claimant. It was not and should not have been the claimant's call to make because the subjective views of the claimant are irrelevant to the conclusion of whether the discriminatory conduct was, objectively speaking, based on a protected characteristic. The act of discrimination, objectively speaking, was therefore wrongful per se, and the court was right to make the non-compensatory award of nominal damages.

[610] *Alexander v Home Office* [1988] 1 WLR 968 (CA) 973F.
[611] ibid 977A–977B.
[612] ibid 977E.
[613] ibid 977D-F.
[614] ibid 979B.
[615] ibid 979E.
[616] ibid 975E.

In accord with the cases discussed so far in this section, the objective aspect of wrongdoing in *Alexander* can also be analysed as an infringement of the right *qua* category. It is wrongful that the defendant had discriminated against the claimant (the objective aspect), and this wrongdoing was an affront on the right against discrimination as a category that is protected for the public benefit and an affront against equality as a public interest that the claimant cannot control and cannot waive.

In another leading case concerning nominal damages, *Constantine v Imperial Hotels Ltd*, Birkett J seems to have taken a similar approach to the protection of public interests. To repeat the facts of the case (see also section II of chapter four), a sportsman of colour brought a claim against a hotelier who had wrongfully refused to check him in. In this case, the very act of discrimination could have been regarded as wrongful even if the cricketer had waived his private right to be accommodated in the hotel. The duty not to discriminate against customers was arguably not a duty grounded wholly or predominantly in the reciprocal freedom between parties, and the private claimant thus would not have been able to waive his right not to be discriminated against. This suggests that the interest at stake was public and that a non-compensatory award – nominal damages – could have been justly made by the court in this case, as indeed it was.

In *Lumba*[617] – which is often cited as a leading case on vindicatory damages (because it arguably bans this kind of award), but which has resulted in an award of nominal damages only – the events in dispute concerned the application of an unpublished detention policy. The defendant thus engaged in an unlawful exercise of the Home Secretary's power to detain, even though the claimants could have been detained under the published lawful policy.[618] Interestingly, the claimants' detention itself did not amount to consequential damage to interests because the claimants would have been detained anyway. Of course, the claimants' detention was a necessary condition for them to be able to bring a claim and have standing against the defendant, but the interesting aspect of this case was that there was no real harm to the claimants' private interests. We can see that the claimants' own interest in not being detained had no significant bearing on the court's conclusion about the wrongfulness of the defendant's conduct, because there was a good (although unapplied) legal ground to detain the claimants. The imprisonment was deemed wrongful because the application of an unpublished policy was procedurally wrong. The procedure violated the fundamental requirement of the rule of law to exercise state powers on the basis of and within the remit of express legal authorisation. Thus, we can say that the chief reason for the detention being considered harmful was not the adverse result (that the claimants were detained for some time) but the adverse procedure (that the decision was made on an unlawful basis). The procedure (not the result) was harmful.

[617] *Lumba* (n 18).
[618] ibid [64]–[72], [88], [89], [175], [195], [207], [208], [238], [239], [242], [243] and [251].

On the hypothetical waiver analysis, we can see that the claimants were in no position to determine whether the application of an unpublished policy was wrongful or not. Even if the claimants had expressly consented to their detention, the detention procedure would have been wrongful. Accordingly, and to the extent that a lawful detention procedure is for the benefit of a functioning society, the case involved a violation of public interests and warranted a non-compensatory response. Baroness Hale and Lords Collins, Kerr and Dyson would thus have been right to make an award of NCDs in *Lumba* even if they had used the hypothetical waiver method.

C. Contemptuous Damages Cases

In *Grobbelaar*[619] – a central case of the supposed category of contemptuous damages – the court made a derisory award of £1 in response to a libellous publication which had harmed, at least nominally, the already worthless reputation of the claimant. On one reading of the case, we can say that the award was compensatory (even if the measure was only nominal) since it was justified by correlative interests in the claimant's nominal reputation. The alternative reading, presented in chapter four, was that the derisory sum is in fact a hidden penalty awarded against the claimant and, as such, does not amount to damages in any meaningful sense.

But for the sake of the present analysis, let us assume (contrary to the conclusion I have reached in chapter four) that contemptuous damages are indeed a kind of NCDs. If that is the case, then the hypothetical waiver would suggest that the award in this case is based as if it were a case of nominal damages awarded for libel (which is actionable per se). In *Grobbelaar*, the court found against the defendant, and by making the derisory award, it marked the fact that the libellous and false publication was wrongful regardless of the claimant's reputation worth. The marking of a wrong closely resembles the role of nominal damages. It is hard to imagine that the claimant would have been able to waive the protection against false journalism.

Indeed, the conclusion in *Grobbelaar* was based on the publisher's interference with what we may call the public interest against false journalism. We can argue that had the court not made any award against the defendant, the protection of this interest against false journalism would have been put in doubt. Could the false and libellous publication have been regarded as wrongful even if Mr Grobbelaar had waived his interest in not being subjected to a false publication? Here the answer would have been in the affirmative. By way of the hypothetical waiver, we can thus surmise that the underlying interest was protected for the public benefit. In effect, it was thus confirmed in *Grobbelaar* that reputation as a category is worthy

[619] *Grobbelaar v News Group Newspapers Ltd* (n 316).

of protection from false journalism even if the claimant has none.[620] By implication, we can read *Grobbelaar* as a case that protected the public interest that no one publishes untrue defamatory allegations. This approach explains why the false allegations against Mr Grobbelaar could have resulted in the non-compensatory award rather than in a complete dismissal of his claim.

Alternatively, one may formulate an even more demanding argument in support of the same conclusion. It is generally in the public interest that news publishers release information that is not false because that would lead to general mistrust in our public discourse and, as a result, would undermine the very possibility of a meaningful exchange of information that is vital for the functioning of a democratic society. This is all the more true in situations where the false publication attacks one's personal reputation and hence one's credit in society. Publishers often act as if they were servants of the public interest; they inform the public, and their publication powers should thus be restricted by the public interest. The public clearly has an interest in not reading fake news, and one should not be able privately to waive the protection of this public interest. Arguably, thus, Mr Grobbelaar's hypothetical waiver of his right not to be defamed by libel would have no implication for the wrongfulness of the defendant's action per se.

D. Vindicatory Damages Cases

In English law, there are no leading cases that would result in awards of vindicatory damages expressly so labelled. In *Lumba*,[621] the House of Lords ruled that there is 'no justification for letting such an unruly horse loose on our law'.[622] That said, I argued in chapter four that there may nevertheless be some hidden awards of vindicatory damages in English law, referring to *Rees*[623] as the main example. It will suffice to say here that it would not be right for Ms Rees to waive the protection of reproductive autonomy, because the right to reproductive autonomy (as a category) is protected for the public benefit. We saw in previous sections of this chapter how similar matters of public interest justify the awards of NCDs and there is no need to repeat those arguments again.

E. Disgorgement Damages Cases

The key case cited when it comes to disgorgement damages is *AG v Blake*.[624] Mr Blake, a former British secret agent, published a memoir on the basis of his earlier

[620] See also the concept of reputation as 'dignity' in RC Post, 'The Social Foundations of Defamation Law: Reputation and the Constitution' (1986) 74 *California Law Review* 691, 707–19.
[621] *Lumba* (n 18).
[622] ibid [101] (Lord Dyson). Similarly, ibid [237] (Lord Collins).
[623] *Rees v Darlington Memorial Hospital NHS Trust* (n 403).
[624] *Blake* (n 8).

unlawful endeavours involving disclosure of state secrets and his escape from prison to Russia. The claimant successfully argued that had Mr Blake not been such an infamous traitor, people would not have been interested in his memoir. Mr Blake's unlawful actions thus spilt over into his profits from the book and made the profits wrongful as well. The publication of the memoir was a direct attack on the public interest because Blake was a convicted criminal and yet decided to profit from it by releasing the publication.

There is no doubt that the wrongdoing in *Blake* was constituted by a violation of a public interest.[625] The question here is whether we can identify the 'publicness' of the underlying interest by the hypothetical waiver method. Had the state waived its contractual right that it held against Mr Blake, ie, the right not to have its state secrets disclosed, would the profit still have been wrongful? I think this answer would be in the affirmative. This is because a waiver of that right is in contradiction with the concept of a state secret. Once a state secret can be freely disclosed, it is no longer a state secret. It is vital for the very concept of state secret to be non-disclosable at all. 'An absolute rule against disclosure, visible to all, makes good sense',[626] stated Lord Nicholls and added that '[s]ecret information is the lifeblood of these [intelligence] services'.[627] All this supports the conclusion that the court could have awarded a non-compensatory remedy in *Blake* under the hypothetical waiver method.

Another often cited case, *AG v Observer Ltd, AG v Guardian Newspapers Ltd (No 2), AG v Times Newspapers Ltd (No2)*,[628] also concerned disclosure of state secrets. It was made clear in that decision that the public interest in the protection of state secrets must prevail over any private interests of the parties. 'Important issues of principle … remain. The Crown has established the principle that members of the Security Service owe a lifelong duty of confidence, the upholding of which is vital to preserve the effectiveness of the Security Service and the protection they afford the nation.'[629] As summarised by Aplin in her article exploring the links between breach of confidence and breach of privacy, the House of Lords 'held [in this case] that when it came to protection of confidential *government* information, an additional requirement had to be satisfied, namely, a public interest in *maintaining* the confidentiality of the information'.[630] Indeed, the House of Lords stated that '[t]he exceptions to this lifelong duty of secrecy are extremely limited',[631] because '[t]he purpose of that duty is to preserve intact the secrets of the service which it would be against the public interest to disclose.'[632] Once disclosed to the public, any subsequent publication of the secret is not capable of causing

[625] See more in ch 4, section VI.
[626] ibid 287F (Lord Nicholls), see also ibid 289B, 289C and s 1(1) of the Official Secrets Act 1989.
[627] *Blake* (n 8) 286F.
[628] *AG v Observer* (n 468).
[629] ibid 234A–234B.
[630] Aplin (n 464) 147 (emphases in original).
[631] *AG v Observer* (n 468) 235G.
[632] ibid 265F–265G.

any further damage to the public interest, because it is no longer secret. 'Thereafter such duty is incapable of existing quoad the matter disclosed.'[633]

We may therefore argue that the state (represented by the Attorney General) should not be allowed to waive the duty to protect state secrets. At best, the state may determine that the specific information is no longer secret, but that is something different than surrendering the overarching duty to protect state secrets. To explain, the duty to protect state secrets will remain intact, because the surrender would apply only to the duty to protect that specific information and not to the protection of state secrets at large. In this light, it seems that the hypothetical waiver would have supported the conclusion that infringed interests were protected for the public benefit and that the court was thus right to grant the non-compensatory remedy and disgorge any wrongful benefit stemming from the breach.[634]

VI. Testing the Method: Cases not Concerning Damage to Public Interests

Let us now turn to cases concerning awards that are, or recently were, difficult to conceive of in compensatory terms, but that are nonetheless underpinned by correlative reasons and by protection of interests which the claimant could have waived.

A. Restitutionary Damages Cases

As was explained in chapter four, restitutionary damages are sometimes classified as NCDs because, like disgorgement damages or like awards of restitution of unjust enrichment, they are measured by reference to the defendant's gain and not by the claimant's loss. Nevertheless, as I also showed in chapter four, restitutionary damages are designed to remedy damage to the claimant's private interests, and, in this sense, they compensate the claimant for the correlative harm suffered (although measured by reference to the wrongful gain at the expense of the claimant). In this regard, the difference between compensatory damages and restitutionary damages lies in how the quantum of compensable damage is assessed, whether by reference to the claimant's loss or the defendant's gain.

In *Experience Hendrix LLC v PPX Enterprises Inc*,[635] discussed several times throughout the book,[636] the court awarded gain-based damages by depriving the defendant of profits gained by their selling of Jimmy Hendrix recordings, which

[633] ibid 265G.
[634] eg, ibid 259, 262, 266.
[635] *Experience Hendrix LLC v PPX Enterprises Inc* (n 143).
[636] See especially ch 2, section II and ch 4, section VI.

profits were obtained by breach of a contract. Amongst other things, the contract had obliged the defendant not to grant a licence to third parties in respect of recordings not listed in a schedule to the agreement. One purpose of that agreement was to protect the claimant's interest in not having unlisted recordings on the market. Absent the claimant's consent, however, 'PPX did do the very thing it had contracted not to do'[637] and 'well knew that the [claimant] would not consent thereto'.[638]

In theory, had the claimant waived the relevant rights to the recordings, the defendant's profit would not have been wrongful. The protected interest was created and specified by the contract, and the claimant was therefore in a position to waive its protection. In other words, we can say that the specific interest in removing the unlisted recordings from the market was private to the claimant. This explains why, even though the award was measured by reference to the defendant's profits (and therefore was open to a restitutionary gain-based analysis premised on the fact that the defendant has taken something for nothing[639]), the remedy can be said to have in effect compensated the claimant for damage to the company's private interests. This is further supported by the ruling in *Hendrix* according to which the award of gain-based damages could have been refused if, unlike in *Esso Petroleum*,[640] the claimant would not have any correlative 'legitimate interest in preventing the defendant profiting'.[641] Had there been no correlative interest, the gain-based remedy would not have been available.[642] All this clearly indicates that the court was right to award correlatively justified damages in this case and that the waiver method would have probably led to the same result. This does not undermine the conclusion that nominal damages would have been available for the breach of the contract, because the justifications for that award would be different to the justification for the restitutionary damages.

B. Other Difficult Cases

There are other cases that are (or were) difficult to square with the existing doctrinal categories of damages and might have been regarded by some lawyers as non-compensatory. This subsection looks at three such leading cases.

[637] *Experience Hendrix LLC v PPX Enterprises Inc* (n 143) [36].

[638] ibid [36].

[639] ibid [26]. See also D Campbell and P Wylie, 'Ain't No Telling (Which Circumstances are Exceptional)' (2003) 62 *CLJ* 605, 606 and 607; Edelman, Varuhas and Higgins (n 5) para 15-017.

[640] *Esso Petroleum Co Ltd v Niad Ltd* [2001] EWHC Ch 458, [2001] All ER (D) 324. See also *Novoship (UK) Ltd v Mikhaylyuk* (n 474) [64], [119] and [124].

[641] *Experience Hendrix LLC v PPX Enterprises Inc* (n 143) [31].

[642] ibid [32] (referring to *WWF (World Wide Fund for Nature) v World Wrestling Federation Entertainment Inc* [2001] EWHC Ch 482, [2002] FSR 32).

The first case is *Wrotham Park*.[643] The defendants in *Wrotham Park* had erected buildings in breach of a covenant, and the claimant sought a mandatory injunction for the demolition of those buildings and to restrain further building works on the land. It was thought that full restoration to a position as if the covenant had been duly observed would not be a reasonable solution, because that solution would imply demolition of the existing construction and because purchasers would need to be evicted from the houses. Wrotham Park damages were thus assessed by way of a hypothetical negotiation concerning a price for a release from the breached obligation.

Prior to the Supreme Court decision in *One Step*, which has clarified that negotiating damages are compensatory,[644] the award in *Wrotham Park* was sometimes characterised as non-compensatory.[645] The quantum of damages was animated by what would have been negotiated by reasonable parties in the position of the parties. Part of the analytical challenge, therefore, was whether the 'lost' negotiation represents some kind of compensable loss.[646] Clearly, the award was not assessed by reference to loss in any traditional sense, and so it seemed that it may be analysed as a non-compensatory remedy.

In *One Step*, it was clarified that this kind of damage will generally amount to infringement of the claimant's interest in the control over the use of an asset or a proprietary right. According to Lord Reed, the user principle applies here that 'the person who makes wrongful use of the property prevents the owner from exercising his right to obtain the economic value of the use in question'.[647] In property cases, the measure is (in line with the logic of contractual damages)[648] based on 'the value of the right to control the use of the property as it had been wrongfully used',[649] which may be sensibly seen also as restitution of the wrongdoer's benefit obtained by the wrongful use.[650] The hypothetical negotiation is merely 'a tool'[651] for arriving at the relevant sum to compensate for that damage.

Using the hypothetical waiver method, it seems that the analytical challenge could have been resolved as well. It is clear that the claimant in *Wrotham Park* would have been able to waive the protection of the specific restrictions pertaining to the land. Accordingly, we may see why the Wrotham Park (negotiating) damages would not have been regarded as a non-correlatively justified kind of NCDs on the hypothetical waiver analysis. As stated by Brightman J, the award

[643] *Wrotham Park Estate Co Ltd v Parkside Homes Ltd & Ors* (n 46).

[644] *One Step (Support) Ltd v Morris-Garner* (n 15).

[645] A Burrows, 'Are "Damages on the *Wrotham Park* Basis" Compensatory, Restitutionary or Neither?' in D Saidov and R Cunnington (eds), *Current Themes in the Law of Contract Damages* (Oxford, Hart Publishing, 2008).

[646] *Wrotham Park Estate Co Ltd v Parkside Homes Ltd & Ors* (n 46); Burrows (n 643).

[647] *One Step (Support) Ltd v Morris-Garner* (n 15) [30].

[648] ibid [31]–[35].

[649] ibid [79].

[650] ibid [79].

[651] ibid [91].

was simply 'a just substitute … as might reasonably have been demanded by the plaintiffs from Parkside as a quid pro quo for relaxing the covenant'.[652] We can conclude that the hypothetical waiver method seems to perform accurately in relation to *Wrotham Park* as well.

The second leading case that was often seen to be at the borderline between compensatory and non-compensatory damages is *Vercoe v Rutland Fund Management Ltd.* In this case, Sales J awarded a remedy in relation to breach of contract and in relation to breach of confidence 'by reference to the notional reasonable price which the Defendants should have paid to buy release from the rights'.[653] In modern parlance, this would be labelled as an award of negotiating damages. The obvious conclusion thus is that the private parties would have been able to waive the protection of the violated rights, because these rights were justified based on their correlative private relationship. In other words, the underlying rights and protected interests were clearly thought to be up for negotiation. The court would thus most likely not award NCDs *qua* public interest damages in this case. Note, however, the distinction between *Vercoe* and *Blake*. In *Vercoe* the hypothetical waiver would have been made in respect of the reciprocal right not to release the other party from the contractual obligations. In *Blake*, by contrast, the hypothetical waiver would have been made in respect of the contractual right to non-disclosure of state secrets as such. As we can see, framing of the analysis matters greatly. While the first framing might imply that the right is waiverable, the latter framing might imply the exact opposite.

Another interesting aspect of *Vercoe*, which often makes it understood as a case that is difficult to conceive in loss-based compensatory terms, is that the case discusses the issue of election between alternative remedies. Traditionally, the claimant will implicitly waive a tort if he elects a gain-based (rather than loss-based) award for the defendant's wrong. The rationale for the election is that the two remedies are alternatives – responding to the same underlying damage – and so they cannot be recovered concurrently. If the claimant chooses the gain-based remedy, he effectively waives the loss-based alternative. In *Vercoe*, however, Sales J clarified that not all gain-based remedies are alternatives to loss-based compensation. In particular, he rejected the claim for an account of all the profits made by breach of obligations of confidence, although the confidential information allowed the defendants to complete a profitable transaction.

What is interesting about *Vercoe* is the basis for the ban on the claimant's election of the best remedy. Sales J thought that sometimes the need to elect does not arise in the first place because, as I think Sales J's position might be understood, the two remedies – loss-based and gain-based – do not always protect the same type of interest. This may be, according to Sales J, when the availability of gain-based

[652] *Wrotham Park Estate Co Ltd v Parkside Homes Ltd & Ors* (n 46) 815D.
[653] *Vercoe & Ors v Rutland Fund Management Ltd & Ors* [2010] EWHC 424 (Ch), [2010] Bus LR D141 [361].

damages would be underpinned by non-correlative damage. While the judge did not use this terminology, he clarified that:

> in relation to a claim based on breach of confidence there are circumstances in which the claimant will not be allowed to choose a remedy in the form of an account of profits, and may be confined to an award of [loss-based] damages (which will often be assessed by reference to the value of a notional reasonable agreement to buy release from the claimant's rights, as in relation to the breach of contract claim in this case). Recent developments in the law and wider considerations of justice tend to reinforce this approach.[654]

Sales J then referred to the exceptionality of disgorgement damages as set out in *AG v Blake*[655] and highlighted that the *Blake* exceptionality and the wider considerations of justice only kick in when it comes to

> [rights and interests] of a kind where it would never be reasonable to expect that it could be bought out for some reasonable fee, so that it is accordingly deserving of a particularly high level of protection (such as the promise to keep state secrets … and rights to protection under established fiduciary relationships, where trust … rather than a purely commercial relationship is regarded as central to the obligations in question).[656]

This confirms that some rights and interests are not up for sale, and as such, they should be 'non-waiverable'. Some interests are mandatorily protected, and the court can deem their violation wrongful even if the claimant had tried to waive their protection. In other words, these interests are public. Here the hypothetical waiver thus also seems accurately to identify whether a non-correlative interest could have been at stake.

You may object that Sales J also stated that 'the test is whether *the claimant's interest* in performance of the obligation in question … makes it just and equitable that the defendant should retain no benefit from his breach of that obligation'.[657] This would suggest that those interests that could have in theory justified the disgorgement remedy were private to the claimant. Yet I think this reading of *Vercoe* would be plainly wrong, as it would confuse the exceptional reasons in *Blake* with the entirely ordinary correlative interests of the claimant. The root of this confusion seems to be the fact that the claimant in *Blake* (ie, Attorney General) was already a representative acting in defence of the non-correlative public interest. But I think that we can reconcile the judge's words in *Vercoe* with the public interest analysis of *Blake* by highlighting that Sales J pointed to some additional reasons 'and wider considerations of justice'[658] that could justify the total disgorgement and that are not at par with the correlative justification of loss-based compensation.

[654] ibid [334].
[655] ibid [337].
[656] ibid [340].
[657] ibid [339] (emphasis added).
[658] ibid [334].

The third case to which I will turn is *Mosley*.[659] Mr Mosley was a former president of the Formula 1 governing body. He was secretly recorded engaging in very private BDSM sexual activities. His family life was ruined after the release of the footage by the defendant newspaper. A punitive award was expressly considered in this case,[660] but in the end the court only awarded what some may view as an over-inflated quantum of compensation totalling £60,000. This award was made 'for the purpose of acknowledging the infringement and compensating, to some extent, for the injury to feelings, the embarrassment and distress caused'.[661] The claim in this case was based on breach of confidence and unauthorised disclosure of personal information in violation of Mr Mosley's rights of privacy as protected by Article 8 of the Convention.[662]

As was shown in this case, the law affords protection to information in respect of which there was a reasonable expectation of privacy, even if there was no pre-existing duty of confidence, because the law protects autonomy, dignity and self-esteem as the relevant interests in such situations. These interests were considered worthy of protection per se, and rightly so because we can argue that the protection of the fundamental right to privacy (as a category) should not be reliant on one's private waiver. One can consent to being filmed and to having that footage published, but one cannot waive the right to consent with privacy interferences. We can also argue that the extreme facts of this case make it all the more urgent that the courts stand up for the public importance of the underlying right, or else the very protection of privacy would be put in doubt.

Indeed, a non-compensatory award was expressly considered as an option in *Mosley*, but since the affront to Mr Mosley's privacy has resulted in such devastating private damage to Mr Mosley's personal life, the court thought that by awarding a greater amount of compensation and 'some degree of *solatium* to the injured party',[663] these public interests would be sufficiently protected. This argumentation has rendered it unnecessary (though not unjust) to make the award for punitive or vindicatory purposes and for the purposes of protecting those interests *qua* public interests. Presumably, the award of punitive damages could have been made had the compensation in this case not been at such a high level (which level had made the eventual punitive award unnecessary and disproportionate), as the court argued.[664] The judge stated that '[t]here is no "pressing social need" for this [punitive remedy]'.[665] The basic award of £60,000 was already intended to acknowledge 'the infringement'[666] and 'the intrusion on the personal privacy of the Claimant … in the light of modern rights-based

[659] eg, *Mosley v News Group Newspapers* [2008] EWHC 1777, [2008] EMLR 20 (Mosley case).
[660] ibid [172ff] and [235].
[661] ibid [235].
[662] ibid [3].
[663] ibid [231].
[664] ibid [193], [197].
[665] ibid [173].
[666] ibid [235].

jurisprudence'.[667] Overall, here it seems that although the court made only an award of compensatory damages (by label), the nature of the interests protected by that award was at least partly also public – but did not result in a formally distinct award of NCDs.[668]

This begs an important question: how can we make sure that awards labelled as compensatory are not in fact being made in a non-compensatory measure that protects violations of public interests? My response to this challenge would be simple – we can do so by identifying the public interests in the relevant cases and therefore by facilitating a transparent debate about the types of reasons that are intended to justify the measure of the award. This implies that if we want to bring the relevant public interest considerations into sharp focus, the hypothetical waiver method has a useful role to play.

VII. Conclusion

In this chapter, we saw that the concept of public interest is widely used but not well defined. In particular, it was argued that the relevant sources often confuse claims about: (i) the concept of public interest, (ii) the methods by which public interests are identified, and (iii) the specific matters which are protected in the public interest. In order to examine whether all non-correlatively justified NCDs are justified by violations of public interests, this chapter thus defined the concept of public interest and then suggested a method to identify whether the events in dispute could be protected in the public interest. I showed that matters of public interest may be protected regardless of private interests in those matters, because private individuals should not be allowed freely to control whether protecting some matters is in the public interest.

Based on this understanding of the concept of public interest, the so-called 'hypothetical waiver' method to determine whether something is to be protected *qua* public interest was suggested. The gist of the waiver method of identifying public interests in the law of damages is that we can determine public interests by asking whether, at the time of the events in dispute, the claimant was not allowed or should not have been allowed to waive the protection of the matters in dispute. If the answer is in the affirmative, then those matters may only be protected *qua* public interests. It was argued in sections III and IV that all non-acquired private rights are arguably non-waiverable in the relevant sense and that this would imply that nominal damages should be available more broadly than they currently are (including in relation to a breach of duty in negligence).

The advantage of the method over an abstract ethical and political argumentation regarding what is good for the functioning of our society is that the method

[667] ibid [233].

[668] *cf Ashley v Chief Constable of Sussex* (n 19) [22] (Lord Scott): '[T]here is no reason in principle why an award of compensatory damages should not also fulfil a vindicatory purpose'.

provides an easy-to-implement benchmark for determining matters of public interest in concrete private disputes. As such, the method allows the courts to avoid the difficult ethical and political questions about which matters deserve a full-scale legal recognition as public interests and how best to achieve such recognition. Such questions are probably best answered outside the judiciary that, in cases of individual damages disputes, has a very limited view of what publicly important matters might be at stake and how the law might respond to those challenges. If implemented, the waiver method would thus call for a more targeted debate about why something is good for the public and whether we should protect it by way of damages. If this were the ultimate impact of the proposed method, it should be put to its credit because it is intrinsically good to have debates about whether and why something should be protected for the public benefit.

Sections V and VI demonstrated how the hypothetical waiver method could work in practice. The method was tested against the leading damages cases, focusing primarily on cases concerning NCDs awards and awards that are (or were) difficult to square with compensatory interpretations. We saw that there is a strong correlation between the specific matters that were protected by NCDs awards in those leading cases and the courts' ability to identify those matters as matters of public interest. In other words, had the courts decided to award non-correlatively justified NCDs only when the events in dispute caused some damage to public interests, they would have reached the same decisions as they did in those leading damages cases. The hypothetical waiver method thus proved to be sufficiently accurate and supports the conclusion that all non-correlatively justified measures of damages can be defined as public interest damages.

This examination of the leading cases showed the strength of the waiver method because it allowed us to reinterpret the piecemeal area of non-correlatively justified NCDs as a coherent domain of public interest damages without compromising the established doctrines and the existing legal principles. A collective approach to NCDs *qua* public interest damages would therefore still give effect to the underlying justifications of those awards, which is a strong argument against those who would oppose the introduction of the public interest analysis of damages. Furthermore, the hypothetical waiver method, it seems, would also allow us to distinguish between compensatory and non-compensatory aspects of global awards of damages. This is important because in relation to such awards, it is typically difficult to ascertain what their true function is.

Overall, we can conclude that the idea of damages that stand in contrast with compensation on the *restitutio in integrum* principle (ie, the idea typically referred to as NCDs) is best defined as damages the measure of which is justified by damage to public interests. Or better, if we do not want to change the way in which the term NCDs is (sometimes loosely and incoherently) used in the literature, we should start using the phrase 'public interest damages' to refer to all non-correlatively justified measures of damages. This reinterpretation of the law of NCDs would help us to highlight the fundamentally distinct justificatory reasons on which all such public interest damages are based and contrast them with compensatory remedies.

To be sure, the overarching claim does not mean that compensatory damages awards are not justified by public interests. The very institution of all kinds of damages and the possibility of their award are, of course, justified by reasons of public interest because damages facilitate commerce, support the institution of property, etc, and these things are considered good for the society. However, my claim is not about reasons for the existence of damages awards at large. It is about reasons that positively justify damages awarded in a non-compensatory (as opposed to compensatory) measure. In other words, it is about the reasons that justify the content of those remedies. If we maintain this distinction, then the suggested reinterpretation of the law of NCDs allows us to produce a theory that is coherent and fits with the primary sources as well as with major parts of the literature.

The claim that NCDs are justified by violations of public interests has both theoretical and practical value. The public nature of the violated interests *positively* informs us what the non-correlative justifying reasons are (as opposed to what they are not). Thus, the public interest definition of NCDs informs us about the nature of such awards independently of our understanding of compensatory awards. As such, this definition allows us to focus on why something is beneficial for the public, rather than why it does not give effect to individual rights. The public interest definition also helps us to appreciate the similarities amongst NCDs and thus better to co-ordinate their award, which is an important doctrinal issue that will be addressed in chapter six.

Besides, unlike the analytical idea of non-correlative reasons, the concept of public interest is familiar to judges. The courts are used to deploying reasons of public interest in their judgments. The concept of 'non-correlativity' was a necessary analytical vehicle to describe an aspect of those interests that is prescribed by the 'publicness'. This has helped to make the claim in chapter four, but that claim is now no longer needed. If we decide to develop NCDs as a category, it is thus desirable that we do so by reference to the 'publicness' rather than 'non-correlativity' of the justifying reasons. The question to which we will turn next is whether it is desirable to develop NCDs collectively at all.

6

The Case for a Collective Approach

This chapter argues that public interest damages should be approached collectively and as a distinct class of awards. Currently, the law views NCDs as independent and possibly unrelated remedies and, in accordance with that view, has no express motivation to apply the doctrines governing the award of NCDs coherently across the board. However, this chapter argues that the significant overlap amongst the various forms of public interest damages (section I) and the distinctive ethical concerns that such awards collectively attract (section II) demand that we approach them collectively. It is desirable that we co-ordinate the doctrines governing their availability and assessment so that the distinctions between individual forms of public interest damages can be either justified or challenged.

The collective approach and the co-ordination of the relevant legal doctrines do not mean that we should collapse all the various forms of public interest damages into a single remedy. Rather, as is argued in section III, the different forms of public interest damages – and the doctrines governing such measures – should be seen as different methods of assessment of the quantum of these awards. A specific aspect of the co-ordination of such assessment methods concerns the inconsistency of remedies: the co-ordinated approach raises the question as to which measures of NCDs are (or should be) incompatible with each other and why. This is addressed in section IV. Section V concludes and prepares the ground for chapter seven which will elaborate further on how the collective approach might look in practice and what doctrinal implications it would have if we acknowledged the distinctive justificatory ground for public interest damages.

I. Overlaps Amongst the Various Forms of Public Interest Damages

The traditional view regards NCDs as independent and possibly unrelated categories of damages. Yet this book shows that the various forms of non-correlatively justified NCDs overlap very significantly in terms of their justifications – they are all justified by violations of various public interests. That said, chapter five has incidentally revealed a striking feature of public interest damages, namely that some of these awards sometimes protect the same matters of public interest. In such situations, the stated distinctions between different types of NCD are hardly explicable on any principled ground. This, I think, gives us a compelling reason to explore the availability conditions and assessment techniques associated with these awards more systematically.

To substantiate this claim, let us look again at some of the cases discussed in chapter five. Given the seemingly close connection between the public interest in the regulated market competition in *2 Travel Group*[669] and the public interest in the market monopoly in *Stoke-on-Trent City Council*,[670] we may ask what separates the two cases. This question is important because it helps us to see whether individual measures of NCDs substantively differ from each other under the public interest analysis. Why did, in the first case, the violation of competition rules trigger a punitive response, whereas the violation of another market-protecting principle only triggered a nominal award? After all, setting aside the specific doctrinal rules and adopting the public interest analysis, the damage to public interest in *2 Travel Group* does not look that different from the damage in *Stoke-on-Trent City Council*.

One could suppose that the major distinction between punitive and nominal damages in these two cases is that the defendant flagrantly violated the competition interests in *2 Travel Group* and that this makes the infringement all the more serious. But the trouble is that in nominal damages cases, defendants also often violate the underlying interests knowingly, with a level of disregard for the monopoly right in question. In *Stoke-on-Trent City Council*, for example, the town clerk protested against the defendants' intention to hold the market, but '[u]ndeterred by that protest … the company went ahead with the operation of its market'.[671] Indeed, Nicholls LJ noted in *Stoke-on-Trent City Council* that '[c]ertainly the defendants' conduct in persisting in holding their market despite the plaintiffs' objections, is not conduct calculated to attract much sympathy'.[672] His Lordship even opined that it is not clear whether 'a claim for exemplary damages … if such a claim had been made … would have been well-founded'.[673] And while the company's 'deliberate breaches of the law [were] not material to the question which arise[d]' in *Stoke-on-Trent City Council*,[674] there does not seem to be any reason to believe that a claim for a punitive remedy would be founded on materially different reasons from the reasons behind the nominal remedy awarded. This suggests that if the same justification could result in different types of NCDs (nominal vs punitive), then the law should have some way to deal with this overlap.

Similarly, we can see an overlap between nominal damages and other non-compensatory measures in *Alexander v Home Office*,[675] for example. In that case, the court discussed the vindicatory function of the nominal award made in respect of the defendant's wrongful discrimination, as if the two measures (or functions of damages) belonged to the same family of remedies that can be meaningfully

[669] *2 Travel Group Plc (in liq) v Cardiff City Transport Services Ltd* (n 242).
[670] *Stoke-on-Trent City Council v W & J Wass Ltd* (n 602).
[671] ibid 1408H (Nourse LJ).
[672] ibid 1419H (Nicholls LJ).
[673] ibid 1419H (Nicholls LJ).
[674] ibid 1409C (Nourse LJ).
[675] *Alexander v Home Office* (n 610).

explored alongside each other. Further, and similarly to the situation in *Alexander*, the court felt that the wrongful discrimination in *Constantine* may sometimes attract only nominal damages, and sometimes it may rightly elicit the question of whether some form of punishment would also be deserved if other conditions are met.[676]

Further, in *Lumba*,[677] a lot of ink was spilt on whether the award should be vindicatory or nominal, as if the two categories were mutually exclusive. This suggests that the gist of the polemic was that the two awards overlap and fulfil (at least in part) the same function. And we saw in chapters four and five that this function was the need to rectify damage to public interest. An interesting question thus is why the claimants in *Lumba* obtained only nominal damages and whether other public interest awards could have been made in that case. We can argue, for example, that if the defendant in *Lumba* had proceeded arbitrarily, then some kind of punishment under Category 1 punitive damages could have been in order. The specific doctrinal conditions for Category 1 punitive damages could have made a significant difference to the final assessment of the non-compensatory remedy even though the public interests at stake would remain the same and the type of the underlying damage would be almost identical. One may doubt whether such a distinction is justified.

Notably, there is a stark contrast between *Lumba* and another unlawful detention case, *Muuse*, where 'the conduct of those acting for the Home Secretary had been so bad that it was worthy of punishment'.[678] In *Muuse* punitive damages (£27,500) were awarded for imprisonment which was initiated and maintained in a 'high handed and oppressive way … in complete disregard of laid down procedures'.[679] Thus, the claimant and others could have seen that there is not only a violation of the public interest but also a complete disregard for that interest – which demonstrates a much greater impact on the public interest involved. In *Lumba*, by contrast, the infringement of the public interest was rather nominal because the defendant did not proceed with disregard to the claimants' rights and because the unlawfulness of the detention was rather formal – both the published policy according to which the detainment decision should have been made and the unpublished policy according to which the detainment decision was actually made would lead to the claimants being detained. The public interest infringement in *Lumba* therefore did not justify more than a nominal award. But in principle, the kind of damage caused by the defendants in *Muuse* and *Lumba* seems to be identical under the hypothetical waiver method.

Overall, these examples cast doubt on the strict doctrinal distinctions amongst individual types of public interest damages. In particular, these examples illustrate

[676] *Constantine v Imperial Hotels Ltd* (n 281) 702, 704.

[677] *Lumba* (n 18).

[678] *Abdillaahi Muuse v Secretary of State for the Home Department* [2010] EWCA Civ 453 (Muuse case) [65].

[679] ibid [66], referring to para 117 of the first instance judgment.

that the same reasons of public interest that justify one type of NCDs could, if advanced as part of a re-framed legal argument, also justify an alternative non-compensatory remedy. The doctrinal distinctions between the different non-compensatory awards thus call for a better justification than we currently have, or at least better co-ordination. If, for example, nominal and punitive damages are justified by the same reasons, it seems we should seek to quantify these measures in a more principled and coherent fashion. Besides, once we accept that all public interest damages are justified by the same sort of considerations, there is a real danger that their awards will overlap[680] and result in double-counting for the defendant or an unjust windfall for the claimant. The recommendation that follows from these observations is that the law should pay more attention to the substantive overlaps between the reasons that justify different types of NCDs and, where such overlaps exist, that the law should approach the different awards in a coherent way in order to explain the differential treatment or, alternatively, to justify a more uniform treatment of these remedies.

II. Distinctive Ethical Concerns

This section argues that unless we accept and maintain the distinction between public and private interests in their role of justifying reasons for damages awards, we are unlikely to separate the relevant considerations from those which are irrelevant. As a result, not only do we have good reasons to approach public interest damages collectively, but – as this section claims – we should also approach them as a collectively distinct class of awards. This is because public interest damages are underpinned by distinctive ethical concerns in relation to all the various forms of such damages. Unless we acknowledge the distinctiveness of these 'public interest' concerns, we are likely to err in our reasoning in that we would employ arguments or draw conclusions which are properly only made or drawn when an individual right or private interest in the disputed matters justifies the availability of the award.

As was argued earlier, matters of public interest are not in the interest *of* all the members of the public, but rather *for* the benefit of all these members. The question about whether the disputed matters are of private or public interest is thus not something that shall be determined by empirical evidence. Rather, it is a question of law or – since the law does not always provide a perfect answer – a question of ethical judgment. In order to exercise this ethical judgement correctly and properly to interpret and apply the law, we thus need to know which considerations are relevant to it and which are not.

If it is indeed the case that 'publicness' of interests points to those interests being *for* the benefit of the public, then we should ask this question: 'Why do we

[680] *cf* S Watterson, 'Alternative and Cumulative Remedies: What is the Difference?' (2003) *Restitution Law Review* 7; Burrows, *Remedies for Torts, Breach of Contract, and Equitable Wrongs* (n 575) 13–15.

think that something is good for the public?' Some considerations will be clearly irrelevant to this judgement. For example, if public interests are protected regardless of one's private wishes or assertions, then those private wishes or assertions cannot have a legitimate role to play in ascertaining the 'publicness' of the disputed matters. The point is that, from their correlative standpoints, neither the claimant nor the defendant is entitled to determine whether it is legitimate to protect the disputed matters *qua* public interests. It simply is not their call to make. The legitimacy of public interests (as non-correlative interests) is not grounded in the reciprocal freedom between the parties, and so their correlatively justified arguments cannot be at the forefront here.

Take the following example: a court is invited to create a new tort of queue-jumping and to award punitive damages for that tort. If someone jumps a typical English queue, say a bus queue, it may well be that this violates many people's perceptions of what decency in the public sphere requires and what many think is important for the functioning of our society. Hence, the queue-jumping might constitute damage to some public interests, and such damage could, in theory, justify a non-compensatory award. As the law stands, there is of course no tort of queue-jumping, let alone the possibility to award punitive damages for such conduct.[681] But the key point is that it would be problematic if the court accepted that the events in dispute are of public interest solely on the basis of the claimant's submissions concerning his own interests. While it may be acceptable to do so when it comes to ascertaining the 'privateness' of the disputed matters, it would be extremely difficult to justify the same approach when it comes to the 'publicness' of the disputed matters.

Surprisingly perhaps, even though public interest damages will be awarded in disputes between private individuals, the relevance of the parties' arguments will need to be benchmarked against something else than the norms of corrective justice. This follows from the conclusion in chapter three. In particular, if we accept the fundamental distinction between rights-based and non-rights-based justifications for measures of damages – and chapter three suggests we should do so – then it follows that public interest damages are governed by norms of distributive justice and that we should thus disregard the parties' arguments that are underpinned by norms of corrective justice.

The argument in support of this claim is straightforward. I accept that there are two and only two types of particular justice that are concerned with the (re)allocation of resources in private relationships: corrective and distributive justice. Thus, if non-correlative reasons are not underpinned by one of those two kinds, then they must be underpinned by the other kind, provided, of course, that NCDs are governed by *some* allocative norms of justice.[682]

[681] No 'legal' claim-right of proper queuing has yet been recognised in common law, but proper queuing can already be considered a relevant factor for assessing the wrongdoer's negligent conduct. See *Grealis v Opuni* [2003] EWCA Civ 177.

[682] See also pp 75–76 (ch 3).

The division between corrective and distributive justice has a long tradition originating from Aristotle's *Nicomachean Ethics*.[683] Aristotle understood justice to be one of many virtues, ie, ethical goods that we shall pursue in our life. He distinguished between a complete virtue (meaning universal or legal justice) and a partial virtue (meaning particular or ethical justice). Particular justice, on his view, is justice regarding individual situations or individual juridical relationships. Aristotle's illuminating idea was that there are essentially two different types of situation that demand two distinct, yet related, types of particular justice – corrective and distributive justice.[684]

The role of these two types of justice has been widely debated and contested.[685] It is not my ambition to contribute to these debates here. For the present purposes it suffices to say that corrective justice is concerned with a relationship between two formally equal persons, whereas distributive justice applies to relations amongst society at large or to a relationship between an individual person and the distributing society.[686] Both corrective and distributive justice are, however, based on the axiomatic assumptions of free and equal individuals, and both are concerned with fair (re)allocations.

Corrective justice demands that, as between two ideally equal parties, unjust losses and gains (ie, damage to correlative rights) be (re)allocated back.[687] 'To say a rule is one of corrective justice is to say that it is a rule that allocates in such a way as to correct (put right, undo) some prior injustice or other misallocation.'[688] So, for example, '[t]he rule that a defendant must make restitution of mistaken payments can be identified as a rule of corrective justice'.[689] But as we have seen, NCDs are not justified by correlative reasons between the two conflicting parties and thereby cannot pursue corrective justice as their goal. In this sense, NCDs do not correct nor allocate back. Instead, they allocate anew, ie, they distribute.[690]

683 Aristotle, *Nicomachean Ethics* (H Rackham tr, rev edn, Cambridge, MA, Harvard University Press, 2014).

684 ibid 1130b.6ff (corrective justice) and 1131a.10ff (distributive justice).

685 A comprehensive analysis, covering historical and modern accounts of these two types of justice can be found in I Englard, *Corrective and Distributive Justice: From Aristotle to Modern Times* (Oxford, OUP, 2009). See also EJ Weinrib, 'Aristotle's Forms of Justice' (1989) 2 *Ratio Juris* 211; JL Coleman, *Risks and Wrongs* (Cambridge, CUP, 1992); Gardner, 'What is Tort Law For? Part 1. The Place of Corrective Justice' (n 202); A Beever, *Forgotten Justice: The Forms of Justice in the History of Legal and Political Theory* (Oxford, OUP, 2013); Gardner, 'What is Tort Law For? Part 2. The Place of Distributive Justice' (n 202).

686 This interpretation is, of course, very rough and it comes mostly from Aquinas (T Aquinas, *Summa Theologiae*, SS.Q61). In more detail, see, AJ Lisska, 'The Philosophy of Law of Thomas Aquinas' in FD Miller and CA Biondi (eds), *A History of the Philosophy of Law from the Ancient Greeks to the Scholastics*, 2nd edn (Cham, Springer 2015) 305–09. See also Beever (n 685) 85.

687 Aristoteles (n 683) 1132a.2–7 and 1134a.28.

688 Webb (n 432) 56–57 (referring to P Saprai, 'Restitution without Corrective Justice' (2006) 14 *Restitution Law Review* 41, 52–54; Gardner, 'What is Tort Law For? Part 1. The Place of Corrective Justice' (n 202) 6–10 and 14–16).

689 Webb (n 432) 56.

690 Other authors put the idea in moderately different terms. Cane, for instance, wrote that 'corrective justice provides the structure of tort law within which distributive justice operates' (P Cane,

Distributive justice seeks to achieve justice according to some distributive criteria, ie, to achieve equality based on an external measure of merit and it has its role in the law of obligations as well.[691] The relevant ethical arguments concerning why it is legitimate to protect some interests *qua* public interest can thus also serve as the considerations of merit, according to which the distribution takes place. These distributive criteria can then be applied to the society of free and equal individuals by way of merit.

We can thus say that the protection of public interests in the law of damages is legitimate because, just like the protection of corrective justice considerations, it is rooted in the axiomatic values of freedom, equality and individuality.[692] Of course, such meritocratic distribution of public interest damages does not guarantee optimal fairness. One could argue that the distributive justifications fail to account for the role of lack, social status and history in the distribution of valuable goods in society.[693] But this is not an objection to the deployment of distributive criteria in awarding damages. My claim here is not that public interest damages are perfectly just, but that they are sufficiently justified by distributive justice arguments.

So what are the relevant arguments? Ethically speaking, we could justify something as good for the public if it maximises welfare, respects individual autonomy, or promotes justice in the public sphere. In other words, we could justify the public interest protection from each of the consequentialist, deontological and virtue ethics standpoints, and we could pragmatically combine and counterbalance the insights offered by these normative ethical positions. This observation, and I fully endorse it, comes from moral philosophy, specifically from normative ethics, where consequentialist ethics, deontological ethics and virtue ethics represent the three main approaches to ethical issues. I guess many readers will already be well versed in this ethical tradition, but if not, then a good place to start is in the Stanford Encyclopedia of Philosophy.[694]

'Distributive Justice and Tort Law' (2001) 2001 *New Zealand Law Review* 401, 413). Gardner's aim was 'to develop and finesse' this book (Gardner, 'What is Tort Law For? Part 2. The Place of Distributive Justice' (n 202) 338). *cf* Englard (n 685) 210, who shows that historically 'some scholars started from the political book that the (absolute) ruler is above the law. Consequently, it was assumed that the violation of distributive justice, as such, does not entail a legal sanction of compensation. The logical result of that view was that in any case where a duty of compensation was to be recognized, its foundation had to be in commutative justice.'

[691] See *McFarlane v Tayside Health Board* (n 408) 83 (Lord Steyn). See also T Keren-Paz, *Torts, Egalitarianism and Distributive Justice* (Aldershot, Ashgate, 2013); P Shaunessy, 'A Matter of Choice: Rethinking Legal Formalism's Account of Private Law Rights' (2017) 37 *OJLS* 163. For an opposing view, see, eg, Weinrib (n 60); Weinrib (n 83).

[692] See the literature in n 205.

[693] See, eg, MJ Sandel, *The Tyranny of Merit: What's Become of the Common Good* (London, Penguin Random House, UK 2020).

[694] R Hursthouse and G Pettigrove, 'Virtue Ethics' in EN Zalta and U Nodelman (eds), *The Stanford Encyclopedia of Philosophy* (Fall 2023 Edn); W Sinnott-Armstrong, 'Consequentialism' in EN Zalta and U Nodelman (eds), *The Stanford Encyclopedia of Philosophy* (Winter 2023 Edn); L Alexander and M Moore, 'Deontological Ethics' in EN Zalta and U Nodelman (eds), *The Stanford Encyclopedia of Philosophy* (Winter 2024 Edn).

In normative ethics, it is generally accepted as uncontroversial that what is ethically good does not need to be recognised by members of the public on the basis of the *same* ethical reasons or on the basis of the *same* individual interests. As put by Wolff, for example, any large-scale social change requires that the public is ready for that change in the sense that a public value of that change is recognised by 'many people, from different backgrounds and with different interests, arguing for similar conclusions, perhaps even for different reasons'.[695] The same argument can be made about the significance of certain matters for the functioning of our society – it is not necessary that there would be a single reason why something can be regarded as being in the public interest. In this light, it is not difficult to see why something cannot be in the public interest simply because of what a particular claimant asserts about his own interest or because of what the subject matter of his interest is. Rather, something may be in the public interest because judges would draw a reasoned conclusion regarding the significance of that matter for the functioning of our society and regarding the type of legal protection with which this 'something' should be provided.

Almost any matter can, in principle, be pronounced to be in the public interest, but the key question is when such a pronouncement is justified. In some societies and their legal systems, only certain kinds of justification are permissible. A society politically organised as a liberal and representative democracy will have different views on which interests are important for the functioning of our society from a society organised as a totalitarian autocracy. The prescriptive notion of 'public interest' may thus vary across these societies because the 'publicness' is necessarily contextual: it is an interest that is good for members of the public when viewed from the perspective of a particular political society. And the courts, as functioning units within that society, will understandably give preference to interests advanced by the legitimate political forces in that society. This is because judicial decision-making is typically conservative and protects the values that are already embedded in a given political system. That some interests are to be protected *qua* public interests is thus akin to a pronouncement along these lines: 'We want to live in a society that protects these interests no matter what concrete individuals may think!' or 'The functioning of our society is underpinned by these interests, and we will protect them!'

Crucially, whether something amounts to a public interest may differ across cultures, geographical locations and times. Take, for instance, same-sex marriage, seduction of a wife, sexual intercourse between siblings, privacy, or discrimination. All these are but examples of interests in relation to which our position has changed over time. What is good for the public thus cannot be enumerated up front, and it would be a futile exercise to try to create a settled list of protected public interests, the violation of which can give rise to awards of NCDs. In specific cases, the various ethical arguments may lead the courts to different conclusions regarding whether the protection of the matters in dispute is of public interest. But

[695] J Wolff, *Ethics and Public Policy: A Philosophical Inquiry* (Abingdon, Routledge, 2011) 208.

if the 'publicness' of the disputed matters were to be based solely on the parties' private arguments, it would be difficult to take into account all this wider context because the parties are unlikely to be concerned with (or even aware of) this wider context.

As a result, if the 'publicness' of the disputed matters were to be based solely on the parties' private arguments, relevant arguments and considerations would probably be omitted and irrelevant arguments and considerations would be taken into account. We would be likely to base the decision about the availability of NCDs on correlatively justified considerations, which would be wrong. It would be wrong in relation to the recognition of public interests in novel cases (such as in our queue-jumping example) but also in relation to the interpretation and application of the existing doctrines governing the award of NCDs. In both the novel cases and established situations, the 'publicness' of the protected interests requires us to exercise a distinctive ethical judgment – a judgment that fundamentally differs from how we would justify compensatory awards.

A private individual can himself point to some 'public interest' arguments and evidence in his submission to the court, but if the claimant wishes to rely on it, then the arguments and evidence should be expressly identified and framed as something that is intended to substantiate the public, not private, interest in the disputed matters. In practice, this would mean that the legitimacy of those considerations will need to be derived from non-correlative grounds. In the London public transport system, for example, a queue-jumper may be fined up to £1,000 under the TfL Byelaws.[696] Such a non-correlatively based sanction supports the argument that queue-jumping is against a public interest. As a private claimant – if you wanted the court to create a new tort and award punitive damages – you may thus refer to the TfL Byelaws in order to establish the validity of your submission that the interest should be protected for the benefit of the public by way of a non-correlative penal response. Here, you could say that the public interest in the disputed matters was already recognised by our society in the past and that it should thus be protected by the common law too.

Such argument or evidence could be persuasive but probably not binding. As was noted, even in relation to established cases of NCDs, the court's ethical judgment is unlikely to be fully settled by any clear precedent. This is partly because the courts do not (as yet) typically discuss the relevant non-correlative evidence in terms of public interest violations, and so it would be difficult to make a doctrinal conclusion that certain public interest considerations are the *ratio* for the judgment and should be applied to all future cases. Admittedly, if the theory of public interest damages is accepted, then this may change.

But even if courts started consistently to articulate the public interest justification of NCDs awards, the *ratio* would still be best described as *a* public interest reason, rather than as a *concrete matter* of public interest. This is because the court's

[696] See, eg, the TfL Road Transport Premises Byelaws 2011, ss 2 and 14 in conjunction with s 37(2) of the Criminal Justice Act 1982.

judgment regarding the specific public interest protection would be, by definition, exercised *de novo* every time. The purpose of making an NCDs award is not to set in stone a general truth about which matters should be protected in the public interest. In other words, even if established NCDs cases can be interpreted as cases of damages, the measure of which is justified by violations of specific public interests, it would be a stretch to say that this means that those cases have firmly established that any interferences with those precise public interests are contrary to the public interest. Rather, we would say that those precedents establish that the matters in dispute, if relevantly infringed, may be regarded as harmful to the public interest and may thus justify the non-compensatory remedy.

This is where the hypothetical waiver method will help. The hypothetical waiver method was introduced as one way to operationalise the relevant ethical judgement and to achieve consistent and well-grounded conclusions regarding the availability of public interest damages: they should only be available in cases where the matters in dispute are 'non-waiverable'. By relying on the waiver method, the courts might thus relatively easily separate the relevant from the irrelevant considerations. If the waiver method is accepted as the preferable way forward, it then makes perfect sense to approach all public interest damages collectively and to apply the waiver method consistently across the board.

The high-level observations about the ethical reasons and political contexts concerning why something is to be protected *qua* public interest may be disappointing to the reader, but I do not believe we can provide any more detail than that. Blackstone famously wrote that law is the most perfect form of ethics,[697] but in relation to NCDs it is very difficult to find the perfected answer ex-ante. This is because there are (as yet) no firm legal reasons why something should be regarded as a matter of public interest. And absent this kind of legal grounding, the best we can say is that these reasons should be fact-sensitive, for it is the specific matters in dispute that raise the question of public interest in the first place, and these reasons should be rooted in one or more ethical positions (the consequentialist, deontological and virtue ethics standpoints) and in the political reality of the society to which these reasons should apply. It will be for one or more of these ethical reasons why we can say that the matters in dispute are 'non-waiverable'. Such distinctive ethical reasoning is applicable to all NCDs *qua* public interest damages, and so we should approach them as collectively distinct, in order to control and develop the doctrines that govern these awards in a fair, principled and transparent manner.

III. Co-Ordination without Unification

The ethical judgment and the waiver method discussed above are applicable to all forms of public interest damages and support the case for a collective

[697] 1 Bl Comm 27.

approach to these remedies. And while the identified 'publicness' of the interests in question does not dictate any specific quantum of damages, it still implies that we should start comparing and contrasting public interest damages awards with each other. Surely, it would be hard to justify any material difference in the sums of NCDs awarded in situations where the same or similar public interests would be infringed and where those interests would be infringed in a similarly grave manner.

Does it mean that we should doctrinally unify the awards of public interest damages, ie, that we should collapse all NCDs into a single remedy? Certainly not. Just like compensatory awards are not a single remedy, as is clear from the doctrinal contrast between aggravated and negotiating measures of compensatory damages, for example,[698] we should also view non-compensatory awards as an amalgam of distinct measures to achieve the same goal: to respond to damage to matters of public interest. As this section shows, the collective approach requires us to co-ordinate but not necessarily to unify the doctrines governing the award of public interest damages. This is because the fact that all public interest damages are assessed by reference to the severity of the infringement to the public interest does not necessarily mean that the tools we use to arrive at the value of that infringement must be identical. It is in this sense, that we can expect some of the core distinctions between different forms of public interest damages to be retained, although the collective and co-ordinated approach is likely to cast doubt on some of the existing differences as regards availability and quantification of specific NCDs awards.

So how can the assessment of NCDs be co-ordinated without a doctrinal unification? It seems to me that the law would not need to radically change in order to give effect to a co-ordinated approach to NCDs *qua* public interest damages. Let me demonstrate this. In principle, one could argue that there are four main techniques that can transparently, and in this sense non-arbitrarily, quantify the damage to the public interest in the disputed matters.

The first assessment technique would be a direct or analogical application of the orthodox NCDs doctrines and assessments prescribed by existing authorities. Thus, if the court awarded £10,000 in punitive damages in one case, it should award an equal amount in a factually similar case. Similarly, if there is existing guidance as to the quantum of damages, the court should follow it. An example of this technique is *Thompson*, which provides guidance as to the quantum of punitive damages.[699] At first glance, this assessment technique seems attractive, because it sticks conservatively with the existing valuations of the relevant public interest infringements. The trouble with this approach is, however, that once we start discussing the underlying damage in terms of damage to public interests, then the established precedents may start losing their justificatory appeal. This is

[698] For other examples, see the text to nn 40–47.
[699] See *Thompson v Commissioner of Police of the Metropolis* (n 273) 516.

because, on the public interest analysis, inconsistencies and unequal quantifications of NCDs may surface. The relevant precedents could thus quickly become unconvincing in view of the new justificatory framework, but it is possible to imagine that the courts will find ways to justify the existing differences even if they accept the public interest account of NCDs.

The second assessment technique would measure the monetary value of the damage to the underlying public interest by analogy from other areas of law, ie, areas which transparently protect the same kind of public interest, against similar violations. The analogical assessment in non-civil disputes would guide the courts as a persuasive authority only. So, for example, if criminal law imposes a monetary sanction of £2,000 on certain criminal behaviour that violates the same matters of public interest that are subject to a civil dispute, then the civil courts might determine the quantum by analogy to that criminal case.[700] The problem with this technique might be that it would not allow the courts to question the legitimacy of the measure. Instead, they would need to accept it as given. We may presume, though, that the legitimacy of the analogous sanction and its measure would be, in most cases, grounded in the legislative decision behind the sanction, and so this need not be a big issue. That said, as was discussed in chapter five, the 'publicness' of protected interests is contextual, and so the context of the analogy would be critical for our conclusion regarding the legitimacy of this assessment technique. On the bright side, from a practical viewpoint, this technique would not require us to abandon the existing doctrines regarding individual types of NCDs.

The third technique would determine the value of the damage to public interest by focusing on the defendant's actual gain made at the expense of that public interest. So, if we can put our finger on some pecuniary gain that was consequent upon the defendant's wrongdoing against the public interest, then such wrongful gain might be a solid proxy for the value of the non-correlative damage. Insofar as the defendant's activity or the consequences of that activity are wrongful *because* that activity or those consequences violate some public interest, then the defendant's gain so achieved can be legitimately disgorged. The existing category of disgorgement damages fits relatively well with this technique, although it is important to note that, under this proposed new technique, the defendant's gain can legitimately be disgorged only to the extent that it is made at the public's expense. In other words, it is not necessary to disgorge the defendant's gain in full (which still seems to be the current understanding of the law regarding disgorgement damages and account of profits).[701]

[700] A similar reasoning can be found in, eg, *Original Beauty Technology Co Ltd & Ors v G4K Fashion Ltd & Ors* (n 244) [154].

[701] Although a recent criminal case (*R v Andrewes* [2022] UKSC 24) suggest that the English law is turning to a more nuanced position in this regard. Mr Andrewes lied about his credentials to the victim, St Margaret's Hospice, to gain a position of Chief Executive Officer, but while his original act amounted to fraud, the services provided by Mr Andrewes to the hospice for over 10 years were not themselves illegal. Hence, it was ruled by the Supreme Court that in a full disgorgement of Mr Andrewes's net earnings

Unfortunately, there will be many cases where such gain would be only normative and hence difficult to measure. Probably the most frequent scenario would be one in which the defendant will cause damage to the public interest but where there will be no precise factual (including purely financial) indicator by reference to which we could assess the award. Yes, there will be various other aspects of the wrongdoing, such as the importance of the protected interests, the claimant's culpability (if any) and own disregard for the protected interest, the claimant's position and wealth, etc. These aspects will typically aggravate or mitigate the supposed extent of the damage caused to the public interest in question, but they would not give us a specific figure. As put by Lord Hope in *Lumba*, in such cases '[w]e have no yardstick by which that sum can be measured to test its accuracy'.[702]

Accordingly, the fourth assessment technique would rely on a conventionally presumed pecuniary value of the non-correlative damage. This assessment technique closely resembles how nominal, vindicatory and punitive damages are currently assessed, except that the proposed technique would require us to standardise the value of the expressly labelled public interest in question, combined with any aggravating or mitigating factors. So just as there is a conventionally presumed quantum in relation to nominal awards, or just as there is a conventionally agreed quantum of criminal or administrative penalties, the quantum of public interest damages would be conventionally stipulated.

The conventional quantum may be basic (as in the case of nominal damages or vindicatory damages) or adjusted, taking into account any aggravating or mitigating factors (as in the case of vindicatory, punitive or disgorgement damages). On this account, vindicatory damages turn out to be a redundant category that straddles between two assessment techniques. This further supports the claim that vindicatory damages do not have any rightful place in English law, but it does not support this claim by authority or by the argument that they are functionally superfluous.[703] Rather, it supports this claim by the argument that the vindicatory measure does not offer any distinct quantification method in relation to the supposed value of the public interest infringed. If there are any hidden awards of vindicatory damages in English law, as was suggested in chapter four, it might thus be sensible to try to explain them as cases of hidden nominal or punitive awards (using the same conventional assessment techniques). In any event, given that the English law has never expressly recognised vindicatory damages as a separate type of damages, it proves feasible to implement the suggested organisation of measures of public interest damages

would amount to 'double disgorgement' (at [41]), because unlike in relation to earnings obtained by illegal services which have 'no value that the law should recognise as valid' (at [42]), Mr Andrewes's services 'did not constitute a criminal offence' (at [42]) and the earnings were thus not made at the public's expense. By contrast, Mr Andrewes's services brought the victim some real 'value' (at [44]) and the correct sum to be confiscated should reflect that by way of deduction.

[702] *Lumba* (n 18) 304 (Lord Hope).

[703] *cf* Baker (n 400) 86.

without significantly altering the existing system of NCDs. This feature of the analysis should be put to its credit.

There may undoubtedly be other ways of organising the measures of public interest damages, but discussing those variants is not the objective of this book.[704] Besides, given that there is no literature on public interest damages, such discussion would be highly speculative. That said, the preceding fourfold systemisation of public interest damages measures could be defended by an argument that it most likely exhausts the universe of possibilities when it comes to the conceivable types of measurement of the relevant damage. These four assessment techniques – in no particular order of priority – would enable us to adopt the public interest interpretation of NCDs as a group of distinct measures designed to achieve the same broad goal: rectification of damage to public interest. Importantly, this fourfold organisation of NCDs measures shows that we need not invent new categories of award in order to bring to life the broader interpretive idea of public interest damages and to operationalise that idea in a principled and consistent manner across various measures of NCDs. It seems sufficient that our understanding of the existing categories of NCDs changes and that we approach their assessment collectively, as indeed we should.

IV. Inconsistency of Remedies

The realisation that NCDs fight over the same terrain implies that we should co-ordinate not only their assessment (the quantification techniques), but also their availability. Otherwise, there is a risk that the defendant will pay twice for the same 'damage' to the public interest. Prescriptively, it is thus important that we understand when NCDs should not be available next to each other. In other words, it is important that we articulate when different forms of NCDs should be inconsistent with each other and whether this theory of inconsistency aligns with the law as it is today.

Inconsistency of remedies is well established in the law of damages, though not expressly in relation to NCDs. Thus, we know that the claimant cannot obtain both compensatory damages and gain-based damages in respect of a single wrong – '[t]he two bases of claim are mutually exclusive', ruled Hoffmann LJ.[705] Thus, a claimant will often have to elect between a loss-based and gain-based remedy.[706] The election will, for strategic reasons, be often 'made at the conclusion of trial once the claimant has sufficient information about the quantum of each remedy'.[707]

[704] *cf* Cane (n 41) 311–12 and R Stevens, 'Damages for Wrongdoing in the Absence of Loss' in J Varuhas and NA Moreham (eds), *Remedies for Breach of Privacy* (Oxford, Hart Publishing, 2018) 121–24.

[705] *Ministry of Defence v Ashman* (n 120) 519.

[706] See, eg, *Tang Man Sit (Deceased) v Capacious Investments Ltd* (n 145) 521.

[707] Edelman, Varuhas and Higgins (n 5) para 16-060.

The incompatibility of loss-based and gain-based remedies is arguably supported by the functional overlap between loss-based and gain-based remedies, both of which aim to address damage to the claimant's private interests. If different measures of damages are underpinned by the same rationale, it follows that they likely serve the same overarching function. Similarly, for example, wasted expenditure cannot be claimed in addition to loss of bargain damages. These two measures are regarded as alternatives between which the claimant must elect because these are two measures to redress the same damage, when damage is seen at a certain level of abstraction.[708] Consequently, awarding both types of damages concurrently would risk duplicating compensation, amounting to double-counting.

The same argument could be applied to NCDs. As was demonstrated in section I, there are overlaps as to the justificatory reasons behind different forms of NCDs. In those cases, it would thus be unjust to permit any cumulation of NCDs awards, especially since the different forms of NCDs can be seen as different assessment techniques for the same kind of damage. So, NCDs should be seen as alternative (not cumulative) remedies, insofar as they respond to the same resulting damage.

That said, the law does not (yet) expressly recognise various forms of NCDs as being underpinned by a common rationale, and so it stands to reason that the law also does not contain any clear rules on their mutual incompatibility – which indeed it does not. Thus, we need to infer the doctrines on incompatibility of NCDs from the cases more indirectly.

One ground of incompatibility concerns punitive damages: punitive damages present a danger that the defendant will be subjected to a double sanction – which is why the courts should systematically mitigate this risk by checking whether the civil remedy does not overlap with a sanction already imposed outside the private law dispute.[709] *Borders*,[710] for instance, shows that where the remedy in question responds to a violation of public interests, there would normally be a risk that the damages award may amount to a duplicate sanction. This would be the case, for example, where a public law sanction such as a confiscation order or an administrative penalty would be paid by the defendant (or its payment enforced) and where the claimant would ask for punitive damages for the same wrongful conduct.[711]

Borders also demonstrates that this test need not be limited to punitive damages claims. The claim in *Borders* was formally made for punitive damages, but, in essence, seemed more like a claim for disgorgement damages because the purpose of the award was to strip the wrongful gain made by the defendant. The reason for the punitive award here was not just the defendant's profit-seeking intention

[708] *Anglia Television Ltd v Reed* [1972] 1 QB 60 (CA) 64, 65.

[709] eg, *Archer v Brown* (n 271) 421; *AB v South West Water Services Ltd* (n 271) 527, 531; *Borders* (n 249) [17], [23], [46]; *Devenish Nutrition Ltd v Sanofi-Aventis SA* (n 9) [20], [28] and [102]; *AT & Ors v Dulghieru & Anor* (n 271) [69] and [71].

[710] *Borders* (n 249).

[711] ibid [17], [23] and [46].

(as Category 2 punitive damages requires) but the actual profit made by the illicit activity.[712] Arguably thus, the public interest violations which underpin disgorgement damages also require us to test any potential overlap of this remedy with public law sanctions. In *R v Andrewes*, for example, the Supreme Court ruled that a full disgorgement of Mr Andrewes's net earnings would amount to 'double disgorgement', because his services 'did not constitute a criminal offence'.[713] And given the overlapping between disgorgement, as exemplified by confiscation orders in *AT & Ors v Dulghieru & Anor*,[714] it could be argued that the same incompatibility we see between punitive damages and criminal sanctions, *should* apply to the relationship between punitive and disgorgement damages: they should be incompatible with each other.

Further, if punitive damages are only available when compensation payable is not sufficient to punish the defendant, then it follows that punitive damages cannot be compatible with nominal damages. That is because nominal damages and compensatory damages are never available in tandem (see chapter four). A fortiori, if the declaratory goal of nominal damages is *ipso facto* discharged by compensatory damages, then the same goal must be discharged by punitive damages. And if punitive and disgorgement damages *should not* be available alongside each other, then the same *should* apply to the mutual compatibility of nominal and disgorgement damages. In short, nominal damages arguably are and normatively should be incompatible with punitive damages and disgorgement damages, although there is no express pronouncement in the cases to this effect.

There is no apparent reason to believe that the same test should not be applicable to public interest damages across the board. Rather, it seems that public interest damages should always be regarded as mutually exclusive remedies insofar as they respond to the same damage (see also sections I, III and IV) and that they should not be seen as incompatible with compensatory awards. We know from *Rookes*, for example, that compensatory damages are compatible with punitive awards (indeed, they are baked into the availability of punitive damages), and we know from cases cited earlier in this section that they are incompatible with restitutionary damages. Thus, we should correct the law's own unhappy (but luckily only sparse) language to the contrary. In *Rees & Ors v Commissioner of Police of the Metropolis*,[715] for instance, the court thought there was a 'potential overlap between the factors which provide justification for … aggravated and exemplary awards [and which] require the court to be aware of double-counting'.[716] But if aggravated damages protect private interests in the disputed matters and if punitive (ie, exemplary) damages protect

[712] ibid [25]–[27].
[713] *R v Andrewes* (n 701) [41] and [42].
[714] n 271 [69]–[73].
[715] *Rees & Ors v Commissioner of Police of the Metropolis* (n 118).
[716] ibid [12].

public interests in the disputed matters, then the risk of double-counting does not arise and the court does not need to engage in this line of difficult reasoning at all.

This line of reasoning also sheds light on the compatibility of compensation with disgorgement. Traditionally, as we saw, gain-based and loss-based remedies are mutually incompatible alternatives. Still, in *Vercoe*,[717] Sales J clarified that not all gain-based remedies are alternatives to loss-based compensation. This case was analysed at length in section VI.B of chapter five and there is no need to repeat the points made there. The key message is that the two remedies – loss-based and gain-based – do not always protect the same type of interest and are therefore not always mutually incompatible. This will be where, in particular, the availability of the gain-based award would be underpinned by non-correlative damage and would therefore amount to a disgorgement (rather than restitutionary) remedy.[718]

When it comes to the compatibility of vindicatory awards with other remedies, the law is rather unclear – in part because vindicatory damages hardly exist as an available remedy in English law. That said, there is an indication in *Mosley*, for example, that the large quantum of compensation for non-material damage (£60k) was regarded as sufficient to serve not only the punitive but also the vindicatory goals.[719] And there is an indication in *Lumba*, that other damages, including various forms of compensatory and non-compensatory awards, can fulfil the vindicatory function and thereby make a separate award of vindicatory damages redundant.[720] This would suggest that vindicatory damages are unlikely ever to be available next to compensatory damages, and possibly also next to any other non-compensatory award in English law.

The law is relatively unclear also in relation to the compatibility of nominal and contemptuous damages, both of which can in fact serve as awards of nominal compensation, as was explained in chapter four. Where this is the case, it should be uncontroversial for the law to demand election between those remedies and to declare such remedies incompatible with each other as well as with compensatory awards generally. Where this is not the case, nominal as well as contemptuous damages should arguably be available next to compensatory awards because they would respond to a different kind of damage: damage to public (not private) interests. In the case of contemptuous damages, however, we would need to adopt a strange analysis whereby the contemptuous awards would be a kind of penalty against the claimant, who would obtain compensation less the contemptuous penalty. This interpretation of the case law was explained in chapter four as well. In the case of nominal damages, the award should in principle be available on top of the compensatory sum, but this is not what the law currently does.

[717] *Vercoe & Ors v Rutland Fund Management Ltd & Ors* (n 653).
[718] ibid [334], [337], [340].
[719] *Mosley v News Group Newspapers* (n 206) [235].
[720] See the text to nn 388–392.

V. Conclusion

The case for a collective approach to public interest damages is strong. This conclusion supports the claim made in chapter three. It was argued in chapter three that the law *should* expressly recognise the two fundamental justifications (justifications giving effect to individual rights and non-rights-based justifications) because the distinction between them is theoretically sound and could have positive doctrinal implications that would not strengthen the law's internal consistency. Four arguments were made in support of this claim. First, that the distinction could help to confirm or deny the stated contrast between compensatory and non-compensatory awards and, hence, their mutual (in)compatibility. Second, that it could help to confirm or deny the stated unrelatedness between individual types of NCDs and, hence, their mutual (in)compatibility. Third, that it could help increase the law's transparency, and such transparency could help better identify areas ripe for a doctrinal change. And fourth, that it could imply whether certain measures should be available as of right or not.

Here we can add a fifth argument, namely that the analysis of damages presented in this book implies that we have good reasons to approach all public interest damages collectively and as a distinct class of awards. This concerns both the availability and quantum of public interest damages. Building on the findings from chapter five, this chapter showed that the statedly distinct types of NCDs can sometimes be analysed as awards that protect the same matters of public interest. If distinct NCDs protect the same interests and are based on the same ethical considerations, then we should arguably approach them in a similar way or provide compelling reasons to explain the distinctions. The traditional doctrinal distinctions drawn between individual types of NCDs thus call for a careful re-examination and the collective approach is an appropriate way to do that. As Jansen puts it, '[i]t would be misleading to take doctrinal categories as a given, pre-existing structure, into which legal rules and policies can then be placed. Doctrine must respond to the law's normative structure, to its basic principles and rules, and not vice versa'.[721] In this regard, the collective approach promises to achieve a fairer and more coherent and principled application of the relevant doctrines. Some brief observations were made as regards how this co-ordinated approach could influence the availability and assessment techniques relating to different forms of public interest damages.

We saw in this chapter that the determination of the 'publicness' of the interests in dispute and, relatedly, the availability of public interest damages requires the courts to exercise an ethical judgement. And that judgment cannot be legitimately based on certain types of argument which are legitimate in the context of compensatory damages. We also saw that the public interest protection of the relevant

[721] N Jansen, 'The Concept of Non-Contractual Obligations: Rethinking the Divisions of Tort, Unjustified Enrichment, and Contract Law' (2010) 1 *Journal of European Tort Law* 16, 33.

interests is underpinned by the norms of distributive justice. This too calls for a co-ordinated approach that contrasts public interest damages with compensatory damages and that applies the comparable distributive criteria to comparable events in disputes. Thus, to separate the relevant from irrelevant arguments, it was argued, that we should acknowledge the distinction between public and private interests in their role of justifying reasons for measures of damages and approach public interest damages collectively. The hypothetical waiver method (see chapter five) is one way to exercise the ethical judgement in relation to all public interest damages.

In relation to the quantification of public interest damages, it was argued that if our aim is to give better effect to the public interests which such NCDs protect, then we might want to revise the existing assessment techniques. This is because if we want expressly to discuss the quantum of public interest damages as an issue of the size of damage to the underlying public interest, then it is desirable to quantify such damage on a co-ordinated basis so that the awards across all public interest damages are consistent and fair. Four co-ordinated assessment techniques were suggested: (i) quantification by reference to specific NCDs precedents; (ii) quantification by reference to analogous cases in other areas of law that protect the same public interest (eg, criminal sanctions); (iii) quantification by reference to gain obtained at the expense of the public (and not necessarily *all* of the gain, as is the case in relation to disgorgement damages); and (iv) quantification by reference to the conventionally presumed value of the non-correlative damage. The last, conventional method would be nothing new in relation to nominal, vindicatory and punitive damages. Yet unlike the traditional doctrines, the collective approach and the public interest analysis would allow us effectively to compare and contrast these different types of damages with each other. To this end, it was suggested that vindicatory damages are redundant – even if only as an idea – under this organisation of assessment techniques. The same conclusion seems to follow from the exploration of mutual (in)consistency of damages measures. While the law does not contain clear rules on mutual (in)consistency of NCDs, vindicatory damages should arguably be inconsistent with other awards which, ultimately, can fulfil their function and give effect to the same underlying justifications.

There are also good reasons to believe that punitive, disgorgement and nominal damages are incompatible with each other; and that disgorgement (unlike restitutionary) damages can be awarded in tandem with compensatory awards. By contrast, the position in relation to nominal damages and contemptuous damages is less clear, largely because the awards under these categories include both awards of nominal compensation (which should be incompatible with compensatory damages, but compatible with NCDs) and awards of a non-compensatory nominal sanction (which should be compatible with compensatory damages, but incompatible with NCDs).

As a side benefit, this collective and co-ordinated approach to public interest damages would help us not only to compare their own internal availability and measures and, therefore, to achieve higher consistency and predictability in their application, but also to appreciate the justificatory overlaps amongst public interest damages and monetary awards, such as criminal or administrative fines.[722] After all, NCDs, if defined as monetary awards that are justified by infringements of public interests, invite questions about how to co-ordinate and compare them with other public sanctions. The potential benefits of the collective approach are thus clear. As Lord Neuberger and Baroness Hale recently put it, '[p]articularly at a time when costs of litigating are very substantial, clarity and consistency are very precious commodities in the law'.[723] And in relation to an area of law so complex and so under-theorised as is the area of NCDs at large, the public interest analysis of NCDs and the collective approach to public interest damages offer this precious quality.

[722] See, eg, M Dyson, 'Challenging the Orthodoxy of Crime's Precedence over Tort: Suspending a Tort Claim Where a Crime May Exist' in SG Pitel, JW Neyers and E Chamberlain (eds), *Tort Law: Challenging Orthodoxy* (Oxford, Hart Publishing, 2013).

[723] *Knauer v Ministry of Justice* [2016] UKSC 9, [2016] AC 908 [21].

7

The Way Forward

If public interest damages are approached collectively, how exactly should we treat them? What are the specific doctrinal implications of such a collective approach? We already saw how the 'publicness' of the disputed matters might be determined in practice and what types of argument and ethical concerns may be accepted as relevant and legitimate when justifying public interest awards. We also saw how one might co-ordinate the various forms of assessment technique concerning damage to the public interest and how one might go about the inconsistency of NCDs. The chief aim of this chapter is to outline the way forward by identifying further doctrinal implications and by dealing with possible objections to the introduction of the public interest analysis of NCDs into our law.

Section I argues that public interest damages should be awarded only exceptionally because it is inconsistent to hold that the public interest remedy is owed to the claimant as of right and at the same time justified by non-correlative damage to public interests. Thus, it is argued that if the public interest analysis of NCDs is correct, then all the non-correlatively justified damages should not be available as of right. This claim is then evaluated against the law's own position concerning the 'as-of-right' nature of different types of damages.

Section II argues that the 'publicness' of the interests in dispute requires the courts to play an unusually proactive role in civil disputes concerning public interest damages and that they should often be going beyond the parties' own arguments and submissions. However, it is also argued that this judicial activity should not be confused with unconstrained judicial discretion. The controversies associated with this proactive role are then discussed alongside the safeguards against the risk that the courts would abuse (even if inadvertently) their power when adjudicating public interest damages disputes.

Section III explains five very specific doctrinal implications that emerged from the testing of the hypothetical waiver method against leading damages cases.

Section IV explains how the public interest analysis could operate alongside the existing doctrines. It also deals with several objections to public interests damages theory. The purpose of that section is to show that there are no apparent reasons to resist the proposed public interest analysis of NCDs.

Section V concludes and outlines the recommended way forward.

I. Not Available as of Right

The picture of NCDs *qua* public interest damages portrayed thus far showed that in many important respects these remedies are nothing like compensatory awards. This is not particularly surprising. Even under the traditional view, it is sometimes suggested that NCDs are exceptional remedies.[724] To paraphrase Lord Nicholls's statement in *AG v Blake*, it 'is axiomatic … [that with] the anomalous exception of [public interest damages] …, damages are compensatory'.[725] But what exactly does it mean? In what sense are NCDs *qua* public interest damages exceptional? Relatedly, in what sense are compensatory damages ordinary, ie, unexceptional?

Exceptionality in law can have at least two different meanings: descriptive and prescriptive exceptionality.[726] At the descriptive level we may say that judges *do* exceptionally award public interest damages. To give an example, we could say, in a descriptive mode, that the frequency or the quantum of public interest damages is exceptional relative to the frequency and quantum of all damages awards.[727] Such empirical claims, however, describe the judicial practice and not some intrinsic characteristics of public interest damages as a category. Exceptionality in this sense will not be discussed here. At the prescriptive level, we can say that judges *ought* only exceptionally to award damages in any other than the ordinary measure.[728] Such a normative claim assumes that NCDs *qua* public interest damages are exceptional in nature, regardless of how often or in what quantum they are awarded. We will focus here on the exceptionality of public interest damages in this prescriptive sense.

This section argues that unlike in relation to compensatory damages, the courts' duty to award NCDs *qua* public interest damages should not be owed to the claimant as of right, because the courts' public duty to protect the public interest in the disputed matters is not grounded wholly or predominantly in the claimant's interests. Accordingly, public interest damages should be awarded only exceptionally, and not whenever the claimant successfully establishes his claim and asks for the public interest remedy. In this sense, public interest damages are exceptional because the courts ought normally not to award them.

Cane's work on exceptional measure of damages provides a useful background for thinking about these issues.[729] To understand why a measure is exceptional, it

[724] eg, Cane (n 41) 304; Edelman, Varuhas and Colton (n 33) para 1-008. But *cf* Edelman, Varuhas and Higgins (n 5) para 1-010, where such remedies are now more accurately described as 'additional types of damages, rather than as exceptional'.

[725] *Blake* (n 8) 282.

[726] Similarly, Cane (n 41) 303–04.

[727] *cf* Goudkamp and Katsampouka (n 69) (reporting and discussing the results of a study that captures every UK decision in which punitive damages were sought that was delivered between 1 January 2000 and 31 December 2015).

[728] *cf* Cane (n 41) 304. See also Zipursky (n 58) 151 (offering a prescriptive reading of non-compensatory punitive damages).

[729] Note that Cane's study on the exceptional measure of damages was published in 1996, ie, before *Blake* (n 8) which first used the term in the black-letter law.

is necessary to know which of the basic measures are ordinary (unexceptional), argues Cane.[730] Thus, if we accept that the ordinary rule governing the correlative relationship between the claimant and the defendant is that damages awards should only be justified by correlative reasons and awarded to the claimant as of right, then all the non-correlatively justified damages should, by implication, be treated as an exception to this rule. It would follow that, insofar as correlative reasons do not (and cannot) justify the measure of public interest damages, then the judges ought not to award them in ordinary circumstances, ie, on the basis of the claimant's private claim and evidence of the claimant's correlative loss or the defendant's correlative gain. On this account, public interest damages would thus be exceptional.

Indeed, according to Cane, the ordinary measure of damages in private law is embedded in correlative justifying reasons, whereas the exceptional measure expresses a greater 'degree of disapproval of particular conduct and give[s] deterrent signals of [bigger] strengths in relation to such conduct'.[731] In this regard, we can say with Gardner that the correlatively justified damages are 'a remedy of first resort'.[732] The reason why such damages (Gardner calls them 'reparative damages') are a remedy of first resort is that 'this is the only remedy against a [defendant] that the successful [claimant] enjoys *as of right*'.[733] In relation to such remedies, the court is obliged to give effect to the individual rights and correlatively justified protected interests by awarding the remedy whenever the successful claimant asks for it. As Gardner explains, in relation to reparative damages (typically an award of compensation for loss), the court is 'legally bound to make a reparative award of some kind if one is sought by the successful plaintiff, because [the claimant] has a right to such an award'.[734] Gardner then contrasts this view with an observation about certain NCDs. In particular, he writes that 'the court is not legally bound … to order any kind of disgorgement of profits, or to award any kind of exemplary or punitive damages (even at common law)'.[735]

The same implication flows logically from the analysis of NCDs *qua* public interest damages. Since the non-compensatory measures of public interest damages are not grounded wholly or predominantly in an individual right or in the rights arising from the infringement of that individual right, then it would be internally inconsistent to hold that such damages are both non-rights-based and available as of right. It thus follows that public interest damages cannot be available to the claimant as of right, because they are not rights-based. Accordingly, the courts should regard themselves as legally free to deny the award of public interest damages, because the refusal to award such damages cannot (by implication) cause any injustice to the claimant. At most, the decision not to award public interest

[730] Cane (n 41) 303.
[731] ibid 304.
[732] Gardner (n 322) 53.
[733] ibid 53 (emphasis in original).
[734] ibid 55 (footnote omitted).
[735] ibid 55.

damages would let the defendant get away with the public interest infringement, which is a different problem.

Let us now consider the law's own position on the matter to see how the claim that public interest damages should not be available as of right fits with that position. The following text will first consider the law's position in relation to: (i) compensatory damages, before it will turn, to (ii) the current legal position in relation to individual types of NCDs.

A. Compensatory Damages

The courts do not discuss the 'as of right' availability of damages very often. This is understandable if we consider that most damages (ie, the ordinary compensatory measure) give effect to individual rights. Since compensatory damages are justified by correlative reasons, it is self-evident that they should be available as of right. In this light, the current legal position – namely that they are available as of right – probably is not pointed out specifically in the cases because it is believed to be self-evident. Thus, the as-of-right nature of compensatory damages seems to be mentioned by the courts as a matter of course. For example, in *President of India v La Pintada Compania Navigacion SA*, the House of Lords stated that '[compensation] at common law [is awarded] … as of right since once a breach of contract and damage caused by that breach are proved a court has no discretion but must award the damages claimed in full'.[736] Similarly, in *One Step*, the Supreme Court stated that '[c]ommon law damages for breach of contract are not a matter of discretion. They are claimed as of right'.[737] In relation to negligence then, '[t]he general rule is that where a breach of duty has been established and a causal link between the breach and the loss suffered has been proved the injured party is entitled as of right to damages'.[738] In a case concerning damages for personal injury caused by medical negligence, the Court of Appeal stated that '[t]he claimant was entitled as of right to an award of general damages including the 10 per cent uplift and the judge had no discretion to depart from that'.[739] When it comes to conversion, the Court of Appeal confirmed that the claimant (whose two expensive sports cars were converted) is entitled 'as of right, by way of damages for detention, to the [rise in the price of the cars] … where property is wrongfully detained and is still held by the defendant and the price has risen meanwhile'.[740] And in a harassment case, the as-of-right nature of compensatory damages was confirmed in relation to the civil remedy under the Protection from Harassment Act 1997.[741] This last example

[736] *President of India v La Pintada Compania Navigacion SA* [1985] AC 104 (HL) 112.
[737] *One Step (Support) Ltd v Morris-Garner* (n 15) [95].
[738] *R v Secretary of State for Transport, Ex parte Factortame Ltd & Ors (No 5)* [2000] 1 AC 524 (HL) 550 (Lord Hope).
[739] *Summers v Bundy* [2016] EWCA Civ 126 [26].
[740] *IBL Limited (formerly IBL Plc) v Philip Arthur Coussens* [1991] 2 All ER 133 (EWCA Civ) 142.
[741] *Majrowski v Guy's and St Thomas's NHS Trust* [2006] UKHL 34, [2006] ICR 1199 [21] and [22].

is interesting because section 3(2) of the Act merely states that 'damages *may* be awarded for (among other things) any anxiety caused by the harassment and any financial loss resulting from the harassment' (emphasis added). Regardless of this specific wording, it was held in *Majrowski* that compensatory damages are available as of right.[742] Overall, these cases confirm the self-evident conclusion that compensatory damages are available as of right.

There is also one case which would seem to suggest a contrary view. In *D v Commissioner of Police of the Metropolis*, the Court of Appeal noted a 'contrast between damages as of right and compensation at the court's discretion'.[743] In this case, the Court was referring to the provision for 'just satisfaction' under the Convention and the Human Rights Act 1998, which was characterised by the Court of Appeal as 'essentially discretionary'.[744] However, once we remember that 'just satisfaction' can serve both compensatory and non-compensatory functions,[745] then the statement by the Court of Appeal starts making good sense. We can, of course, criticise the Court for using the word 'discretion' in this context, but the point remains the same: non-correlatively justified remedies should not be available as of right, and, in relation to 'just satisfaction', the Court of Appeal confirms that view.

B. Non-Compensatory Damages

Turning to NCDs, the law is relatively clear when it comes to the as-of-right nature of punitive damages. As stated by Lord Devlin, a decision on whether punitive damages will be awarded is 'one of discretion in which all the surrounding circumstances should be taken into account'.[746] A successful claimant, even if he establishes a cause of action, thus cannot obtain punitive damages as of right, because the courts always have some measure of discretion as to whether such an award is necessary to serve the punitive aims and whether it is necessary to protect the relevant public interest. Similarly, the High Speed Rail (London – West Midlands) Act 2017 states that '[a] court may award exemplary damages against the person if the court thinks it appropriate to do so in the circumstances'.[747] The wording of this provision shows that such a punitive award is not available as of right. It can thus be argued that the public interest analysis well explains and justifies the current legal position.

The fact that punitive awards are not available as of right under English law is also supported by a case concerning recognition of a foreign judgment for multiple

[742] ibid.
[743] *D v Commissioner of Police of the Metropolis* [2015] EWCA Civ 646, [2016] QB 16 [67].
[744] ibid [66] (interpreting the House of Lords decision in *R (Greenfield) v Secretary of State for the Home Department* [2005] 1 WLR 673 (HL)).
[745] *Cyprus v Turkey* (n 235) [13].
[746] *Rookes* (n 97) 1160.
[747] s 51(10) of the High Speed Rail (London – West Midlands) Act 2017.

(triple) damages awarded pursuant to US antitrust law (Sherman Act 1980). As put by the Court of Appeal in that case, 'the antitrust litigation procedure in the United States is oppressive and unjust … in particular with regard to the mandatory triple damages'.[748] These triple damages under what was described by the Court of Appeal as 'foreign penal legislation'[749] are 'awarded as of right' according to the US law,[750] yet under the Protection of Trading Interests Act 1980, section 5(2)(a), 'no court in the United Kingdom shall entertain proceedings at common law for the recovery of any sum payable [under a judgment] for multiple damages'.[751] This clearly suggests that even if the penal award of multiple damages is available as of right in other jurisdictions, it will not be so available in the UK.

Nominal damages (and contemptuous damages, insofar as they serve the same function as certain awards of nominal damages[752]) are more difficult in this regard because the nominal damages label is sometimes used for both correlatively and non-correlatively justified awards, as was demonstrated in section II of chapter four. According to Gardner, for example, nominal damages are 'nominally reparative damages … [and their existence] confirms rather than refutes the primacy of reparative damages as a remedy in the law of torts'.[753] However, as was argued in chapter four, this correlative conception of nominal damages is problematic and fails to explain, for example, why nominal damages are not available for all claim-right violations. It was thus argued in chapter four that nominal damages should not be understood (or at least not always understood) as a liminal case of compensatory damages. Instead, we saw that they can be convincingly explained as damages justified by violations of public interests. This would mean that they cannot and should not be available as of right because their award is not grounded wholly or predominantly in the claimant's individual right. Let us have a look at what the authorities say about this.

Rather than positively saying that nominal damages are available as of right, the turn of phrase typically used by the courts is that a successful claimant cannot obtain more than nominal damages in relation to certain causes of action, unless he proves some loss. Thus, in *One Step*, Lord Reed observed that where the claimant has not suffered any loss, 'he cannot be awarded more than nominal damages'[754] for breach of contract. Sometimes, the authorities state that the claimant is entitled to 'no more than nominal damages',[755] that certain wrongs 'would give rise to nominal damages only',[756] or that the claimant 'can only recover, at most, nominal

[748] *British Airways Board v Laker Airways Ltd & Ors* [1984] QB 142 (CA) 176.
[749] ibid 201.
[750] ibid 155.
[751] See also the text to n 22.
[752] In more detail, see ch 4, section III.
[753] Gardner (n 322) 57.
[754] *One Step (Support) Ltd v Morris-Garner* (n 15) [95]; applied eg, in *Priyanka Shipping Ltd v Glory Bulk Carriers Pte Ltd* [2019] EWHC 2804 (Comm), [2019] 1 WLR 6677 [187] and [200]–[203].
[755] eg, *Neville v London 'Express' Newspaper Ltd* [1919] AC 368 (HL) 393; *Lumba* (n 18) [71].
[756] *Salt Ship Design AS v Prysmian Powerlink SRL* (n 487) [223] (emphasis added).

damages'.[757] While these words can be construed to mean that nominal damages are available as of right, there is no definitive judicial pronouncement that nominal damages (as a category) would be so available.

Despite the widespread belief that nominal damages are available as of right, the current legal position on the matter is thus not as clear-cut as one might think. The public interest analysis presented throughout this book might well explain the courts' reluctance to make any generic statements about nominal damages, especially when we contrast this with the express acknowledgement of the as-of-right nature of compensatory damages by the judiciary.

At least part of the judicial practice of awarding nominal damages might, of course, be seen as giving effect to the claimant's rights and thus resulting in awards made as of right. For example, if we broaden our understanding of damage to include interferences with protected interests, then at least some nominal damages awards are explicable as compensatory.[758] This would also easily explain why they are (and should be) available as of right. But there is also evidence to the contrary. For example, how are we to explain the statement by Sedley LJ that unless the defendant's conduct concerns something 'obviously off the limits … [then t]he claim for a shilling in damages in order to prove a point and obtain an award of costs is history'?[759] It would seem that in Sedley LJ's view, the nominal remedy is not owed to the claimant as of right.

Similarly, the change introduced to the law of defamation by the Defamation Act 2013 seems to have, to say the least, significantly weakened the link between libel and nominal damages being available as of right. According to the Defamation Act 2013, '[a] statement is not defamatory unless its publication has caused or is likely to cause serious harm to the reputation of the claimant'.[760] Prior to the Act, '[t]he common law rule was that damage to reputation was presumed, not proved, and that the presumption was irrebuttable … [but now the law requires] evidence of the actual impact of the publication'.[761] Against this background, it is now difficult to imagine that a court would award nominal damages for defamatory publication because no publication will be regarded as defamatory unless it causes some serious correlative damage to the claimant. Indeed, the reported post-Defamation Act cases that award nominal damages are relatively rare, and when nominal damages are awarded, they seem to be awarded by way of liminal compensation for the worthless reputation of the claimant rather than by way of non-compensatory nominal damages. An example of this is 'the deliberately false case on serious harm advanced by Dr Wright

[757] *Albacruz v Albazero* [1977] AC 774 (HL) 791 (citing *Den of Airlie Steamship Co Ltd v Mitsui and Co Ltd* (1912) 17 Com Cas 116 (KB) 122–23).

[758] Similarly, see Varuhas (n 176) 270.

[759] *White v Withers LLP* (n 292) [72] (Sedley LJ); see also ibid [67] (Ward LJ).

[760] s 1(1) of the Defamation Act 2013.

[761] *Lachaux v Independent Print Ltd & Anor* (n 326) [20]. See also *Thornton v Telegraph Media Group Ltd* [2010] EWHC 1414 (QB), [2011] 1 WLR 1985 [90] ('whatever definition of "defamatory" is adopted, it must include a qualification or threshold of seriousness, so as to exclude trivial claims').

[in *Wright v McCormack* which] … requires more than a mere reduction in the award of damages'.[762]

The broader principle behind this statutory provision is stated to be derived from *Jameel v Dow Jones & Co Inc*, in which the court confirmed the 'potential for trivial cases to be struck out on the basis that they are an abuse of process because so little is at stake'.[763] This is fully in line with the overriding objective of the Civil Procedure Rules, namely that the courts are required 'to deal with cases justly and at proportionate cost'.[764] For example, when a warehouseman converts a few steel coils by holding on to them for longer than he should, but the owner suffers not a penny of loss in consequence, there is a legitimate claim, but the courts would probably strike out a statement of such case.[765] Besides, the courts are always free to strike out a claim, if it appears to them that the claim would amount to 'an abuse of the court's process or is otherwise likely to obstruct the just disposal of the proceedings'.[766]

To be sure, it is not automatically an abuse of process to bring a claim for nominal damages. The key question is whether there is a proportionate procedure to deal with the claim.[767] If there is no such procedure available, then it would be right to strike out the claim.[768] It should be acknowledged that defamation claims are a special case, because section 15(2) of the County Courts Act 1994 precludes county courts from hearing actions for libel or slander. So the proportionality between the size of the claim and the cost of the procedure needs to be managed more carefully.

But the key point is that if all nominal damages – regardless of the cause of action – are always small, then nominal damages should be viewed as disproportionate across the board, not just in relation to defamation cases, and their 'as of right' nature cannot change that. In this light, the public interest analysis of nominal damages better explains why it may be justified for the courts to deny the claimant the award of nominal damages unless some strong public interest is at stake – usually a major point of principle. In the absence of such reason which justifies the use of the court resources, the claim should be struck out. By contrast, the private interest and the supposed 'as of right' nature of nominal damages would not explain why the right sometimes is and sometimes is not good enough to justify the use of the court resources. In this light, by the way, the public interest analysis helps also to explain and justify why nominal damages are not and should not be awarded for all violations of non-acquired private rights (as discussed in section IV of chapter five).

762 *Wright v McCormack* (n 348) [144].

763 See para [12] of the Explanatory Note to s 1(1) of the Defamation Act 2013 and *Jameel v Dow Jones & Co Inc* [2005] QB 946 (CA).

764 CPR r 1.1.

765 Thanks for the suggestion of this example are due to an anonymous reviewer for the *Modern Law Review*.

766 CPR r 3.4(2)(b). See also the text to n 360.

767 *Sullivan v Bristol Film Studios Ltd* [2012] EWCA Civ 570, [2012] EMLR 27.

768 *Shaw v Leigh Day (A Firm)* [2017] EWHC 825 (QB) [19], [36]–[38].

Another reason why it is difficult to make any generic statement about the 'as of right' nature of nominal damages comes from the remedy's historical roots. In relation to nominal damages, it may sometimes be difficult to separate the successful claim from the remedy. And while the victim may be entitled as-of-right to his substantive claim, the as of right nature of nominal damages is not so clear. The source of this complexity appears to be the reverse historical relationship between the remedy and the right (the breach of which justifies the remedy).

The law of damages had for long been shaped as the law of actions, which has caused it to be pragmatically indifferent to the divide between private and public interests that those remedies protect.[769] This makes it difficult to ascertain whether the remedy of nominal damages was indeed made as of the claimant's private right. For example, a classic work – *McGregor on Damages* – which has been 'the first, and often also the last, port of call for any academic, practitioner or judge who encounters a problem on damages',[770] was first published in 1854[771] as a treatise on a specific subset of the law of actions. This was typical also of other treatises of the early nineteenth century. However, subsequent editions of the book by Harvey McGregor (12th to 19th edn) increasingly emphasised the reasons that justify damages. Harvey McGregor sought to rationalise the law of damages by emphasising the substantive laws behind damages awards and hence by also focusing more on the overwhelmingly private interests and rights that justify most damages awards. He highlighted a legal wrong as the premiere justifying reason for damages and as the key defining perspective for our understanding of these awards. But it is not entirely obvious how nominal damages fit this picture.

Prior to *Mediana*,[772] for example, it was not uncommon to see cases where nominal damages were sought merely to establish a private right. The purpose of the claim was thus merely to obtain a judgment, not to seek the remedy. As put in *Godefroy v Jay*, 'nominal damages are sufficient to entitle the Plaintiff to judgment. This is the rule of law and it has recently been recognised and acted on in *Marzetti v. Williams*.'[773] Similarly, in *Leader v Moody*, the judge acknowledged that 'the object of the Plaintiff [was] merely to establish his rights (as he has sh[o]wn by directing his counsel to ask for only nominal damages in case I wish to give him damages instead of an injunction)'.[774] The relationship between the entitlement to damages and entitlement to the judgment was thus different from how we think

[769] See, eg, JH Merryman, 'The Public Law-Private Law Distinction in European and American Law' (1968) 17 *Journal of Public Law* 3; G Samuel, 'Public and Private Law: A Private Lawyer's Response' (1983) 46 *MLR* 558, 558–64; Samuel (n 56) 277–84; JWF Allison, *A Continental Distinction in the Common Law: A Historical and Comparative Perspective on English Public Law* (Oxford, OUP, 2000) ch 2; D Priel, 'The Political Origins of English Private Law' (2013) 40 *Journal of Law and Society* 481.

[770] S Todd, 'Publication Review: Edelman, James, McGregor on Damages' (2018) *Journal of Business Law* 633, 636.

[771] JD Mayne, *A Treatise on the Law of Damages: Comprising Their Measure, the Mode in Which They Are Assessed and Reviewed, the Practice of Granting New Trials, and the Law of Set-off, and Compensation under the Lands Clauses Act*, 1st edn (London, H Sweet, 1856).

[772] See the discussion to nn 310–313 above.

[773] *Godefroy v Jay* (1831) 7 Bingham 413, 131 ER 159 (Comm Pl) 161–62.

[774] *Leader v Moody* (1875) LR 20 Eq 145 (Ch) 154.

about damages today: claimants sought nominal damages because they wanted to establish their rights, not because they were awarded nominal damages because they had established the infringement of their right and because they secured the judgment they wanted. Indeed, if the latter were true, nominal damages would have been available for all civil wrongs.

The modern role of nominal damages is different. Given that the nominal remedy has practically no value to individual litigants, it is understandable why claimants do not expressly seek 'nominal' damages; especially since the remedy of declaration is now available. In practice, the courts often award nominal damages on their own motion and not in response to a claim for nominal damages expressly so identified. Put in other words, the courts often award nominal damages instead of the remedy originally sought.

Thus, the current law's approach to nominal damages seems to be stuck between two competing perspectives: the law of actions' perspective, where nominal damages are available as of right for certain actions, and the law of wrongs' perspective, where nominal damages are the maximum that the courts are ready to award in response to certain wrongs. The wrongs-based analysis of NCDs advanced in this book shows that if nominal damages are indeed justified by public interests, then the courts should regard themselves legally free not to award nominal damages as of right. In other words, a successful claimant should not have the automatic right to nominal damages.

Vindicatory damages can be dealt with very swiftly here. They are currently not available as a separate category under English law, and, as such, they are not available as of right. In any case, for reasons explained earlier, vindicatory damages *qua* public interest damages (for example, in their hidden form – see section IV in chapter four) should not be available as of right.

Finally, let us turn to gain-based damages. If we look at the cases of exceptional gain-based damages, such as disgorgement damages in *AG v Blake*,[775] it seems clear that the law does not automatically award them. Under the current law, there needs to be some exceptional reason to justify this kind of remedy. This view fully conforms with the public interest analysis of disgorgement damages. While there is no conclusive evidence that the exceptional reasons would mean the damages are not available as of right, it seems to be a sensible conclusion. It can be argued that disgorgement damages should not be, and probably already are not, available as of right.

By contrast, restitutionary damages are possibly available as of right, although, again, there is no definitive rule on this point in the cases. One example to support this conclusion can be found in *Hollister*[776] – a case concerning trademark infringement. The Court of Appeal stated in *Hollister* that '[a] claimant who has succeeded in an action for infringement is entitled to damages as of right'.[777] However, the

[775] *Blake* (n 8) 282.
[776] *Hollister Inc, Dansac A/S v Medik Ostomy Supplies Ltd* [2012] EWCA Civ 1419.
[777] ibid [54].

Court also added that the claimant can seek an alternative remedy of 'an account of the profits made by the infringer … [, which is] an equitable remedy, and the court has a discretion whether to order it. It may be refused if, for example, the infringer was entirely innocent'.[778] It is not entirely clear whether the Court had in mind restitutionary or disgorgement damages here.

There thus seems to be a slight tension in gain-based damages cases, which tension is probably more driven by the distinction between common law and equity, than by the nature of the harm suffered and by whether the remedy gives effect to the claimant's private rights or not. Besides, we saw in chapter four that the dividing line between restitutionary and disgorgement damages does not perfectly map onto the doctrines. This helps us to understand why the courts do not necessarily appreciate the important contrast between the two fundamental justifications that underpin these two types of gain-based remedies. If the law accepts the divide and acknowledges the public interest analysis, it would in any event be desirable also to accept that disgorgement damages should not be available as of right, whereas restitutionary damages should be so available. Similarly, in Gardner's view, we *should* contrast at least some restitutionary remedies with disgorgement of profits, because disgorgement is discretionary, whereas restitutionary remedies are owed to the claimant as of right.[779]

C. Evaluation

Overall, we saw why NCDs *qua* public interest damages should not be available as of right to the successful claimant and that this recommendation does not necessarily contradict the current law. This implies that the courts can and should regard themselves as legally free not to award such damages unless some special reasons of public interest would justify the award.

Perhaps, we should echo what Lawton LJ once famously stated about difficult decisions where it is the court that ultimately decides what is just in a given scenario:

> What is just is what the trial judge thinks is just. That being so, an appellate court is not entitled to interfere with his decision unless it is so plainly wrong that it cannot be just. The concept of what is just is not an absolute one. Opinions among right thinking people may, and probably will, differ as to what is just in a particular case. No one person enjoys the faculty of infallibility as to what is just.[780]

If the same applies to the role of public interests in the law of damages, then the awards of public interest damages are always dependent on the court's view as to the convincingness of the ethical and legal reasons that are relevant to the public interest determination and to the non-compensatory award.

[778] ibid [55].
[779] Gardner (n 322) 55.
[780] *BP Exploration Co (Libya) Ltd v Hunt (No 2)* [1981] 1 WLR 232 (CA) 238.

We can look at public interests protected by previous NCDs awards as proxies of what will probably be protected by future judgments. For example, if the protection of the matters in dispute has been firmly established by precedent, the courts will be inclined to award NCDs, such as is the case in relation to nominal damages (although we saw above that this is not as straightforward as it traditionally seems). But we cannot say for certain when interferences with certain matters will attract the award of public interest damages. The previous cases can help us identify the relevant public interests, but this identification does not, on its own, dictate whether an interference with that interest will attract the damages remedy. Such identification is a necessary first step for the award of public interest damages, but it is not a sufficient step for the public interest award. The claim that public interest damages should not be (or that they already are not) available as of right helps us to make better sense of this dynamic between the claim, the precedent, and the decision to award or not to award the remedy.

For example, in a case of kidnapping, rape and murder committed by a police officer during one of the national Covid-19 lockdowns, Fulford LJ stated that there are important public interests such as police trustworthiness that make up 'different aspects of the fundamental underpinnings of our democratic way of life'[781] and they are of the utmost importance. Likewise, in *Drane v Evangelou*, Lord Denning argued that punitive damages could have been awarded for the defendant's '[m]onstrous behaviour'[782] even if such damages were not pleaded by the unlawfully evicted claimant. Does it mean the courts *must* award punitive damages in similar cases because they have identified a relevant public interest in the disputed matters? Clearly not, because even if the categories test in *Rookes* is satisfied, the courts have a discretion not to award punitive damages. The courts may have strong reasons to make the award when the defendant's wrong is so outrageous and unforgivable that it deserves to be responded to by way of public interest damages,[783] but they should not regard themselves to be under a legal duty to do so whenever the successful claimant asks for this remedy.

In conclusion, it can be said that there is a two-step process behind public interest awards. First, the court needs to recognise that the matters in dispute are of public interest. This is where existing precedents and the hypothetical waiver method can help the courts to exercise the relevant ethical judgment. Second, once this is established, the court needs to decide whether the non-correlative damage resulting from the events in dispute merits an award of public interest damages. And while the courts ought to award compensatory damages when the successful claimant asks for them, they ought not to make the same conclusion in relation to public interest damages unless additional reasons are found.

[781] Fulford LJ, Sentencing remarks of 30 September 2021 in case against Wayne Couzens, Central Criminal Court [perma.cc/3JGP-ZAYZ], [19].

[782] *Drane v Evangelou* (n 240) 457.

[783] ibid 457–59. See also *Broome v Cassell & Co* (n 600) 378G–378H, 399H.

The decision whether to make the award could hinge on whether a denial of the public interest remedy would put the damaged interest at risk. In other words, we may argue that the courts should consider whether, by not awarding public interest damages, the public importance of the underlying interest would be somehow compromised. Indeed, while the refusal to award public interest damages would not cause any injustice to the claimant (because it is, or should not be, owed to him as of right), there may still be a risk that the wrongful conduct (if left unremedied) would cause some permanent damage to the public interest in question. Maybe, thus, the courts have some public-regarding duty to protect those interests when they think it is just to do so, but the duty would not be owed to the claimant as of right.

The considerations that could be taken into account in such cases might include the significance of the interest in dispute for the functioning of our society,[784] the prominence of the particular dispute and its likely impact, the need to uphold public confidence in the law concerning that particular interest and the degree of risk that by not awarding the remedy the existence and protection of that interest would be disputed or irreversibly damaged and therefore undermined. As Potacs argues, for instance, 'some public interests have a greater weight than others'[785] and fundamental public interests such as the guarantees of life, health and safety have more significant weight than debatable interests such as consumer protection, employee protection, environmental protection and other forms of welfare.[786] The general criteria that may be taken into account when courts decide for or against a particular form of public interest protection are, according to Potacs, 'the empirical evidence and the seriousness of *danger* for the affected public interest in concrete cases'.[787]

And if it is to be concluded that the protection of the underlying public interest would be put in doubt if the damage were left unrecognised in the court judgment, then the court has a strong reason to award the public interest remedy. As argued by Potacs, once the public interest in the disputed matters becomes non-debatable,[788] it justifies stronger interferences with other, potentially competing or conflicting interests and private rights.[789] The non-debatable character of the relevant interests might speak strongly in favour of the award. After all, we would probably not want some non-debatable public interests to be put in doubt by the defendant's wrongful action. And we would probably not want the public interest violation to be left unnoticed in the dispute. Notably, this kind of reasoning might

[784] See *Pfeifer and Plankl v Austria* (1992) 14 EHRR 692 [37], cited with approval in *Millar* (n 568) [22].
[785] Potacs (n 537) 54.
[786] ibid 55.
[787] ibid 56 (emphasis in original).
[788] Though even the fundamental rights and legal institutions can be in principle always limited or displaced by weightier considerations in the particular case (by way of example, *cf* Art 52 of the Charter of Fundamental Rights of the European Union [2012] OJ C 326/391).
[789] Potacs (n 537) 55.

be applied by the courts across all forms of public interest damages because it is not dependent on the specific non-compensatory measure sought or awarded. In this regard, such reasoning could help the courts to apply the law of public interest damages more consistently.

II. Pro-Active Courts

The public interest analysis of damages also implies that we should want the courts to be more proactive when determining whether the matters in dispute are in the public interest. Given that the parties' own arguments and claims based on their correlative standpoint have (at best) limited relevance for the conclusion about whether the disputed matters are in the public interest,[790] it can be argued that the judiciary owe it to the public that relevant public interests are identified and eventually protected when a dispute comes to a court.

Some of the leading cases on punitive damages already seem to fit this view. For instance, many arguments employed by Lord Devlin to establish the categories test for punitive damages in *Rookes* were most likely based on the court's own active research,[791] rather than just the parties' own arguments. More generally, after the House of Lords decision in *Kuddus*,[792] the courts are expected to consider the underlying substantive reasons for the award, even if the claimant would invite them to follow the formalistic approach taken in *AB*.[793] '[T]here is nothing in Lord Devlin's analysis which requires that … a claim … should also constitute a cause of action which had before 1964 been accepted as grounding a claim for exemplary damages', stated Lord Slynn in *Kuddus*.[794] To this extent, one may argue that when dealing with the matters in dispute, the courts are expected to actively identify the 'publicness' of those reasons, rather than simply to rely on the list of protected interests in the previous authority.[795]

The proactive role of a judge may be controversial because judicial activism is not generally regarded as acceptable or desirable.[796] The courts do not normally actively dig up facts, identify relevant arguments or specify which interests are

[790] For more detail see ch 6, section II.

[791] *cf* the summaries of the parties' arguments in *Rookes v Barnard* [1961] 3 WLR 438 (QB); *Rookes v Barnard* [1963] 1 QB 623, [1962] 3 WLR 260 (CA); *Rookes* (n 97).

[792] *Kuddus v Chief Constable of Leicestershire Constabulary* [2002] 2 AC 122 (HL). See also Goudkamp and Katsampouka (n 69).

[793] *AB v South West Water Services Ltd* (n 271).

[794] *Kuddus v Chief Constable of Leicestershire Constabulary* (n 792) [8].

[795] A similar set of principles according to which the court is bound to identify and eventually to enforce legally protected interests regardless of the parties' claims, interests and assertions is called '*iura novit curia*' and the 'officiality' principle on the Continent (*cf* C Cavallini, 'Why is the Iura Novit Curia Principle not Applied Yet in English Law?' (2017) 17 *Global Jurist* 1).

[796] As for instance Mulcahy noted, it appears 'to be the case that judges are reluctant to engage in identifying [even] the collective interest in a dispute where the parties are unwilling or unable to do so' (L Mulcahy, 'The Collective Interest in Private Dispute Resolution' (2012) 33 *OJLS* 59, 68).

in dispute. Instead, they rely on how parties argue their case, what they submit as relevant to the dispute and so on, although they of course do certain things of their own initiative. For example, they ask the parties to identify the issues in dispute and sometimes strike out a statement of case or exclude an issue from consideration.[797]

The nature of the activity required by the 'publicness' of the disputed matters should be seen as belonging to the second camp, ie, activities that are permissible and can be done by the courts' own motion. The courts would actively determine whether certain facts of the case interfere with legally protected public interests. And this kind of activity need not be seen as such a controversy because, if the activity is properly constrained, then it may be harmless and even beneficial. As put by Jolowicz, while judicial activism is 'contrary to the normal English rule that it is the parties alone who formulate the issues in an action, the court must [sometimes] of its own motion take the point [demanded by the public interest]'.[798]

Indeed, unlike in the pre-CPR system where 'the prevailing view was that under the common law adversarial system, it was primarily for the parties rather than the court to control and progress the litigation process up until the trial itself',[799] the courts now have a duty to further the overriding CPR objective, ie, to deal with cases justly and at proportionate cost,[800] meaning that the courts should try to find ways to resolve the dispute quickly. And if the dispute raises questions of public interest protection, then it makes sense to expect of the courts that they will advance the process in relation to this aspect of the case more than they would do so in relation to aspects of the dispute which, unlike the protection of public interests, are legitimately to be controlled by the private parties.

That said, the risks associated with the courts' active role and the 'not-as-of-rightness' of public interest damages are not to be treated lightly. In practice, it might be difficult to tell if courts are approaching the issues at hand on any principled basis or simply based on a very wide discretion to identify relevant public interests and to make the award. Indeed, we saw that Lord Devlin described the awards of punitive damages as discretionary.[801] Similarly, in *2 Travel Group* it was stated that the court has an 'inherent discretion to award exemplary damages' in such cases.[802] Zakrzewski writes in this context about discretionary remedies,[803]

[797] CPR r 3.4.

[798] JA Jolowicz, 'Active Role of the Court in Civil Litigation' in M Cappelletti and JA Jolowicz (eds), *Public Interest Parties and the Active Role of the Judge in Civil Litigation* (New York, Oceana, 1975) 171 (referring to *Snell v Unity Finance Co Ltd* [1964] 2 QB 203).

[799] A Zuckerman, *Zuckerman on Civil Procedure: Principles of Practice*, 4th edn (London, Sweet & Maxwell, 2021) para 1.7.

[800] See more in ibid paras 1.71–1.90.

[801] *Rookes* (n 97) 1160.

[802] *2 Travel Group Plc (in liq) v Cardiff City Transport Services Ltd* (n 242) [448], referring to *Devenish Nutrition Ltd v Sanofi-Aventis SA* [2009] 1 Ch 390 [56].

[803] Zakrzewski (n 61) 97.

and Gardner too asserts that awards not justified correlatively 'are only available in the discretion of the court'.[804]

So, how should we constrain the activity of the courts in order to minimise the risk of impermissible judicial activism? To answer this question, we need to understand that this active courts' role and the 'not-as-of-rightness' of public interest damages do not imply full discretion. It is not the case, under the public interest analysis, that courts would be free to award NCDs entirely of their own motion. Indeed, if they were free to do so, then the result of a judicial process could be viewed as '*ex post facto* legislation affecting the rights of the parties'.[805] This form of discretion, effectively amounting to impermissible judicial law-making, is problematic for at least two reasons.

First, one may object that the courts should never have an unconstrained discretion to decide what is in the public interest because, in democratic societies, the key decisions about public interests must rest with the 'political community (or citizens, for short)'.[806] Citizens typically express their general views through a representative body such as a parliament, the government or a local council. On this view, we may argue that judges should refrain from autonomously determining public interests because they do not have the democratic mandate to do so. Some may argue that the judges' privileged position may be legitimised by the judges' experience, knowledge of the law, skill and the authority of reason used in their judgments.[807] But this argument does not overcome the objection that judges lack the democratic mandate.

Second, one may object that the courts should never be allowed to recognise public interests with retroactive effect, because such retroactive lawmaking would be arbitrary and unjust in the sense of uncontrolled use of the power.[808] On the one hand, the courts cannot avoid making decisions – they must adjudicate the disputes in front of them. On the other hand, there is often no express or precise legal ground as to why something should be protected *qua* public interest.[809] It may thus seem that the courts are free to create new retroactive rules when recognising the relevant public interests. But that would be a misunderstanding. Similarly to how private individuals should not be allowed freely to control public interests, the courts too should be limited in their determination of which matters are, in their view, in the public interest. The public interest analysis of damages therefore implies both that the courts should be more active and that we should want to have ways to control this activity.

Paradoxically perhaps, in civil disputes, the issue of retroactivity does not typically call for a close scrutiny because, as argued by Zipursky, the defendant's

[804] Gardner (n 322) 54.
[805] J Steiner, 'Judicial Discretion and the Concept of Law' (1976) 35 *CLJ* 135, 135. See also Gardner (n 106) 416 and 417.
[806] Bezemek and Dumbrovský (n 508) 22–23.
[807] ibid 23.
[808] See T Endicott, 'Adjudication and the Law' (2007) 27 *OJLS* 311, 317.
[809] See ch 5, section III and ch 6, section II.

liability in tort law is 'not a sanction for what the state has announced to be [against the public interest, but is] rather the court's ratification of a plaintiff's assertion of a right to redress against someone who wronged her'.[810] In other words, the tortfeasor's liability is based on a retrospective (not retroactive) legal recognition of the claimant's private interests, ie, recognition of a reason that had transparently existed at the time of the events in dispute, even if that reason was not sufficiently specified in any posited legal rule. Zipursky goes on to explain that '[i]t is the wrongful injuring of the plaintiff, not the violation of an announced rule, that generates liability in tort'.[811] This explanation shows why the court's decision to recognise the claimant's private protected interests in the dispute need not be problematised further – it is not retroactive in the strict sense of the term. It goes almost without saying that the private interests protected by contract damages are, by virtue of the contract being entered into by the parties, deemed to be sufficiently transparent at the time of the events in dispute.

In relation to public interest damages, however, the problem of retroactive imposition of a remedial duty looks different. Imagine, for example, that the claimant wanted to argue that the defendant's interference with an environmental covenant is contrary to the public interest. The public interest in the covenant would need to be sufficiently transparent to both of the parties at the time of the events in dispute. Otherwise, the recognition of this protected interest can be criticised as retroactive lawmaking, because the parties would not be able to know (based on their correlative relationship alone) that the relevant reasons of public interest may apply to them. Typically, the public interest reason would thus need to be specified in a non-correlative source such as a statutory provision or in a prior case.[812]

The courts' judgments are often equivocal when it comes to distinguishing between: (i) the imposition of liability in damages on the basis of positive law that existed at the time of the events in dispute, and (ii) the imposition of liability retroactively, ie, on the basis of the law that did not transparently exist or was not legally binding at that time. The courts simply write in their judgments that the defendant is held liable, without mentioning and sometimes perhaps even without considering the distinction, thinks Endicott.[813] Thus, to determine whether the court's decision violates the rule against retroactivity, it is useful to have a test. According to Endicott, we should ask 'which of the court's reasons for decision the institutions of the legal system had already committed the court to act upon, before the time of decision'.[814] This question can help us to determine whether the award of damages is made with retroactive effect or not.

[810] BC Zipursky, 'Torts and the Rule of Law' in LM Austin and D Klimchuk (eds), *Private Law and the Rule of Law* (Oxford, OUP, 2014) 149.
[811] ibid 149.
[812] See the text to n 255 in ch 4, section I. See also J Goudkamp and J Murphy, 'Tort Statutes and Tort Theories' (2015) 131 *LQR* 133.
[813] Endicott (n 808) 311.
[814] ibid 312.

As Endicott convincingly shows, 'uncontrolled judicial law-making *would* violate the rule of law, [but] retroactive judicial law-making need not be uncontrolled'.[815] He goes on to explain that the judicial authority to change the law and to create new legal rules 'with retroactive effect is not necessarily contrary to the ideal of legality',[816] because sometimes it is perfectly acceptable to argue that the *reasons* for the new law or the change were sufficiently transparent at the time of the events in dispute. So, even if those reasons were not binding on the court by virtue of the existing posited laws, these reasons could still be relied on by the court in a controlled manner, argues Endicott.[817]

Endicott's work presumes that some reasons can be accepted as valid reasons for the court's decision even if the posited sources of the law do not yet formulate them as valid reasons. Accordingly, we may advance Endicott's argument by distinguishing between *retrospective* acceptance of some reasons and *retroactive* lawmaking in the strict sense of retroactive imposition of reasons that were not transparent at the time of the events in dispute. And this is, arguably, how we should go about controlling the judicial activism in this arena.

Retroactive judicial lawmaking is arbitrary and uncontrolled. By contrast, retrospective acceptance of some reasons can be relatively well controlled and does not need to result in arbitrariness. The key question thus is whether the reasons in question could have been perceived as legitimate by the disputing parties at the time of the events in dispute and whether there is acceptable evidence that they should have been perceived as such. In other words, the question is whether the disputed interests were sufficiently transparent at the time of the events in dispute. This transparency question will need to be answered differently in relation to private interests than in relation to public interests because of the distinct ethical concerns that justify the protection of those interests (see also section II in chapter six). In relation to public interests, this evidence might be a previous case or a posited legal rule which clearly supports the court's judgment about the 'non-waiverability' of the protection of the matters in dispute. By contrast, the non-waiverability (and therefore the publicness) of the disputed interests will not be evidenced by the claimant's assertion about the relevance of the disputed matters for his wellbeing or by the fact that the relevant reasons were transparent to both parties but no one else.

So, for example, if you were to claim damages for queue-jumping, you would probably be able to prove that your private interests in catching the bus on which you were queuing were legitimate, that they could have been perceived as such, and (with no evidence to the contrary) that they should have been perceived as legitimate by the queue-jumper. From both yours and the queue-jumper's correlative standpoints, these private interests as potential reasons for the award would thus not be arbitrary, and the award would not be uncontrolled. It is another question

[815] ibid 318 (emphasis in original).
[816] ibid 317.
[817] *cf* ibid 325.

whether the reasons are good enough to change the law, but the court would not act unreasonably if it resorted to those reasons and retrospectively accepted them. This is because the existence of your private interest in the disputed matters and the legitimacy of their protection will ultimately be based on interpersonal correlative reasons.

If, however, you submitted that the court should hold the defendant liable for queue-jumping on the basis of non-correlative reasons of public interest, you or the court would need to identify some evidence not based on the relationship between the claimant and the defendant. And you would need to prove that such public interest in the disputed matters existed at the time of the defendant's queue-jumping and that the public interest could have been perceived as such by any member of the public. As shall be clear, this burden will be typically much harder to discharge. Once we start looking at non-correlative considerations, there can be many arguments on both sides. For example, we can argue that whilst queuing is considered publicly beneficial, people jump queues all the time and are not sued or even held liable for such behaviour. Besides, not everyone who lives in the UK is familiar with the social habit of queuing, and since this habit is not clearly posited anywhere in the law,[818] it would be hard to prove that a legitimate public interest against queue-jumping existed at the time of the alleged wrong.

This example illustrates a crucial difference between private and public interests in their role of retrospectively accepted reasons for the award. The public interest in the disputed matters must be transparent at the time of the events in dispute regardless of the private relationship between the parties. Without evidence that those interests were, at least in principle, sufficiently transparent to any member of the public (and not just the two disputing parties), their retrospective acceptance as valid reasons for the award would probably amount to arbitrary and, in this sense, impermissible retroactive law-making.

Overall, we can thus see that while the courts may be expected actively to identify public interests, this does not mean that such judicial activity is to be unconstrained or uncontrolled. Neither does it mean that the courts should be allowed to award public interest damages entirely of their own motion. At best, we can say that these awards are discretionary in the sense that there is always an element of deliberation involved in the decision of whether the matters in dispute merit the remedy. As put by the House of Lords in *George Mitchell (Chesterhall) Ltd v Finney Lock Seeds Ltd*, albeit in a slightly different context,

> [i]t would not be accurate to describe such a decision as an exercise of discretion. But a decision [which will have] in common with the exercise of a discretion, that, in having regard to the various matters, … the court must entertain a whole range of considerations, put them in the scales on one side or the other, and decide at the end of the day on which side the balance comes down. There will sometimes be room for a legitimate

[818] One may argue that the TfL Byelaws (n 696) only express a local social habit of queuing in London.

> difference of judicial opinion as to what the answer should be, where it will be impossible to say that one view is demonstrably wrong and the other demonstrably right. It must follow, in my view, that, when asked to review such a decision on appeal, the appellate court should treat the original decision with the utmost respect and refrain from interference with it unless satisfied that it proceeded upon some erroneous principle or was plainly and obviously wrong.[819]

This means that the courts may decide not to award public interest damages in situations where the 'publicness' of the matters in dispute was not sufficiently transparent at the time of the events in dispute or, building on section I, whenever the court would conclude that the public interest in those matters would not be irreversibly damaged or put in doubt if the award was not made.

III. Further Implications

While some implications of the public interest analysis of NCDs have already been discussed, the impact of the public interest analysis of NCDs on English law still deserves attention. The testing of the hypothetical waiver method in sections V and VI of chapter five gave rise to further questions and complexities which, if left without any commentary, could present a puzzle for those who will want to adopt the public interest account of NCDs but would not have the time to think those implications through. Let us therefore now turn to five very specific implications that emerge from the analysis in those sections and from the interpretive theory of NCDs *qua* public interest damages.

First, the analysis implies that the courts may in theory award public interest damages even if the successful claimant did not advance that specific remedy in the claim. For example, in *Drane v Evangelou* Lord Denning argued that punitive damages can be awarded even if not pleaded by the successful claimant.[820] In the light of CPR r 16.4(1), which requires the claimant to state exactly whether and why he thinks punitive damages should be awarded, Lord Denning's statement seems highly controversial and outdated. But one may argue that the CPR requirement to ask for punitive damages does not imply a prohibition from awarding punitive damages if those are not pleaded.[821] Indeed, the CPR do not explicitly prevent the court from making a judgment in a form different than the form pleaded by the claimant, provided that the claimant successfully establishes a cause of action. In fact, most of the recent awards of nominal damages and all awards of contemptuous damages (if we accept their existence as a separate category – which was rejected in chapter four) are also not the result of what was originally pleaded by

[819] *George Mitchell (Chesterhall) Ltd v Finney Lock Seeds Ltd* [1983] 2 AC 803 (HL) 815, 816.

[820] eg, *Drane v Evangelou* (n 240) 458, 459. See also *Broome v Cassell & Co* (n 600) 378G–378H, 382, 399H (Lord Denning MR).

[821] But *cf* s 36(5) of the Crime and Courts Act 2013, which may be regarded as a special rule: 'Exemplary damages may be awarded under this section only if they are claimed.'

the claimant in those cases. Besides, as we have seen, the courts may be expected to be more active in identifying the 'publicness' of the relevant reasons. Arguably, they may also be expected to be more active in deciding when a public interest award should be made. At the very least, on the public interest analysis, there is no obvious a priori reason why such a form of proactive approach by the court would be unjust, provided that the constraints identified in section II are observed.

Second, by implication, the claimant should not be allowed to obtain interest on the award from the time between the events in dispute and the payment of the public interest award. This is because one cannot plausibly claim to be kept out of money in relation to public interest damages. Indeed, the courts do not seem to award interest on public interest damages. A case law survey suggests, for instance, that there are no orders of interest on nominal or punitive damages.[822] In *2 Travel Group*, this question was addressed explicitly. The tribunal asked whether the claimant should be entitled to interest on the sum of punitive damages. The answer was in the negative, because the tribunal thought that it cannot possibly compensate the claimant for being kept out of his money in relation to the award of punitive damages.[823] It may thus be argued that whenever the courts would award pre-judgment interest on public interest damages, then such an award would be unjustified and, at least in relation to punitive damages, conflict with the authority in *2 Travel Group*.

Third, if public interest damages and compensatory awards are driven by distinct ethical concerns and respond to distinct kinds of damage, then one may wonder whether the 'if but only if' condition of punitive damages is justified (ie, the condition that requires that punitive damages be awarded only if compensation is not sufficient to punish the defendant). Compensatory damages may produce 'punitive' effects, but the punishment would not respond to the same penalty-worthy damage. So, it follows that the punitive effect of compensatory damages should be irrelevant for the justification of punitive damages, unless of course we admit that compensatory damages can in fact (especially in cases of aggravated and general damages) represent hidden awards of punitive damages. One way to resolve this tension is by distinguishing between the overlapping effects of remedies and their overlapping justifications. The analysis advanced in this book therefore helps us to understand why there cannot be any actual or potential overlap between public interest damages and compensatory awards as regards their justifications, although there may be an overlap as regards their effects. This means, inter alia, compensatory damages should limit the availability of punitive damages only insofar as compensation responds to the public interest

[822] In relation to vindicatory damages, *cf* a recent Privy Council (Bahamas) decision *Ngumi v AG of the Bahamas* (n 368) [3], [88]–[91] where it was confirmed (for different reasons than reasons of public interest) that interest on general damages, including vindicatory damages, should not be assessed from the date when the cause of action arose but rather from the date of the claimant's writ. Otherwise, the Privy Council stated, '[t]he award of interest … would have over-compensated the appellant' (ibid [91]).

[823] *2 Travel Group Plc (in liq) v Cardiff City Transport Services Ltd* (n 242) [597].

damage (which seems unlikely). It also means that nominal damages should be available independently of whether compensatory damages are awarded, even though, pragmatically, compensatory damages can in effect (though not in principle) discharge the declaratory function of nominal damages. Such a change to the conditions of availability of nominal damages would amount to a significant alteration to the existing law, although technically there is no strict ban on nominal damages in addition to compensatory awards.[824]

Fourth, if there are multiple claimants to whom the non-compensatory remedy should be awarded, then the award should in principle always be divided equally between them. The violations of public interests by the defendant imply that the remedy and its quantum should be individualised only with respect to the defendant's position and the gravity of the wrong as such, not with respect to the claimant's position, because the violation of the claimants' liberty rights will typically be uniform. As stated by Lord Dyson in *Lumba*,

> [w]here there is more than one victim of a tortfeasor's conduct, one award of damages should be made which should be shared between the victims, rather than separate awards of exemplary damages for each individual. This is because the purpose of the award is to punish conduct rather than compensate the claimants.[825]

So, if no private interest can justify why any of the claimants would deserve a larger or a smaller share in the total quantum of the non-compensatory award, the award should be split equally. In this sense, the basic compensatory principle that damages are an individual and personal remedy does not apply to public interest damages. For example, in *AT & Ors v Dulghieru & Anor*[826] all claimants were exposed to grave physical violence and trafficked from Moldova to the UK for sexual exploitation and prostitution, and although the story and individual suffering of each of the four exploited women varied, the award of punitive damages was split equally between them. More recently, then, the Court of Appeal in *Rees v Commissioner of Police of the Metropolis*[827] also confirmed that the award of punitive damages should be distributed equally between all claimants.[828]

Fifth, in cases of public interest damages, the courts should be inclined to describe the events in dispute as 'X committed a wrong', rather than 'X committed a wrong against Y' or 'Y was wronged by X'. This seems to be implied by the fact that most public interest damages cases can be explained as cases of wrongdoing against rights *qua* categories, not *qua* individual liberty rights. To put the point more precisely, these are wrongs against the public interest in those rights.

[824] See more in ch 6, section IV.
[825] *Lumba* (n 18) [167] (referring to *Riches v News Group Newspapers Ltd* [1986] QB 256 (CA)). See also *Holownia v Secretary of State for the Home Department* [2019] EWHC 794 (Admin) [77]: 'Unless all claims are quantified at the same time, the true punitive effect of an award of exemplary damages cannot properly be calibrated or assessed.'
[826] *AT & Ors v Dulghieru & Anor* (n 271).
[827] *Rees v Commissioner of Police of the Metropolis* [2021] EWCA Civ 49.
[828] ibid [55].

In *Alexander*, for instance, it was stated that the court should sanction the fact that the defendant had committed an unlawful racial discrimination, ie, that the category had been infringed.[829] The wrongdoing against the right *qua* category was considered worthy of a non-compensatory remedy. Arguably, it would thus be right for the courts to emphasise these defendant-oriented and wrongs-based considerations in all cases of public interest damages in order to avoid any misunderstandings as to the nature of the justifying reasons for the eventual award.

This last implication generally relates to the problem of transparency in the law of NCDs. To the extent that NCDs are justified by damage to public interests, there is a case for the courts and parties to refer to those considerations expressly as 'public interests' because that would allow everyone involved to engage with those considerations properly, on the basis of the correct ethical grounds (see chapter six, section II). Thus, if we want to achieve full transparency, then the CPR should be amended to include a specific requirement that the claimant expressly identifies the relevant public interest considerations in the particulars of his claim whenever he seeks public interest damages.

IV. Possible Objections

There are several objections that need to be addressed before we can conclude that the public interest damages theory is the right way forward. First, commentators such as Sayer might object that damages should not be 'recoverable by a private person for an injury to the publick',[830] because everyone is to some degree injured by an injury to the public, and this could lead to an 'infinity of actions'.[831] Yet as we saw in chapters four to six, public interest damages are only available if the public interest has been infringed in respect of the claimant's private liberty rights. In other words, while everyone is to some degree injured by an injury to a public interest, only those whose rights and liberties have been damaged directly by the defendant's conduct can seek the remedy. A mere bystander who himself did not suffer any civil wrong cannot bring a successful action against the tortfeasor. Thus, Sayer's objection cannot succeed because public interest damages are in fact only available in relation to very specific violations of public interests. The consequentialist objection about the risk that there will be an infinity of actions therefore does not withstand scrutiny.

Second, some would argue that the protection of public interests, and especially the role of punishment in tort and contract, is problematic given the lower

[829] *Alexander v Home Office* (n 610) 979E.

[830] J Sayer, *The Law of Damages* (London, Strahan and Woodfall, 1770) 1. According to J Taliadoros, 'Thirteenth-Century Origins of Punitive or Exemplary Damages: The Statute of Westminster I (1275) and Roman Law' (2018) 39 *Journal of Legal History* 278, 279, the publication by Sayer is the first English textbook on damages.

[831] Sayer (n 830) 2.

procedural safeguards that these areas of private law offer in comparison with the safeguards available in public law disputes. But this objection was rejected in the literature (in my view successfully) because the objection is not sufficiently specific.[832] If we want to criticise punitive damages or other public interest damages on the basis of insufficient safeguards, we should equally criticise a host of other private law tools and institutions that in effect promote some sort of punishment or that protect public interests. At best, this objection would imply that we should *prefer* public law tools when it comes to punishment and protection of public interests. But it does not imply that we should *ban* private law enforcement and private law protection of public interests. The practical implication of this preference could be that the courts should award public interest damages if and only if other public law remedies do not already rectify the public interest infringement (which is in effect an argument that is concerned with double-counting). But this preference does not imply that the courts should not award public interest damages at all.

Besides, given that damages do not impose any harsh physical detriment on the wrongdoer and do not directly deprive the wrongdoer of his liberty (as in the case of imprisonment in criminal law), it is hard to see any convincing reason why the public interests cannot be protected via private claims by individuals. The 'publicness' does not imply any direct use of physical force or other harsh detriment against which the defendant would need to be safeguarded by way of criminal or administrative procedures.

Third, some might object that public interest damages amount to 'an unmerited windfall'[833] to the claimant. This objection, however, also does not justify the conclusion that we should get rid of such awards. The 'windfall' criticism is rooted in the assumption that damages awards cannot be legitimately justified by other than correlative reasons, which assumption was rejected earlier in the book.[834] The question 'Why *should* the claimant (rather than anyone else) obtain the award?' is not in fact a question of unjustified windfall (as the windfall objection would suggest) but a question of regulatory design. So again, we may *prefer* some other remedies and sanctions in response to the public interest violation, but it does not mean that public interest damages are an unjustified remedy or that the award unjustly enriches the claimant.

[832] Goudkamp and Katsampouka (n 416). See also PS Atiyah, *The Damages Lottery* (Oxford, Hart Publishing, 1997) ch 7; R Williams, 'Criminal Law in England and Wales: Just Another Form of Regulatory Tool?' in M Dyson and B Vogel (eds), *The Limits of Criminal Law: Anglo-German Concepts and Principles* (Cambridge, Intersentia, 2020) 220; and E Bant, W Courtney and J Goudkamp (eds), *Punishment and Private Law* (Oxford, Hart Publishing, 2021).

[833] *Broome v Cassell & Co Ltd (No 1)* (n 250) 1114. Similarly, *Thompson v Commissioner of Police of the Metropolis* (n 273) 517; *Hussain v New Taplow Paper Mills* (n 274) 523; *Smoker v London Fire Authority* (n 274) 533. See also *Ashley v Chief Constable of Sussex Police* (n 19) [4] (Lord Bingham) and [24] (Lord Scott), both of them acknowledging that the claimant's right to pursue a damages claim even if this would amount to what others may call a 'windfall' because it cannot bring the claimant any compensation. To the contrary, see ibid [131] (Lord Neuberger).

[834] See ch 2, section II, ch 3, section III and ch 6, section II.

The core question should be whether the claimant *can* justly demand the award for himself (regardless of whether there are better regulatory tools to protect the interests in dispute). In line with the analysis that has been advanced throughout this book, we can answer this question in the affirmative. We can say that the claimant *can* justly demand the award because of the necessary link between the claimant's private interests (liberty rights) and the relevant public interests (the protection of which gives rise to the liberty rights). In other words, the claimant is a victim rather than a bystander, and so he is justified in making the claim and obtaining the award. In this light, we can at least appreciate the force of an argument according to which public interest damages are a good response to violations of public interests because it is justifiable to reward the claimant (on the merits of the case) for his stepping up and advocating for what is beneficial for the functioning of our society. So if a private individual brings an action for public interest damages, the underlying distributive criteria behind the public interest protection justify the obtainment of the award by the claimant.[835] This argument fits well with our understanding of damages and with the idea that monetary sanctions and remedies give effect to the underlying norms of justice, including the norms of distributive justice. The windfall objection therefore also does not withstand scrutiny.

Fourth, even if you agree that important public interests should be protected by *some* remedies and quite apart from the procedural safeguards associated with various regulatory solutions, it is far from clear that the remedy of *damages* is the right response to these public interest violations. In principle, there may be a host of public law sanctions or other remedies that could also protect the public interests infringed. For example, a declaratory judgment could serve the same purpose as nominal damages. So why should we regard damages, and public interest damages in particular, as the right or even the preferred remedy for violations of public interests?

From a regulatory design perspective, public interest damages seem to be a reasonable (even if not necessarily flawless) response to certain public interest violations. It can be pointed out, for example, that public interest damages are typically very low (nominal, contemptuous and vindicatory awards) or relatively infrequent (punitive and disgorgement damages). Thus, it would not be cost-effective to try to set up a public enforcement mechanism that would take over the role of public interest damages. Indeed, Chapman and Trebilcock similarly argue that punitive damages *should* be enforced through private law institutions such as the law of tort, if we accept the argument from administrative efficiency. Their argument goes like this: even if the wrongful conduct warrants state action, there may be 'serious budgetary constraints on public enforcement'[836] which may

[835] KY Törnblom and DR Jonsson, 'Distribution vs. Retribution: The Perceived Justice of the Contribution and Equality Principles for Cooperative and Competitive Relationships' (1987) 30 *Acta Sociologica* 25.
[836] Chapman and Trebilcock (n 287) 779.

justify the second-best enforcement model, ie, the private law model. Chapman and Trebilcock explore that position in more detail and go across various factors that might be relevant to this enforcement architecture to conclude that there are strong law-and-economics reasons to prefer the private law model.[837]

Interestingly, the argument from administrative efficiency seems to have taken root in English law as well. In *Muuse*, for example, it was precisely this argument that was used by the court to explain why it is acceptable to give the claimant the extra money in the form of punitive damages even though it was recognised that the payment could be easily seen as a windfall at the public expense.[838]

Further, the regulatory choice to enforce the protection of public interests via damages has some advantages over other regulatory solutions. In some sense, the non-compensatory measure might be seen as justified prize money, ie, a reward for those who are able and willing publicly to challenge the wrongful conduct. This could also help us to address the 'windfall' objection. The public interest remedy could be seen as a bonus for the claimant's acting 'as guardian of the public interest'.[839] The laws concerning whistleblowing[840] or the historical rules regarding *qui tam* actions and *actiones populares*,[841] are examples where such justifications took hold because the benefits generated by the permissibility of private enforcement of public interests were considered bigger than the eventual downsides. Historically speaking, private individuals were empowered to protect public interests via damages in various forms, including via actions against public service agencies.[842]

The public interest damages theory thus should not be seen as something particularly new in this respect. Indeed, in the US, for example, there is a renewed interest in *qui tam* actions in the context of collective harms to privacy, as a possible vehicle to redress the kinds of injustice that are not wholly or predominantly grounded in individual rights.[843] If we wanted to criticise public interest damages, it would thus make sense to do so on the basis of the motivations they create for individuals when bringing their public interest claims in court, and not on the basis that they amount to a windfall or that they are not the right regulatory design choice.

[837] ibid 786–98. Similarly, see WM Landes and RA Posner, 'The Private Enforcement of Law' (1975) 4 *Journal of Legal Studies* 1, 39 and 40.

[838] *Muuse* (n 678) [64], [77], [82].

[839] *Blake* (n 8) 288G.

[840] See, eg, T Nyreröd and G Spagnolo, 'Myths and Numbers on Whistleblower Rewards' (2019) *Regulation and & Governance* (online). See also D Lewis, 'Stigma and Whistleblowing: Should Punitive Damages be Available in Retaliation Cases?' (2022) 51 *Industrial Law Journal* 62.

[841] See, eg, JR Beck, 'The False Claims Act and the English Eradication of *Qui Tam* Legislation' (2000) 78 *North Carolina Law Review* 539 and PP Mercer, 'The Citizen's Right to Sue in the Public Interest: The Roman Actio Popularis Revisited' (1983) 21 *University of Western Ontario Law Review* 89.

[842] Pound (n 175) 342–44. In more detail on this historical feature of the law, see, eg, J Bessler, 'The Public Interest and the Unconstitutionality of Private Prosecutors' (1994) 47 *Arkansas Law Review* 511, 515–16.

[843] P Ormerod, 'Privacy Quit Tam' (2022) 98 *Notre Dame Law Review* 267.

Fifth, one may object that the theory of NCDs *qua* public interest damages should be rejected because it has no real prospect of being implemented in practice, given the established understanding of the doctrines governing the award of NCDs. However, we do not need to abandon the existing doctrines in order to start applying and developing those doctrines as part of a unitary domain of public interest damages. By implementing the public interest analysis, the courts would be able to give effect to public interests in precisely the same situations as they currently do (as was demonstrated in sections V and VI in chapter five). The consistency of this book's approach with the existing law was also explained in sections III (concerning the co-ordination of different forms of public interest damages), and IV (concerning incompatibility of remedies) of chapter six, and in sections I (concerning the not-as-of-right nature of public interest damages) and II (concerning the limits on the courts' supposed discretion) of this chapter, although we also saw that the public interest analysis suggests that NCDs – especially nominal damages – should in principle be more widely available, including in relation to negligence and in addition to compensatory awards. That said, and coupled with the CPR requirement for managing disputes in a cost-effective way, the courts would still be free not to award public interest damages, if they thought this was the right thing to do in the circumstances. In other words, the courts would not need to make the non-compensatory award whenever they would believe that the events in dispute do not justify the remedy. And so, in effect, the application of the public interest analysis would not require the courts to materially depart from the existing law because the no-as-of-right nature of NCDs gives the courts more room for deliberation than we currently think the courts have in this pocket of the law. This too justifies the claim that if courts started to apply and develop the law of NCDs in line with the public interest analysis, it would not lead to direct confrontation with the principles behind the existing doctrines or with the doctrines themselves.

The public interest account of NCDs is actually consistent with what the courts are already trying to do and thus can be implemented in practice. As was argued in this book, the courts are already giving effect to public interest protection when they award many NCDs, even if they do not always say so expressly. In adopting the public interest analysis and in approaching public interest damages collectively, the courts would merely start discussing the reasons behind these awards in new terms, and this could facilitate a transparent debate about what is good for the functioning society and what should be protected *qua* public interest. By contrast, in adopting the public interest analysis, the courts would not revolutionise the law of damages by creating an entirely new (or unified) doctrinal category of 'public interest damages'. The fifth objection, therefore, also cannot withstand scrutiny.

As was stated in chapter one, the theory advanced in this book is interpretive. Accordingly, the acceptance of public interest damages – as a category – into our law only requires us to reform our understanding of the law of NCDs to make it more compatible with the reasons that justify those awards and to give effect to the implications of the public interest theory of NCDs. We do not need to change the technical doctrines that control the award of NCD in order to start interpreting them as part of a coherent field of public interest damages. Instead, it will suffice to reform our thinking about NCDs and our thinking about the rules that govern those awards and their assessment. And probably the first step to do so would be to acknowledge the foundational distinction between, on the one hand, measures of damages giving effect to non-rights-based considerations and, on the other hand, measures of damages giving effect to individual rights.

V. Conclusion

Once we accept that some NCDs are justified by violations of public interests and that they significantly overlap in their justifications, it makes sense to try to develop them collectively and in contrast with compensatory awards. In this chapter, we saw how we should develop them and how we should translate the findings about public interest damages into the law governing their award. In particular, we saw that:

(i) public interest damages should not be available as of right,
(ii) the courts should play a more active role when identifying the relevant public interests that were sufficiently transparent to members of the public (not only the parties) at the time of the events in dispute,
(iii) and that the public interest analysis should have implications for:
  a. the availability of the remedy even when the claimant does not seek it,
  b. interest on the award,
  c. incompatibility of damages with overlapping justifying reasons, rather than those with overlapping actual or perceived effects,
  d. the distribution of the remedy amongst multiple claimants and
  e. the language used to describe the events in dispute.

Finally, we saw that the main objections to the public interest account of NCDs (infinity of actions, low procedural safeguards, windfall to the claimant, deference to other regulatory solutions, fit with the existing doctrines) can be successfully rejected. Importantly, we saw that it is feasible to implement the public interest analysis in practice without compromising any of the core tenets of the existing doctrines.

In this regard, we need to keep in mind that the public interest analysis only tells us whether and when a non-compensatory award would be justified. It does not tell us whether the courts must award the public interest remedy, let alone whether they must award the remedy in any specific quantum. This means that the courts are free to decide not to award public interest damages in situations where the award would not, in their view, be justified by any relevant public interest violation. Such an approach would give better effect to the true reasons that justify non-compensatory measures of damages, it would not contradict the existing doctrines, and it would not violate the claimant's rights because, as was argued, the measure of public interest damages is not grounded in the claimant's private rights in the first place. So whenever the court would conclude that the 'publicness' of the matters in dispute was not sufficiently transparent at the time of the events in dispute, or whenever the court would conclude that the protection of that interest would not be irreversibly damaged or put in doubt if the award was not made, then no award of public interest damages needs to be made. Similarly, the parties may want to challenge the legitimacy of public interest damages awards from these positions. This would, in effect, help the courts and parties to mirror and achieve the same or substantially the same results that the law arrives at under the current doctrines. The most significant difference would be in how the courts and the parties would rationalise the law and those same results.

8

Conclusion

The book sought to understand non-compensatory damages (NCDs) in the English law of tort and contract. The chief claim of the book is that many types of damages that are traditionally labelled as NCDs can be collectively defined as 'public interest damages'. As such, the book challenges the orthodox view that NCDs are no more than a series of disparate remedies. The definition is based on the insight that NCDs are justified by damage to public interests, that they very significantly overlap in terms of their justifications and that compensatory measures of damages are not justified by the same reasons. To be sure, this insight is largely interpretive because NCDs are only sometimes justified by considerations of public interest expressly so labelled. Yet as this book shows, we can plausibly and accurately describe the law's own stated justificatory reasons as public interest considerations, and so the definitory claim stands.

A few qualifying statements need to be added to the definition of NCDs *qua* public interest damages. A closer inspection of the current usage of the term 'NCDs' shows that this term does not have any stable meaning. That creates a difficulty when it comes to defining NCDs, because it may be unclear what is actually being defined. On the one hand, primary sources use the term NCDs to describe awards that stand largely in contrast with (rather than alongside) compensatory damages – this concerns punitive, nominal, vindicatory and disgorgement damages. On the other hand, secondary sources traditionally associate the term with all non-loss-based awards that stand in contrast with as well as next to loss-based compensation – this concerns all the previous four categories and, additionally, contemptuous and restitutionary damages.

The book only claims that there is some normative unity amongst NCDs in the first sense, not the second. To disambiguate the different understandings of NCDs, it is recommended to use the term 'public interest damages' when referring to the normatively unified class of NCDs. To be sure, the normative unity does not mean that the non-compensatory quantum of punitive, nominal, vindicatory and disgorgement damages would or should be assessed by a single technique or that the doctrines governing the award of such NCDs would or should be identical. Rather, the claim about the normative unity means that all public interest damages give effect to the same types of justificatory reason that clearly separate these awards from compensatory damages. This supports, inter alia, the case for a collective and co-ordinated approach to public interest damages.

Importantly, it was argued that the considerations of public interest attract distinct ethical concerns. The arguments and evidence in support of public interest awards should thus be evaluated against different criteria than those we use to award compensation. This special approach to public interest damages is rooted in a fundamental divide between two types of reason that can justify measures of damages: (i) justifications giving effect to individual rights or rights arising from the violation of such rights (ie, damage to private interests), and (ii) non-rights-based justifications (ie, damage to public interests). This divide, the book contends, should be acknowledged by the law because it is real and because it has important doctrinal implications. In fact, it was suggested that, for the purposes of defining, organising and justifying NCDs, this divide is central.

Interestingly, we saw that damage to private interests is the key justifying reason not only for compensatory damages but also for other awards made on the *restitutio in integrum* principle, including contemptuous and restitutionary damages. The definition of NCDs *qua* public interest damages thus puts NCDs in sharp contrast not only with compensatory damages but also with some other NCDs, depending on how broadly we understand the term NCDs. This internal tension within the NCDs category can be explained by reference to the unstable use of the term NCDs in the literature, meaning that the interpretive theory of NCDs 'fits' the law, although it does not 'fit' the literature. Indeed, the public interest theory of NCDs was shown to be descriptively accurate when it comes to all awards that primary sources discuss as NCDs. To this extent, we might say that the theory meets the 'fit' criterion of a successful theory of an area of law.

However, the fit of the theory of NCDs *qua* public interest damages with the existing law should not be overstated because some other tensions have emerged from the analysis. For example, the label nominal damages proved to vacillate between compensatory and non-compensatory interpretations because the courts sometimes use the label for nominally small awards of compensation. This makes it impossible to claim that the public interest damages theory fits with virtually all 'nominal damages' awards, although it is still true that the theory fits with nominal damages as a category (if we take seriously the claim that this category is not compensatory). The corollary of the public interest theory of NCDs is thus that we need to pay more attention to the internal unity of the existing categories of damages and to focus more on the justifying reasons for individual measures of damages than on how those measures are labelled.

The 'coherence' of the theory of NCDs *qua* public interest damages springs from the analytical framework identified in chapters two and three. That framework allowed us to analyse all damages at the same level of abstraction. Thus, the coherence of the analysis is guaranteed by the research methods deployed in the book. In fact, the requirements of coherence and consistency have led to some interesting doctrinal implications. For example, we saw that the supposed doctrinal boundaries between the existing categories of damages should be re-assessed in view of the significant overlapping among the substantive reasons behind individual kinds of public interest damages. We also saw that some of the existing NCDs categories are not themselves internally unified or clearly delineated. Indeed, if we accept that established categories of damages are not framed (or at least not transparently framed) according to the divide between the two fundamental justifications, it should come as no surprise that the normative unity of some of the existing categories may be put in doubt by the present analysis. According to this book's normative conclusions, this lack of normative unity is problematic and should be fixed because public interest awards attract very distinctive ethical concerns, and they should be approached differently from how we approach compensatory remedies. This concerns not only individual types of NCDs but, for example, also awards of general damages which seem occasionally to operate as hidden awards of NCDs.

If, as the book recommends, we decide to accept the theory of NCDs *qua* public interest damages, we should take on board the doctrinal implications that the coherence of the theory requires. In particular, if we accept the theory, then it seems to follow that: (i) public interest damages should not be available as of right, (ii) their availability and quantum should be co-ordinated to avoid double-counting and unjustified differences between the awards, and (iii) the courts should be more active when determining the public interest in the disputed matters, and they should go beyond the parties' arguments by, for example, employing the hypothetical waiver method when exploring the availability of public interest damages.

Probably the most contentious of these implications is that public interest damages should not be available as of right. It is not clear whether this implication fits with the law as it stands. Section I of chapter seven addressed this tension in more detail by showing that the as-of-right nature of different forms of NCDs is not as clearly established in the primary sources as we may think. This, in turn, has created the possibility to reconcile the stated implication with the existing doctrines by way of showing that the doctrines are still in need of rationalisation and that the public interest theory can help us to satisfy that need. For example, if (at least some) nominal damages are not available as of right, then the public interest analysis of NCDs would be consistent with (at least part of) this doctrinal category, although it would also call for an acknowledgement of the two distinctly justified remedies that can be found behind the 'nominal damages' label: the correlatively and non-correlatively justified awards of nominal damages.

Further, the public interest analysis implies that non-compensatory nominal damages should be available more broadly than they currently are (including in relation to a breach of duty in negligence, provided that the claimant would prove his loss but would only seek nominal damages as a remedy) and that a relevant interference with *any* right not acquired as a result of the claimant's choice should in principle be seen as a good justification for an award of NCDs. This would be a significant alteration to the existing law. That said, given the not-as-of-right nature of public interest damages, the effects of this alteration would hardly result in a material change to the outcomes of legal disputes, as was argued. As such, these potentially revolutionary implications should not pose a difficulty to acceptance of the public interest analysis by the legal community.

Several other implications were identified in this book. Put briefly, the public interest analysis also requires us to re-examine some of the more technical questions, such as the availability of the remedy even when the claimant does not seek it, the availability of interest on the award of public interest damages, the overlapping of public interest damages among each other and their overlapping with public law sanctions, the distribution of the remedy amongst multiple claimants and the correct language used to describe the defendant's harmful conduct. Also, it surfaced that punitive damages should not be constrained by whether or not compensation is capable of achieving punitive *effects*, but only by whether or not compensation is capable of responding to the underlying damage to the public interest (which is unlikely unless we admit that compensation can be a hidden award of punitive damages).

The 'morality' of the theory was largely discussed in chapters six and seven. We saw how the protection of public interests by way of damages awards can be justified and that, unlike compensatory damages, public interest damages are governed by the norms of distributive justice. And while it was acknowledged that public interest damages might not be an optimal regulatory solution, it is still a morally appealing and justified response to violations of certain public interests. For example, thanks to NCDs, private individuals can actively participate in matters of public significance and play an important role in co-determining what is regarded as good for the functioning of our society. This kind of participation is, I think, intrinsically a good thing. And since the objections to the morality of the theory of NCDs *qua* public interest damages and to our acceptance of the theory were dismissed in Chapter 7, it can be concluded that the theory meets the 'morality' criterion.

Finally, let us turn to 'transparency'. Insofar as the theory of NCDs *qua* public interest damages is an interpretive theory, it is inevitable that the suggested interpretation does not simply repeat the law's internal stated explanations and justifications of NCDs and the language used by the law in that context. That said, we saw that some cases use the term 'public interests' when justifying measures of NCDs and that in other cases the relevant justifications for NCDs, even though not expressly labelled as public interests, can be accurately described as public interest considerations. The theory of NCDs advanced in this book therefore does not contradict the law's own language. Rather, it merely finds a common characteristic of the reasons used in the cases and required by the law. Thus, the 'transparency' criterion is also satisfied.

It can be argued, of course, that the law's own transparency should be improved. But this argument does not undermine the theory of NCDs *qua* public interest damages. Rather, it is an implication that stems from the descriptive observation that the law sometimes does not clearly separate the compensatory and non-compensatory aspects of damages awards. To this end, if we want to increase the law's transparency, we should adopt the public interest analysis and justify these damages by express reference to damage to either public or private interests. This, in turn, would help us better to control all the various awards of public interest damages in our law, including the hidden non-compensatory awards that are occasionally made by courts under the banner of general damages, for example. We may even want to amend the Civil Procedure Rules to include a specific requirement that the claimant expressly identifies the relevant public interest considerations in the particulars of his claim.

Once we begin to discuss the relevant considerations in terms of public interests and once the courts begin to be more active in identifying the matters of public interest, we will be in a better position to have a transparent debate about those matters. Importantly, we will also be in a better position to avoid missteps in our arguments about whether the exceptional remedy can indeed serve its non-compensatory function in a given dispute. In any event, to the extent that judges are in effect making pronouncements about what is deemed to be good for the functioning of our society, I believe that we should want to have this transparent debate about public interests.

In conclusion, it is submitted that the theory of public interest damages is a successful interpretive theory of the existing categories of NCDs as it meets the key evaluative criteria of 'fit', 'coherence', 'morality' and 'transparency' as introduced in chapter one. The theory helps us to see how certain measures of damages can protect important public interests. As such, it helps us to see how these remedies reinforce the law's role as a catalyst for societal development and cohesion. Not all publicly important values and interests are captured by the existing legislation, and the appreciation that English law allows citizens and judges to participate in the discourse about these public interests via awards of damages is thus an advantage. Public interest damages can help us better protect various emerging aspects of human well-being, including those facilitated by artificial intelligence systems[844] or those threatened by various forms of large-scale online data processing.[845] In the age of automated systems and online communication, there is now a bigger range of systemic risks which are experienced by private individuals, in everyday interactions, yet which are not within the purview of classical public law. If what it takes to tackle some of these issues is simply that we reinterpret, not change, the law of non-compensatory damages and that we learn how to deploy the hypothetical waiver method, then it should be easy to welcome the public interest analysis of NCDs. Its adoption will be a justified step forward.

My point is not that we should start weaponising NCDs to enforce all sorts of public interests but that we should adopt a collective approach to public interest damages so that we can protect those interests fairly and transparently. After all, it is arguably in the public interest that we do so. Should the courts or others decide to adopt the public interest analysis, there is still a lot to be worked out,

[844] See, eg, FA Pasquale, 'Data-Informed Duties in AI Development' (2019) 119 *Columbia Law Review* 1917 (proposing that punitive damages be awarded for repeated or wilful relying on faulty data in AI development and deployment).

[845] See, eg, J Skillen, 'Exemplary Damages and Misuse of Private Information' (2023) 28 *Comms Law* 158 (arguing in favour of recognising exemplary damages as a head of damages for misuse of private information); LH Scholz, 'Privacy and the Punitive Impulse' (2025) 77 *Baylor Law Review* 336 (arguing that privacy violations are, to a significant extent, similar in kind to crimes, ie, to public wrongs, and that this justifies why they can be remedied by punitive damages or even criminalised).

especially as regards the appropriate quantification techniques that would apply to all these awards and as regards the common conditions for their availability. That is because, in view of the public interest analysis, some of the existing doctrinal distinctions between separate types of NCDs might no longer be seen as desirable or sound. These issues should be addressed after we accept the theory of NCDs *qua* public interest damages. A large portion of this book suggested how we might go about doing that, and so we are in a good place to start.

BIBLIOGRAPHY

Addison, CG, *Wrongs and Their Remedies: Being a Treatise on the Law of Torts*, 2nd edn (London, Stevens and Haynes, 1864)

Alexander, L and Moore, M, 'Deontological Ethics' in EN Zalta and U Nodelman (eds), *The Stanford Encyclopedia of Philosophy* (Winter 2024 Edn)

Allison, JWF, *A Continental Distinction in the Common Law: A Historical and Comparative Perspective on English Public Law* (Oxford, OUP, 2000)

Aplin, T, 'The Future of Breach of Confidence and the Protection of Privacy' (2007) 7 *Oxford University Commonwealth Law Journal* 137

Aquinas, T, *Summa Theologiae*

Aristotle, *Nicomachean Ethics* (H Rackham tr, rev edn, Cambridge, MA, Harvard University Press, 2014)

Atiyah, PS, *The Damages Lottery* (Oxford, Hart Publishing, 1997)

Auckland, C and Goold, I, 'Offsetting Damages in Wrongful Conception and Birth Cases: A Way Through the Post-McFarlane Mire' (2022) 138 *LQR* 407

Ban,t E, Courtney, W and Goudkamp, J (eds), *Punishment and Private Law* (Oxford, Hart Publishing, 2021)

Barker, K, 'Private and Public: The Mixed Concept of Vindication in Torts and Private Law' in SGA Pitel, JW Neyers and E Chamberlain (eds), *Tort Law: Challenging Orthodoxy* (Oxford, Hart Publishing, 2013)

—— 'Punishment in Private Law – No Such Thing (Any More)' in E Bant, W Courtney and J Goudkamp (eds), *Punishment and Private Law* (Oxford, Hart Publishing, 2021)

Barnett, K, *Accounting for Profit for Breach of Contract: Theory and Practice* (Oxford, Hart Publishing, 2012)

Barnett, K and Harder, S, *Private Law Remedies* (Cheltenham, Edward Elgar, 2025)

Barry, B, *Political Argument* (New York, Humanities, 1967)

Barzun, CL, 'Inside-Out: Beyond the Internal/External Distinction in Legal Scholarship' (2015) 101 *Virgina Law Review* 1203

Beale, H, *Chitty on Contracts* (35th edn, incorporating 1st supplement, London, Sweet & Maxwell, 2024)

Beatson, J, '"Public" and "Private" in English Administrative Law' (1987) 103 *LQR* 34

Beatson, J, Burrows, A and Cartwright, J, *Anson's Law of Contract*, 31st edn (Oxford, OUP, 2020)

Beck, G, 'Immanuel Kant's Theory of Rights' (2006) 19 *Ratio Juris* 371

Beck, JR, 'The False Claims Act and the English Eradication of *Qui Tam* Legislation' (2000) 78 *University of North Carolina Law Review* 539

Beever, A, 'The Structure of Aggravated and Exemplary Damages' (2003) 23 *OJLS* 87

—— *Forgotten Justice: The Forms of Justice in the History of Legal and Political Theory* (Oxford, OUP, 2013)

Bell, J, 'Public Interest: Policy or Principle?' in R Brownsword (ed), *Law and the Public Interest* (Stuttgart, Franz Steiner Verlag, 1993)

Bělohlávek, A, 'Public Policy and Public Interest in International Law and EU Law' (2012) 3 *Czech Yearbook of International Law* 117

Bedke, MS, 'Explaining compensatory duties' (2010) 16 *Legal Theory* 91

Benditt, TM, 'The Public Interest' (1973) 2 *Philosophy & Public Affairs* 291

Bessler, J, 'The Public Interest and the Unconstitutionality of Private Prosecutors' (1994) 47 *Arkansas Law Review* 511

Bezemek, C and Dumbrovský, T, 'The Concept of Public Interest' in L Tichý and M Potacs (eds), *Public Interest in Law* (Cambridge, Intersentia, 2021)
Birks, P, 'Civil Wrongs: A New World', *Butterworth lectures 1990–91* (London, Butterworths, 1992)
—— 'Inconsistency between Compensation and Restitution' (1996) 112 *LQR* 375
—— 'Definition and Division: A Meditation on *Institutes* 3.13' in P Birks (ed), *The Classification of Obligations* (Oxford, Clarendon Press, 1997)
—— 'The Law of Restitution at the End of an Epoch' (1999) 28 University of Western Australia Law Review 13
—— 'Rights, Wrongs, and Remedies' (2000) 20 *OJLS* 1
—— *Unjust Enrichment*, 2nd edn (Oxford, OUP, 2005)
Blackburn, R, Tettenborn, A and Wilson, A (eds), *Halsbury's Laws of England*, 5th edn (London, Lexis-Nexis, 2019)
Blackstone, W, *The Commentaries on the Laws of England*, vol 1 in D Lemmings (ed), *The Oxford Edition of Blackstone: Commentaries on the Laws of England, Vol. 1: Of the Rights of Persons* (Oxford, OUP, 2016)
—— *The Commentaries on the Laws of England*, vol 3 in TP Gallanis (ed), *The Oxford Edition of Blackstone: Commentaries on the Laws of England, Vol. 3: Of Private Wrongs* (Oxford, OUP, 2016)
Bowers, RD, *A Treatise on the Law of Waiver* (Dever, WH Courtright Publishing, 1914)
Brennan, C, *Tort Law Concentrate: Law Revision and Study Guide*, 7th edn (Oxford, OUP, 2024)
Brownsword, R (ed), *Law and the Public Interest* (Stuttgart, Franz Steiner Verlag, 1993)
Burrows, A, *Remedies for Torts and Breach of Contract*, 1st edn (London, Butterworths, 1987)
—— *Remedies for Torts and Breach of Contract*, 2nd edn (London, Butterworths, 1994)
—— 'Reforming Exemplary Damages: Expansion or Abolition?' in P Birks (ed), *Wrongs and Remedies in the Twenty-First Century* (Oxford, Clarendon Press, 1996)
—— 'Reforming Non-Compensatory Damages' in W Swadling, GH Jones and RG Goff of Chieveley (eds), *The Search for Principle: Essays in Honour of Lord Goff of Chieveley* (Oxford, OUP, 1999)
—— 'Are "Damages on the *Wrotham Park* Basis" Compensatory, Restitutionary or Neither?' in D Saidov and R Cunnington (eds), *Current Themes in the Law of Contract Damages* (Oxford, Hart Publishing, 2008)
—— *The Law of Restitution*, 3rd edn (Oxford, OUP, 2011)
—— 'Comparing Compensatory Damages in Tort and Contract: Some Problematic Issues' in S Degeling, J Edelman and J Goudkamp (eds), *Torts in Commercial Law* (London, Thomson Reuters, 2011)
—— 'Damages and Rights' in D Nolan and A Robertson (eds), *Rights and Private Law* (Oxford, Hart Publishing, 2012)
—— 'Judicial Remedies' in AS Burrows (ed), *English Private Law*, 3rd edn (Oxford, OUP, 2013)
—— 'One Step Forward?' (2018) 134 *LQR* 515
—— *Remedies for Torts, Breach of Contract, and Equitable Wrongs*, 4th edn (Oxford, OUP, 2019)
—— *A Casebook on Contract*, 7th edn (Oxford, Hart Publishing, 2020)
Campbell, D and Wylie, P, 'Ain't No Telling (Which Circumstances are Exceptional)' (2003) 62 *CLJ* 605
Campbell, CD, 'The Nature of Power as Public in English Judicial Review' (2009) 68 *CLJ* 90
Cane, P, *Tort Law and Economic Interests* (Oxford, Clarendon Press, 1991)
—— 'Corrective Justice and Correlativity in Private Law' (1996) 16 *OJLS* 471
—— 'Exceptional Measure of Damages: A Search for Principles' in P Birks (ed), *Wrongs and Remedies in the Twenty-First Century* (Oxford, Clarendon Press, 1996)
—— *The Anatomy of Tort Law* (Oxford, Hart Publishing, 1997)
—— 'Distributive Justice and Tort Law' (2001) 2001 *New Zealand Law Review* 401
—— *Responsibility in Law and Morality* (Oxford, Hart Publishing, 2002)
Cavallini, C, 'Why is the Iura Novit Curia Principle not Applied Yet in English Law?' (2017) 17 *Global Jurist* 1
Chapman, B and Trebilcock, M, 'Punitive Damages: Divergence in Search of a Rationale' (1989) 40 *Alabama Law Review* 741
Chen-Wishart, M, *Contract Law*, 7th edn (Oxford, OUP, 2022)
Coleman, JL, *Risks and Wrongs* (Cambridge, CUP, 1992)

Colm, G, 'The Public Interest: Essential Key to Public Policy' in CJ Friedrich (ed), *Nomos V: The Public Interest* (New York, Atherton Press, 1962)
Conte, C, 'From Only the "Bottom-up"? Legitimate Forms of Judicial Reasoning in Private Law' (2014) 35 *OJLS* 1
Cunnington, R, 'Should Punitive Damages be Part of the Judicial Arsenal in Contract Cases?' (2006) 26 *Legal Studies* 369
—— 'Changing Conceptions of Compensation' (2007) 66 *CLJ* 507
—— 'Gain-based Damages for Breach of Contract' in D Saidov and R Cunnington (eds), *Contract Damages: Domestic and International Perspectives* (Oxford, Hart Publishing, 2008)
Dagan, H, *Unjust Enrichment: A Study of Private Law and Public Values* (Cambridge, CUP, 1997)
Deakin, SF and Adams, Z, *Markesinis and Deakin's Tort Law*, 8th edn (Oxford, OUP, 2019)
Descheemaeker, E, 'Unravelling Harms in Tort Law' (2016) 132 *LQR* 595
—— 'The Standardisation of Tort Damages' (2021) 84 *MLR* 1
—— 'Pecuniary and Non-pecuniary Loss: A Reinterpretation' (2022) 138 *LQR* 79
Dorgan, T and McKenna, P, *Damages* (Dublin, Thomson Reuters Ireland Limited, 2015)
Drexl, J, 'The Interaction Between Private and Public Enforcement in European Competition Law' in H Micklitz and A Wechsler (eds), *The Transformation of Enforcement: European Economic Law in Global Perspective* (Oxford, Hart Publishing, 2016)
Dworkin, R, 'Hart's Postscript and the Character of Political Philosophy' (2004) 24 *OJLS* 1
Dyson, M, 'Challenging the Orthodoxy of Crime's Precedence over Tort: Suspending a Tort Claim Where a Crime May Exist' in SG Pitel, JW Neyers and E Chamberlain (eds), *Tort Law: Challenging Orthodoxy* (Oxford, Hart Publishing, 2013)
—— (ed), *Unravelling Tort and Crime* (Cambridge, CUP, 2014)
—— (ed), *Comparing Tort and Crime* (Cambridge, CUP, 2015)
Edelman, J and Bant, E, *Unjust Enrichment*, 2nd edn (Oxford, Hart Publishing, 2016)
Edelman, J, *Gain-Based Damages: Contract, Tort, Equity and Intellectual Property* (Oxford, Hart Publishing, 2002)
Edelman, J, Varuhas, J and Colton, S (eds), *McGregor on Damages*, 20th edn (London, Sweet & Maxwell, 2017)
Edelman, J, Varuhas, J and Higgins, A (eds), *McGregor on Damages*, 22nd edn (incorporating 1st supplement, London, Sweet & Maxwell, 2025)
Elliott, SB, 'Restitutionary Compensatory Damages for Breach of Fiduciary Duty?' [1998] *Restitution Law Review* 135
Ellscheid, G and Hassemer, W (eds), *Interessenjurisprudenz* (Darmstadt, Wissenschaftliche Buchgesellschaft, 1974)
Endicott, T, 'Adjudication and the Law' (2007) 27 *OJLS* 311
Englard, I, *Corrective and Distributive Justice: From Aristotle to Modern Times* (Oxford, OUP, 2009)
Erh-Soon Tay, A and Kamenka, E, 'Public Law – Private Law' in SI Benn and GF Gaus (eds), *Public and Private in Social Life* (London, Croom Helm, 1983)
Feintuck, M, 'The Public Interest' in *Regulation* (Oxford, OUP, 2004)
Flathman, RE, *The Public Interest: An Essay Concerning the Normative Discourse of Politics* (Chichester, Wiley, 1966)
Frankfurter, F in HB Phillips (ed), *Felix Frankfurter Reminisces* (New York, Reynal, 1960)
Frauenfelder, S, 'Rewriting history: Lewis v ACT and counterfactual analysis in unlawful imprisonment' (2024) 55 *Australian Bar Review* 92
Friedmann, D, 'The Performance Interest in Contract Damages' (1995) 111 *LQR* 628
Friedrich, CJ (ed), *Nomos V: The Public Interest* (New York, Atherton Press, 1962)
Fulford, LJ, Sentencing remarks of 30 September 2021 in case against Wayne Couzens, Central Criminal Court [perma.cc/3JGP-ZAYZ]
Fulham-McQuillan, S, 'Infringement of autonomy as damage in medical negligence' (2023) 139 *LQR* 126
Fuller, LL and Perdue, WR, 'The Reliance Interest in Contract Damages' (1936) 46 *Yale Law Journal* 52
Gahan, F, (ed), *Mayne's Treatise on Damages*, 10th edn (London, Sweet and Maxwell, 1927)

Gardner, J, 'Torts and Other Wrongs' (2011) 39 *Florida State University Law Review* 43

—— 'What is Tort Law For? Part 1. The Place of Corrective Justice' (2011) 30 *Law & Philosophy* 1

—— 'What is Tort Law For? Part 2. The Place of Distributive Justice' in J Oberdiek (ed), *Philosophical Foundations of the Law of Torts* (Oxford, OUP, 2014)

—— 'Damages without Duty' (2019) 69 *University of Toronto Law Journal* 412

—— *Torts and Other Wrongs* (Oxford, OUP, 2019)

Georgiou, A and Steel, S, 'Remedies and the Public Interest' in A Robertson and JW Neyers (eds), *Private Law and the State* (Oxford, Hart Publishing, 2024)

Giglio, F, 'Restitution for Wrongs: A Structural Analysis' (2007) 20 *Canadian Journal of Law & Jurisprudence* 5

—— 'Pseudo-Restitutionary Damages: Some Thoughts on the Dual Theory of Restitution for Wrongs' (2009) 22 *Canadian Journal of Law & Jurisprudence* 49

Giliker, P, *Tort*, 8th edn (London, Sweet & Maxwell, 2023)

Goldberg, JCP and Zipursky, BC, 'Torts as Wrongs' (2010) 88 *Texas Law Review* 917

—— *Recognizing Wrongs* (Cambridge, MA, Harvard University Press, 2020)

Goudkamp, J and Katsampouka, E, 'An Empirical Study of Punitive Damages' (2018) 38 *OJLS* 90

—— 'Form and Substance in the Law of Punitive Damages' in A Robertson and J Goudkamp (eds), *Form and Substance in the Law of Obligations* (Oxford, Hart Publishing, 2019)

—— 'Punitive Damages and the Place of Punishment in Private Law' (2021) 84 MLR 1257

Goudkamp, J and Murphy, J, 'The Failure of Universal Theories of Tort Law' (2015) 21 *Legal Theory* 47

—— 'Tort Statutes and Tort Theories' (2015) 131 *LQR* 133

Goudkamp, J and Nolan, D (eds), *Winfield & Jolowicz on Tort*, 20th edn (London, Sweet & Maxwell 2020)

Goudkamp, J, 'The Rule Against Bias and the Doctrine of Waiver' (2007) 26 *Civil Justice Quarterly* 310

—— 'Exemplary Damages' in G Virgo and S Worthington (eds), *Commercial Remedies: Resolving Controversies* (Cambridge, CUP, 2017)

Graham, M, 'Restitutionary Damages: The Anvil Struck' (2004) 120 *LQR* 26

Gray, A, 'Disgorgement damages' (2013) 7 *Journal of Business Law* 657

Graziani, AM, *Pascal Paoli: Père de la partie corse* (Paris, Tallandier, 2002)

Green, S and Gardner, J, *Tort Law*, 2nd edn (Oxford, Hart Publishing, 2024)

Häberle, P, *Öffentliches Interesse als juristisches Problem: Eine Analyse von Gesetzgebung und Rechtsprechung* (Frankfurt, Athenäum Verlag, 1970)

Hall, J and others (eds), *The Jurisprudence of Interests: Selected Writings of Max Rümelin, Philipp Heck, Paul Oertmann, Heinrich Stoll, Julius Binder, and Hermann Isay* (MM Schoch tr, Cambridge, MA, Harvard University Press, 1948)

Halliwell, M, 'Profits from Wrongdoing: Private and Public Law Perspectives' (1999) 62 *MLR* 271

Halson, R and Campbell, D (eds), *Research Handbook on Private Law Remedies* (Cheltenham, Edward Elgar, 2019)

Harder, S, *Measuring Damages in the Law of Obligations: The Search for Harmonised Principles* (Oxford, Hart Publishing, 2010)

Harlow, C, '"Public" and "Private" Law: Definition without Distinction' (1980) 43 *MLR* 241

Harper, FV, *A Treatise on the Law of Torts: A Preliminary Treatise on Civil Liability for Harms to Legally Protected Interests* (Indianapolis, Bobbs-Merrill Co Publishers, 1933)

Hart, HLA, *The Concept of Law*, 3rd edn (Oxford, OUP, 2012)

Heck, P, 'Gesetzauslegung und Interessenjurisprudenz' (1914) 112 *AcP* 1

—— *Begriffsbildung und Interessenjurisprudenz* (Tübingen, Mohr Siebeck, 1932)

—— *Interessenjurisprudenz* (Tübingen, Mohr Siebeck, 1933)

Held, V, *The Public Interest and Individual Interests* (New York, Basic Books, 1970)

Hershovitz, S, 'Treating Wrongs as Wrongs: An Expressive Argument for Tort Law' (2017) 10 *Journal of Tort Law* 405

Heuston, RFV, *Salmond on the Law of Torts*, 17th edn (London, Sweet & Maxwell, 1977)

Hohfeld, WN, 'Some Fundamental Legal Conceptions as Applied in Judicial Reasoning' (1913) 23 *Yale Law Journal* 16

Homburger, A, 'Private Suits in the Public Interest in the United States of America' in A Homburger and H Kötz, *Klagen Privater im öffentlichen Interesse* (Frankfurt, Alfred Metzner Verlag, 1975)

Hondius, E and Janssen, A (eds), *Disgorgement of Profits: Gain-Based Remedies throughout the World* (Cham, Springer, 2015)

Hursthouse, R and Pettigrove, G, 'Virtue Ethics' in EN Zalta and U Nodelman (eds), *The Stanford Encyclopedia of Philosophy* (Fall 2023 Edn)

Ibbetson, DJ, *A Historical Introduction to the Law of Obligations* (Oxford, OUP, 1999)

Isay, H, 'The Method of the Jurisprudence of Interests: A Critical Study' in J Hall and others (eds), *The Jurisprudence of Interests: Selected Writings of Max Rümelin, Philipp Heck, Paul Oertmann, Heinrich Stoll, Julius Binder, and Hermann Isay* (MM Schoch tr, Cambridge, MA, Harvard University Press, 1948)

Jaffey, P, 'Liabilities in Private Law' (2008) 14 *Legal Theory* 233

Janeček, V, 'Exemplary Damages: A Genuine Concept?' (2014) 6 *European Journal of Legal Studies* 189

—— 'CPR Pt 36: Enhanced Interest Should Not Function as Punitive Damages for Malicious Defence' (2019) 38 *Civil Justice Quarterly* 168

—— 'Data Protection, the Value of Privacy and Compensable Damage' (2020) 79 *CLJ* 417

—— 'Public Interest Damages' (2020) 40 *Legal Studies* 589

—— 'Three Problematic Assumptions About Public Interests in Law' in L Tichý and M Potacs (eds), *Public Interest in Law* (Cambridge, Intersentia, 2021)

—— 'Mass Compensation Claims for Illegal Online Tracking' (2022) 138 *LQR* 205

Jansen, N, 'The Concept of Non-Contractual Obligations: Rethinking the Divisions of Tort, Unjustified Enrichment, and Contract Law' (2010) 1 *Journal of European Tort Law* 16

Jolowicz, JA, 'Active Role of the Court in Civil Litigation' in M Cappelletti and JA Jolowicz (eds), *Public Interest Parties and the Active Role of the Judge in Civil Litigation* (New York, Oceana, 1975)

Judicial College, *Judicial College Guidelines for the Assessment of General Damages in Personal Injury Cases*, 16th edn (Oxford, OUP, 2022)

Kant, I, *The Metaphysics of Morals* (Cambridge, CUP, 1996)

Katsampouka, E, 'Exemplary Damages and Insurance Fraud' (2019) 135 *LQR* 380

Keating, GC, 'Corrective Justice: Sovereign or Subordinate?' in AS Gold and others (eds), *The Oxford Handbook of the New Private Law* (Oxford, OUP, 2020)

Keren-Paz, T, *Torts, Egalitarianism and Distributive Justice* (Farnham, Ashgate, 2013)

Kramer, A, *The Law of Contract Damages*, 3rd edn (Oxford, Hart Publishing, 2022)

Kramer, MH, 'Refining the Interest Theory of Rights' (2010) 55 *American Journal of Jurisprudence* 31

Kurki, VAJ, 'Rights, Harming and Wronging: A Restatement of the Interest Theory' (2018) 38 *OJLS* 430

Landes, WM and Posner, RA, 'The Private Enforcement of Law' (1975) 4 *Journal of Legal Studies* 1

Law Commission, *Aggravated, Exemplary and Restitutionary Damages* (Law Com No 247, 1997)

Law, J (ed), *A Dictionary of Law*, 9th edn (Oxford, OUP, 2018)

Lee, M, 'The Public Interest in Private Nuisance: Collectives and Communities in Tort' (2015) 74 *CLJ* 329

Lee, PW, 'Contract Damages, Corrective Justice and Punishment' (2007) 70 MLR 887

Lewis, D, 'Stigma and Whistleblowing: Should Punitive Damages be Available in Retaliation Cases?' (2022) 51 *Industrial Law Journal* 62

Liau, T, *Standing in Private Law: Powers of Enforcement in the Law of Obligations and Trusts* (Oxford, OUP, 2023)

Lisska, AJ, 'The Philosophy of Law of Thomas Aquinas' in FD Miller and CA Biondi (eds), *A History of the Philosophy of Law from the Ancient Greeks to the Scholastics*, 2nd edn (Cham, Springer, 2015)

Lobban, M and Moses, J (eds), *The Impact of Ideas on Legal Development* (Cambridge, CUP, 2012)

Lobban, M, 'English Jurisprudence and Tort Theory' in M Lobban and J Moses (eds), *The Impact of Ideas on Legal Development* (Cambridge, CUP, 2012)

Lunney, M and Oliphant, K, *Lunney & Oliphant's Tort Law: Text and Materials*, 7th edn (Oxford, OUP, 2023)

Magnus, U, 'Causation in German Tort Law' in J Spier (ed), *Unification of Tort Law: Causation* (Alphen aan den Rijn, Kluwer Law International, 2000)

Mayne, JD, *A Treatise on the Law of Damages: Comprising Their Measure, the Mode in Which they are Assessed and Reviewed, the Practice of Granting New Trials, and the Law of Set-off, and Compensation under the Lands Clauses Act*, 1st edn (London, H Sweet, 1856)

McBride, M, 'Preserving the Interest Theory of Rights' (2020) 26 *Legal Theory* 3
McBride, NJ, 'Duties of Care – Do They Really Exist?' (2004) 24 *OJLS* 417
McBride, NJ and Bagshaw, R, *Tort Law*, 7th edn (London, Pearson, 2024)
McKendrick, E, *Contract Law: Text, Cases, and Materials*, 11th edn (Oxford, OUP, 2024)
Mercer, PP, 'The Citizen's Right to Sue in the Public Interest: The Roman Actio Popularis Revisited' (1983) 21 *University of Western Ontario Law Review* 89
Merryman, JH, 'The Public Law-Private Law Distinction in European and American Law' (1968) 17 *Journal of Public Law* 3
Micklitz, HW and Reich, N (eds), *Public Interest Litigation before European Courts* (Baden-Baden, Nomos, 1996)
Miller, PB and Oberdiek, J (eds), *Civil Wrongs and Justice in Private Law* (Oxford, OUP, 2020)
Mulcahy, L, 'The Collective Interest in Private Dispute Resolution' (2012) 33 *OJLS* 59
Mulheron, R, *Principles of Tort Law*, 2nd edn (Cambridge, CUP, 2020)
Mulligan, A, 'A Vindicatory Approach to Tortious Liability for Mistakes in Assisted Human Reproduction' (2020) 40 *Legal Studies* 55
Murphy, J, 'The Nature and Domain of Aggravated Damages' (2010) 69 *CLJ* 353
Newhouse, ME, 'Two Types of Legal Wrongdoing' (2016) 22 *Legal Theory* 59
Nolan, D, 'New Forms of Damage in Negligence' (2007) 70 *MLR* 59
—— 'Rights, Damage and Loss' (2016) 36 *OJLS* 1
—— 'Tort and Public Law: Overlapping Categories?' (2019) 135 *LQR* 272
Nyreröd, T and Spagnolo, G, 'Myths and Numbers on Whistleblower Rewards' (2019) Reg & Gov (online)
O'Mahony, LF, 'Eviction and the Public Interest: The Right to Respect for Home in English Law' in RP Malloy and M Diamond (eds), *The Public Nature of Private Property* (Farnham, Ashgate Publishing, 2011)
O'Sullivan, J, *O'Sullivan's & Hillard's The Law of Contract*, 11th edn (Oxford, OUP, 2024) 452
O'Sullivan, R, 'A Scale of Values in the Common Law' (1937) 1 *MLR* 27
Oertmann, P, 'Interests and Concepts in Legal Science' in J Hall and others (eds), *The Jurisprudence of Interests: Selected Writings of Max Rümelin, Philipp Heck, Paul Oertmann, Heinrich Stoll, Julius Binder, and Hermann Isay* (MM Schoch tr, Cambridge, MA, Harvard University Press, 1948)
Ogus, AI, *The Law of Damages* (London, Butterworths, 1973)
Oliphant, K, 'Basic Questions of Tort Law from the Perspective of England and the Commonwealth' in H Koziol (ed), *Basic Questions of Tort Law from a Comparative Perspective* (Vienna, Jan Sramek Verlag, 2015)
Oliver, D, *Common values and the public-private divide* (London, Butterworths, 1999)
Ormerod, P, 'Privacy Quit Tam' (2022) 98 *Notre Dame Law Review* 267
Pasquale, FA, 'Data-Informed Duties in AI Development' (2019) 119 *Columbia Law Review* 1917
Patterson, EW, 'Pound's Theory of Social Interests' in P Sayre (ed), *Interpretations of Modern Legal Philosophies: Essays in Honour of Roscoe Pound* (Oxford, OUP, 1947)
Pearce, D and Halson, R, 'Damages for Breach of Contract: Compensation, Restitution and Vindication' (2008) 28 *OJLS* 73
Peel, WE, *Treitel on The Law of Contract*, 16th edn (London, Sweet & Maxwell, 2025)
Peter, S, *Public Interest and Common Good in International Law* (Basel, Helbing Lichtenhahn Verlag, 2012)
Plunkett, J, 'Principle and Policy in Private Law Reasoning' (2016) 75 *CLJ* 366
Pollock, F, *The Law of Torts: A Treatise on the Principles of Obligations Arising from Civil Wrongs in the Common Law* (London, Stevens & Sons, 1887)
Post, RC, 'The Social Foundations of Defamation Law: Reputation and the Constitution' (1986) 74 *California Law Review* 691
Potacs, M, 'Public Interest in Legal Interpretation' in L Tichý and M Potacs (eds), *Public Interest in Law* (Cambridge, Intersentia, 2021)
Pound, R, 'A Theory of Social Interests' (1921) 15 *Papers and Proceedings of the American Sociological Society* 16
—— 'A Survey of Social Interests' (1943) 57 *Harvard Law Review* 1

—— 'A Survey of Public Interests' (1945) 58 *Harvard Law Review* 909

—— *Jurisprudence*, vols 1–5 (St. Paul, West Publishing, 1959)

Priel, D, 'A Public Role for the Intentional Torts' (2011) 22 *King's Law Journal* 183

—— 'The Political Origins of English Private Law' (2013) 40 *Journal of Law and Society* 481

Raz, J, 'Reasons for Action, Decisions and Norms' (1975) 84 *Mind* 481

—— 'Promises in Morality and Law' (1982) 95 *Harvard Law Review* 916

—— *The Morality of Freedom* (Oxford, Clarendon Press, 1986)

Rotherham, C, 'The Conceptual Structure of Restitution for Wrongs' (2007) 66 *CLJ* 172

—— 'Deterrence as a Justification for Awarding Accounts of Profits' (2012) 32 *OJLS* 537

—— 'Restitution for Wrongs' in E Bant, K Barker and S Degeling (eds), *Research Handbook on Unjust Enrichment and Restitution* (Cheltenham, Edward Elgar, 2020)

Rowan, S, 'The "Legitimate Interest in Performance" in the Law of Penalties' (2019) 78 *CLJ* 148

Sanchez-Graells, A, 'The Procurement Act 2023's Kaleidoscopic View of the Public Interest' (2025) *Legal Studies* (FirstView)

Sandel, MJ, *The Tyranny of Merit: What's Become of the Common Good* (London, Penguin Random House UK, 2020)

Samuel, G, 'Public and Private Law: A Private Lawyer's Response' (1983) 46 *MLR* 558

—— 'Governmental Liability in Tort and the Public and Private Law Division' (1988) 8 *Legal Studies* 277

—— *Law of Obligations and Legal Remedies*, 2nd edn (London, Cavendish Publishing, Ltd 2001)

—— 'Should Jurists Take Interests More Seriously?' (2017) (August) *Law and Method* 1

Saprai, P, 'Restitution without Corrective Justice' (2006) 14 *Restitution Law Review* 41

Sayer, J, *The Law of Damages* (London, Strahan and Woodfall, 1770)

Scholz, LH, 'Privacy and the Punitive Impulse' (2025) 77 *Baylor Law Review* 336

Senu, J, 'Negotiating Damages and the Compensatory Principle' (2020) 40 *OJLS* 110

Shapiro, SJ, 'What Is the Internal Point of View?' (2006) 75 *Fordham Law Review* 1157

—— *Legality* (Cambridge, MA, Harvard University Press, 2011)

Sharkey, CM, 'Punitive Damages as Societal Damages' (2003) 113 *Yale Law Journal* 347

Shaunessy, P, 'A Matter of Choice: Rethinking Legal Formalism's Account of Private Law Rights' (2017) 37 *OJLS* 163

Simpson, J and Weiner, E (eds), *The Oxford English Dictionary*, 2nd edn (Oxford, OUP, 1989)

Sinanis, N, 'The North Briston No. 45 and the Doctrinal Origins of Exemplary Damages' (2023) 82 *CLJ* 321

—— '"Damages, One Farthing": Under-compensation in nineteenth-century tort' in F Bettini and others (eds), *New Directions in Private Law* (London, UCL Press, 2023)

Sinnott-Armstrong, W, 'Consequentialism' in EN Zalta and U Nodelman (eds), *The Stanford Encyclopedia of Philosophy* (Winter 2023 Edn)

Skillen, J, 'Exemplary Damages and Misuse of Private Information' (2023) 28 *Comms Law* 158

Slavny, A, *Wrongs, Harms, and Compensation: Paying for our Mistakes* (Oxford, OUP, 2023)

Smith, S, 'Why Courts Make Orders (and What This Tells us About Damages)' (2011) 64 *Current Legal Problems* 51

—— 'Duties, Liabilities, and Damages' (2012) 125 *Harvard Law Review* 1727

—— *Rights, Wrongs, and Injustices: The Structure of Remedial Law* (Oxford, OUP, 2019)

Sorauf, FJ, 'The Conceptual Muddle' in CJ Friedrich (ed), *Nomos V: The Public Interest* (New York, Atherton Press, 1962)

Stapleton, J, 'A New "Seascape" for Obligations: Reclassification on the Basis of Measure of Damages' in P Birks (ed), *The Classification of Obligations* (Oxford, Clarendon Press, 1997)

Steel, S and Stevens, R, 'The Secondary Legal Duty to Pay Damages' (2020) 136 *LQR* 283

Steel, S, 'False Imprisonment and the Fetch of Hypothetical Warrant' (2011) 127 *LQR* 527

—— 'Private Law and Justice' (2013) 33 *OJLS* 607

—— '*Proof of Causation in Tort Law* (Cambridge, CUP, 2015)

—— 'Damages without Loss' (2023) 139 *LQR* 219

Steele, J, *Tort Law: Text, Cases, and Materials*, 5th edn (Oxford, OUP, 2022)

Steiner, J, 'Judicial Discretion and the Concept of Law' (1976) 35 *CLJ* 135

Stevens, R, 'Torts, Rights and Losses' (2006) 122 *LQR* 565

—— *Torts and Rights* (Oxford, OUP, 2007)
—— 'Rights and Other Things' in D Nolan and A Robertson (eds), *Rights and Private Law* (Oxford, Hart Publishing, 2012)
—— 'Damages for Wrongdoing in the Absence of Loss' in J Varuhas and NA Moreham (eds), *Remedies for Breach of Privacy* (Oxford, Hart Publishing, 2018)
—— *The Laws of Restitution* (Oxford, OUP, 2023)
Street, H, *The Law of Torts* (London, Butterworth & Co Publishers, 1955)
Summers, A, *Mitigation in the Law of Damages* (Oxford, OUP, 2024)
Taliadoros, J, 'Thirteenth-Century Origins of Punitive or Exemplary Damages: The Statute of Westminster I (1275) and Roman Law' (2018) 39 *Journal of Legal History* 278
Tan, W, 'Unpacking the Enigma of Equitable Compensation for Breaches in Equity' [2022] *Journal of Business Law* 407
Tichý, L and Potacs, M (eds), *Public Interest in Law* (Cambridge, Intersentia, 2021)
Tichý, L, 'Public Interest and its Importance in Law' in L Tichý and M Potacs (eds), *Public Interest in Law* (Intersentia 2021)
Todd, S, 'Publication Review: Edelman, James, McGregor on Damages' [2018] *Journal of Business Law* 633
Törnblom, KY and Jonsson, DR, 'Distribution vs. Retribution: The Perceived Justice of the Contribution and Equality Principles for Cooperative and Competitive Relationships' (1987) 30 *Acta Sociologica* 25
Varuhas, J, 'The Concept of "Vindication" in the Law of Torts: Rights, Interests and Damages' (2014) 34 *OJLS*
—— *Damages and Human Rights* (Oxford, Hart Publishing, 2016)
Ventose, ED, 'Damages for Constitutional Infringements: Compensation and Vindication' [2010] *Commonwealth Law Bulletin* 223
Voyiakis, E, *Private Law and the Value of Choice* (Oxford, Hart Publishing, 2017)
Virgo, G, *The Principles of the Law of Restitution*, 3rd edn (Oxford, OUP, 2015)
Wall, J, 'Public Wrongs and Private Wrongs' (2018) 31 *Canadian Journal of Law & Jurisprudence* 177
Ward, J, 'Equitable Compensation – An Overview' in S Degeling and J Varuhas (eds), *Equitable Compensation and Disgorgement of Profit* (Oxford, Hart Publishing, 2019)
Watterson, S, 'Alternative and Cumulative Remedies: What is the Difference?' [2003] *Restitution Law Review* 7
—— 'An Account of Profits or Damages? The History of Orthodoxy' (2004) 24 *OJLS* 471
—— 'Gain-Based Remedies for Civil Wrongs in England and Wales' in E Hondius and A Janssen (eds), *Disgorgement of Profits: Gain-Based Remedies throughout the World* (Cham, Springer, 2015)
Webb, C, *Reason and Restitution: A Theory of Unjust Enrichment*, 1st edn (Oxford, OUP, 2016)
Weinrib, EJ, 'Aristotle's Forms of Justice' (1989) 2 *Ratio Juris* 211
—— 'The Juridical Classification of Obligations' in P Birks (ed), *The Classification of Obligations* (Oxford, Clarendon Press, 1997)
—— 'Punishment and Disgorgement as Contract Remedies' (2003) 78 *Chicago-Kent Law Review* 55
—— 'Two Conceptions of Remedies' in CEF Rickett (ed), *Justifying Private Law Remedies* (Oxford, Hart Publishing, 2008)
—— *Corrective Justice* (Oxford, OUP, 2012)
—— *The Idea of Private Law*, rev edn (Oxford, OUP, 2012)
—— *Reciprocal Freedom: Private Law and Public Right* (Oxford, OUP, 2022)
Weir, T, *A Casebook on Tort*, 1st edn (London, Sweet & Maxwell, 1967)
—— *A Casebook on Tort*, 10th edn (London, Sweet & Maxwell, 2004)
Weisbrod, BA, Handler, JF and Komesar, NK (eds), *Public Interest Law: An Economic and Institutional Analysis* (Oakland, University of California Press, 1978)
Wilken, S and Ghaly, K, *The Law of Waiver, Variation, and Estoppels*, 3rd edn (Oxford, OUP, 2012)
Williams, R, 'Criminal Law in England and Wales: Just Another Form of Regulatory Tool?' in M Dyson and B Vogel, *The Limits of Criminal Law: Anglo-German Concepts and Principles* (Cambridge, Intersentia, 2020)

Winfield, PH, *A Text-Book of the Law of Tort* (London, Sweet & Maxwell, 1937)
Winterton, D, *Money Awards in Contract Law* (Oxford, Hart Publishing, 2015)
Witting, C (ed), *Street on Torts*, 16th edn (Oxford, OUP, 2021)
Wolff, J, *Ethics and Public Policy: A Philosophical Inquiry* (Abingdon, Routledge, 2011)
Woolf, H, 'Public Law – Private Law: Why the Divide? A Personal View' (1987) *PL* 220
Zakrzewski, R, *Remedies Reclassified* (Oxford, OUP, 2005)
Zipursky, BC, 'Civil Recourse, Not Corrective Justice' (2003) 91 *Georgia Law Journal* 695
—— 'A Theory of Punitive Damages' (2005) 84 *Texas Law Review* 105
—— 'Torts and the Rule of Law' in LM Austin and D Klimchuk (eds), *Private Law and the Rule of Law* (Oxford, OUP, 2014)

INDEX

Please note that references to Notes are followed by the letter 'n' and Note number

www.ingramcontent.com/pod-product-compliance
Ingram Content Group UK Ltd.
Pitfield, Milton Keynes, MK11 3LW, UK
UKHW020808290926
15470UKWH00003B/1034

9 781509 981434